EDUCATIONAL POLICIES IN CRISIS

The Praeger Special Studies
Series in Comparative Education

Published in Cooperation with the Comparative
Education Center, State University of New York, Buffalo

General Editor: **Philip G. Altbach**

EDUCATIONAL POLICIES IN CRISIS

Japanese and American Perspectives

Edited by

William K. Cummings
Edward R. Beauchamp
Shogo Ichikawa
Victor N. Kobayashi
Morikazu Ushiogi

Praeger Publishers in association with
The East-West Center

PRAEGER SPECIAL STUDIES • PRAEGER SCIENTIFIC

New York • Westport, Connecticut • London

Library of Congress Cataloging-in-Publication Data

Educational policies in crisis.

Largely based on papers presented at a conference
held at the East-West Center, University of Hawaii at
Manoa, in Aug. 1984.
"Praeger Publishers in association with the
East-West Center."
Includes bibliographies and index.
1. Education – United States – Congresses.   2. Education
– Japan – Congresses.   3. Education and state – United
States – Congresses.   4. Education and state – Japan
– Congresses.   5. Comparative education – Congresses.
I. Cummings, William K.   II. East-West Center.
LA212.E43   1986   370'.952   86-78
ISBN 0-275-92089-5 (alk. paper)

Library of Congress Catalog Card Number: 86-78
ISBN: 0-275-92089-5

First published in 1986

Praeger Publishers, 521 Fifth Avenue, New York, NY 10175
A division of Greenwood Press, Inc.

Printed in the United States of America

The paper used in this book complies with the Permanent
Paper Standard issued by the National Information Standards
Organization (Z39.48-1984).

10 9 8 7 6 5 4 3 2 1

Preface

Hawaii, positioned halfway between Japan and the U.S. mainland, has long served as a lightning rod for new currents that span the Pacific. From the late 1970s academics based in Hawaii began to note the growing number of Japanese educational tourists among the visitors to our homeland, and the thought was born of looking more deeply into its significance. Our plans had already been laid when President Ronald Reagan of the United States visited Japan in November 1983 and proposed to Prime Minister Yasuhiro Nakasone of Japan a comparative study of the two nations' educational systems. With the support of the East-West Center we developed a proposal to examine why these two nations sought to learn from each other and what might come out of the process. The U.S.-Japan Foundation generously funded our proposal, and thus in August of 1984 a conference was convened at which early drafts of most of the papers published herein were presented.

In addition to the authors included in this volume, we wish to thank Richard Rubinger and Glenn Shive, who were members of the core group, and Merry White, S. Luthra, and John Watson, who joined us for the conference. Sumi Makey, dean of the East-West Center, deserves special thanks for her continuing support of this endeavor. And Sandra Ward of the center's Publications Office deserves a purple heart, if not a purple pencil, for her extraordinary effort to save our fractured sentences.

THE EDITORS

Table of Contents

PART III. DECLINE

PART IV. EDUCATION AND WORK

PART V. IMAGES

PART VI. CONCLUSION

List of Figures and Exhibits

Figures

Exhibits

ix

List of Tables

xi

PART I
CRISES

1
REFORM TRADITIONS IN THE UNITED STATES AND JAPAN
Edward R. Beauchamp

Educational reform and the influence of foreign educational models are common, at least to some degree, in all societies. Among the diverse purposes for which nations support education are political integration, economic development, social cohesion, and religious orthodoxy. The passage of time and changing circumstances inevitably require that the "fit" between formal education and the objectives pursued be reformulated in order to achieve better the existing goals or to attain new ones.

Rare is the nation's educational system that, by design or accident, has not been influenced by foreign models, theories, or practices. As for the United States and Japan, both societies owe much of their educational success to their willingness to accept and adapt theories and practices from other lands. Indeed, the current educational ferment in both countries is only the most recent example of their penchant for reform and their willingness to look to others for possible answers to pedagogical problems.

Many elements of the educational systems of both countries have been adapted from abroad. Students of comparative education are acutely aware of the dangers inherent in educational borrowing. There is virtually unanimous agreement that an educational system is essentially an organic outgrowth of a society's unique history and culture and therefore transplantation into a foreign environment is fraught with danger. Yet every educational system is, in a sense, a composite of both domestic and foreign elements. Often the latter

3

have been so well integrated into the system that only the most knowledgeable historian of education is aware of their origins.

It is also commonplace for countries unhappy with their educational enterprise to compare it with a foreign model and to look abroad for answers to their problems. As I have suggested, both Japan and the United States are good examples of this phenomenon. Educational borrowing in the two countries has been both intentional and unintentional, the Japanese being perhaps more willing to search consciously for solutions abroad.

THE JAPANESE EXPERIENCE

One of the outstanding characteristics of the Japanese has been their eagerness to learn from others. This tradition of cultural borrowing is deeply embedded in Japanese history. For example, Buddhism from India was introduced into Japan, by way of Korea, about the middle of the sixth century A.D. At about the same time, Chinese and Korean monks, craftsmen, artists, and scholars carried a superior civilization to Japan, and their lessons were quickly accepted and integrated into Japan's national fabric. In the seventh century Prince Shotoku not only played an important role in the promotion of Buddhism but was also responsible for the importation of a variety of ideas and objects from China that served to enrich Japanese life. One widely used textbook argues that "on the whole, the Japanese government of the eighth century presented an amazingly faithful reproduction of the T'ang system" (Reischauer and Fairbank 1960, p. 486). In addition, Japan's writing system is heavily indebted to Chinese ideographs, which, although pronounced differently by the Japanese, share the same basic meanings in both the Japanese and Chinese languages.

A second great wave of cultural borrowing, once again in the service of reform, occurred during the Meiji period (1868-1912). Opening itself to the West, after more than two and one-half centuries of self-imposed isolation, Japan went on a virtual orgy of borrowing in almost all fields of modern endeavor, not the least of which was education. Setting the stage for this activity was the so-called Imperial Charter Oath, issued on April 6, 1868, which called on the people to eschew old-fashioned ways and proclaimed that "knowledge shall be sought throughout the world and thus shall be strengthened the foundation of the Imperial polity" (Beasley 1972, p. 323).

The response to this clarion call for reform took two basic forms. The first was the dispatch of hundreds, and then thousands, of Japanese students, usually at government expense, to the United States and Europe to learn the secrets of Western power and prestige. The second manifestation of the Charter Oath was the employment of foreign specialists as teachers, technicians, and experts in a wide variety of fields by both the new government in Edo (soon renamed Tokyo, or eastern capital) and several *han* (fief) governments. There was even an impressive number of privately sponsored students who joined the army of young Japanese studying abroad (Jones 1980, pp. xv-xvi, 59).

To their great credit, the Meiji oligarchs quickly recognized the potential of education as a vehicle for reforming the entire society, and to accomplish this enormous task they began to create a modern educational system. Recognizing their limitations, they set out to examine the educational systems of the major Western nations—England, France, Germany, and the United States—in an effort to determine not only which elements of those systems were world class but also, perhaps even more important, which elements were most appropriate for Japan in its present state. Thus they began a practice that still exists today. They sent out intelligent officials, possessing keen powers of observation, to study foreign education, to collect materials bearing on the subject, and upon their return to serve as experts on education in foreign countries. In 1871, for example, Fujimaro Tanaka, a high official in the newly established Ministry of Education, and later minister of education, was sent abroad as part of a team of observers—the Iwakura Embassy—to study educational conditions in the United States and Europe. Upon his return, Tanaka wrote 15 volumes describing Western education as he had observed it.

Yukichi Fukuzawa (1835-1901), and early advocate of Western learning and founder of Keio University, also spent considerable time abroad. He wrote 21 influential volumes, numbering more than 14,000 pages, based on his foreign observations and experiences. His *An Encouragement of Learning* (1876/1969), for example, is estimated to have sold 420,000 copies in the 1870s and a total of 3.4 million copies in 17 editions during his lifetime (Fukuzawa 1969, p. xi). This is an astounding total, even by today's standards, but becomes even more impressive when we consider that Japan's population in the 1870s was about 35 million people. These figures suggest, if nothing else, the extent of the openness of the Japanese to foreign ideas and practices.

The Japanese have always been willing to entertain foreign ideas, but they have been very cautious in choosing those to be adapted to Japanese conditions. More important, they have exhibited nothing short of a national genius in reforming things borrowed into items uniquely Japanese. Sir George Sansom, one of the first and perhaps the most perceptive student of Japan, concluded: "The power and prestige of a foreign culture seems as if they would overwhelm and transform Japan, but always there is a hard, non-absorbent core of individual character, which resists and in turn works upon the invading influence" (Sansom 1962, p. 15). His is an excellent description of what has happened to educational practices borrowed by Japan from the West.

The Japanese decided, for example, to model the administrative structure of public education on France's highly centralized system, creating a Ministry of Education at the center for both policy implementation and day-to-day administration. Much of the financial burden was to be borne by local authorities, however. In both curriculum and educational methodology, the American influence was paramount. A Rutgers University professor of mathematics, David Murray, was brought to Japan to serve as an adviser and, later, inspector of schools. Murray served directly under the education minister from 1873 to 1879 and was an influential voice on educational matters. At the university level, the German model was thought most appropriate for Japanese conditions and shaped the development of Japanese higher education for many years. Foreign influences were somewhat tempered, however, by a conservative resurgence that began to take hold in 1879.

Another brief period of Western influence occurred during the so-called Taisho democracy of the 1920s, when the Japanese evinced significant interest in progressive education in general and in John Dewey's educational thought in particular. But the subsequent rise of the military to national power cut short many promising experiments and plunged the nation into the education morass that would be the target of the next period of Western influence, the 1945-52 Occupation.

In several important ways the American Occupation of Japan was the single greatest experiment in social engineering that the world has seen. In this sense the entire Occupation was an educational enterprise, but the attempts to engender radical social change by reforming the institutions of formal education were, in themselves, virtually unparalleled. The underlying tone was set during the postsurrender planning, which began while the outcome of the war was still in doubt. American planners decided that the U.S. government was committed to the postwar demilitarization, democratization, and decentralization of Japan and its people.

The report of the first U.S. Education Mission to Japan, in the spring of 1946, advised the Occupation authorities how to implement these principles in the education sector. The mission's recommendations ranged from a proposal for greater individualization of instruction to one for a 6-3-3[1] school ladder and nine years of compulsory instruction. That the Japanese were willing to embrace these and other recommendations of the mission is as much a tribute to their continuing openness to foreign ideas as to their inferior role after being defeated on the field of battle.

One of the most important legacies of the Occupation was the creation in late spring 1946 of the Education Reform Committee as an advisory body to the prime minister. This panel evolved in 1952 into the influential Central Council for Education, which, in its early years, was independent of the Ministry of Education, reporting directly to the prime minister. Although today its members are appointed by the education minister, the Central Council for Education has been a major arena for debate over educational reforms.

As the Occupation drew to a close, the "hard, non-absorbent core" of the Japanese character exerted itself and the excesses of the period were corrected in a "reverse course." Even while this was occurring, however, the Japanese tradition of reform continued. Recognizing the need to remain abreast of world trends in education, the Ministry of Education established a National Institute for Educational Research (NIER) to, among other things, "exchange educational information with education and educational institutions in other countries" (NIER 1983, p. 2). Today NIER comprises seven research departments, one of which is charged with collecting information about educational trends throughout the world. In addition, many Japanese schools of education have distinguished researchers studying educational conditions in other countries. The result is that government policymakers have continuous access to an impressive pool of education specialists knowledgeable about worldwide trends in education.

By the mid-1970s there was increasing talk in the Japanese media and in political and educational circles about the need for still another major reform of Japanese education. Rumblings were heard about the need to redress such problems as an overly demanding curriculum, too much rote learning, a dangerous overreliance on the infamous examination system, and a resulting "diploma disease." In October 1975 a Ministry of Education advisory organ, the Educational Curriculum Deliberation Council, suggested that the ministry's national guidelines be revised to reflect (1) a need for each student to develop a well-rounded personality, (2) the development of an integrated framework for grades 1 through 12, and (3) a reduction in both the curriculum content and the number of study hours required of students. Great concern was evidenced over the need to "humanize" education by relieving students of an excessive preoccupation with factual knowledge.

The Current Crisis in Japanese Education

Over the past several years, especially since the publication of Ezra Vogel's *Japan as No. 1* (1979), the excellence of Japanese education has been a popular topic of conversation in the United States. We have been told that the performance of Japanese students on international tests of educational achievement is the highest in the world; that 99.9 percent of all Japanese youngsters successfully complete the nine years of compulsory education through lower secondary school, and almost 95 percent actually complete high school (compared with 78 percent of Americans who accomplish the latter); that at least 35 percent of Japanese in the relevant age cohort go on to some form of higher education; that Japan's national curriculum ensures that all pupils are exposed to a rich and challenging curriculum no matter where they live within Japan; that equality of educational opportunity is substantially assured to all in Japan; that Japan's population of 120 million produces perhaps one-tenth the number of lawyers and twice as many engineers as does the United States, with a population of 236 million. One could go on to discuss the diligence of Japanese students, their willingness to attend special after-school classes (at substantial economic cost), and the infamous entrance examination competition.

Japanese education clearly has achieved an excellent reputation among Americans. Ironically, at the very time when many Americans view Japan's educational enterprise as the sine qua non toward which the United States ought to strive, large numbers of Japanese —politicians and educators, as well as the lay public—are demanding reforms to meet the challenges of the twenty-first century.

During his September 1984 visit to Washington, D.C., Japan's Education Minister Yoshiro Mori experienced firsthand an example of the widespread American ignorance of Japanese education's basic realities. During a meeting with Mori, U.S. Education Secretary Terrel Bell told his visitor that the United States "must have *juku* (cram schools) because the Japanese are so productive. What we need is a continuation of your magnificent example." Bell was reportedly taken aback by Mori's reply that the Japanese were trying to do away with the *juku* as part of a movement to achieve a rebirth of Japanese education. Upon hearing this, Bell lamely replied, "I didn't understand" what the *juku* were; "I thought that maybe the teachers stayed after school" to hold special classes for students. "I was going to ask the minister how he persuaded [teachers] to do

that, since I know that would be a problem in our unionized system"
(*Mainichi Daily News* 1984, p. 1).

Even as Americans regard Japanese education as an ideal to be
emulated, the American system has been under serious attack not
only by U.S. critics at both ends of the political spectrum but also
by many moderate observers. The following statement will have a
familiar ring:

> The . . . educational system enjoyed a rapid, unprece-
> dented, and continuous expansion of enrollment and finan-
> cial resources during the 1960s, which reached a plateau by
> the early 1970s. But in the mid-1970s it entered a period of
> no expansion and even of decline. The population of the
> kindergarten-age cohort has recently reached its lowest level
> . . . since the World War II "baby boom." . . .
>   While enrollments are decreasing, the schools' financial
> problems are increasing. . . . Before the mid-1970s,
> budget officials regarded education and social welfare . . .
> as "sanctuaries," off limits to budget cuts. Since the mid-
> 1970s, however, the increasing deficit in government
> revenue has made these sanctuaries no longer exempt from
> cuts.

These words were written not by an observer of American education, but by a distinguished Japanese scholar, Kazuyuki Kitamura, in his chapter on Japanese education that appears elsewhere in
this volume. As a rule, both U.S. and Japanese scholars tend to see
their respective educational situations in terms quite different from
those of their counterparts. Both also tend to evaluate their own
system against a highly idealized version of the other. Kitamura's
description of an important element of the current reform crisis in
Japanese education illustrates the supreme irony of the widespread
American adulation of Japanese education at a time when virtually all
Japanese policymakers and a large segment of the lay public perceive their system to be in need of fundamental reform; some Japanese even suggest the reform be modeled on the American system.

In the view of many thoughtful Japanese, the educational
problem in Japan has reached almost crisis proportions. In the 1984
national elections, Prime Minister Yasuhiro Nakasone made educational reform a centerpiece of his successful bid for reelection.
In early December 1983 he unveiled a seven-point plan for reforms
that stirred a lively debate in the press. Among Nakasone's proposals were a careful reevaluation of the 6-3-3 school organization,
instituted during the U.S. Occupation; reducing dependence on

national statistical averages in judging scholastic performance and on guiding high school students' future career prospects; and reforming once more the university entrance examination system.

In a policy speech to the Diet in early February 1984, Nakasone emphasized several nonschool elements of education. He told the lawmakers:

> It seems to me that postwar education has been heavily and exclusively dependent upon the schools, and we have tended to neglect the importance of comprehensive education from the broader perspective encompassing family education, social education and other educational forms, and that this imbalance lies behind the explosive increase in violence in the schools, juvenile delinquency and other contemporary problems. . . . I believe that the time has come to institute sweeping reforms across the entire educational spectrum in preparation for the 21st century. (*Japan Times* 1984c, p. 12)

Nakasone would accomplish this goal by "emphasizing home and social education, promoting respect for the individual, [and] encouraging practical hands-on training outside the classroom," as well as several school-oriented reforms.

Nakasone places such importance on the need for reform that in late 1983 he appointed a private advisory council, the Council on Culture and Education, to advise him on how best to reform the educational system. After several months of intensive study and discussion, the seven-member panel submitted its recommendations in mid-March 1984. It concluded that Japan's "educational system must undergo a major reform so that every Japanese will grow more at ease with himself and able to cope with the future independently" (*Japan Times* 1984a, p. 1). The details of the council's reform recommendations constitute a basic framework for Nakasone's projected reforms.

On March 27, 1984, at Nakasone's initiative, a bill to establish an ad hoc commission on educational reform, under the prime minister's direct control was submitted to the Diet. After lengthy debate on August 7, 1984, that body voted to establish the ad hoc Council on Educational Reform for a three-year period. The creation of this body effectively bypassed the existing Central Council for Education and marked a significant departure from the government's long-standing practice of formulating educational policies recommended by the Central Council, which serves as an advisory body to the minister of education. It also suggested

Nakasone's disenchantment with a body that had been long noted for its moderate approach and general satisfaction with the existing system.

An educational conservative, Michio Okamoto, former president of the prestigious Kyoto University and a longtime personal friend of Nakasone, was named chairman of the council on August 17. In addition, Keio University President Tadao Ishikawa and Industrial Bank of Japan consultant Sohei Nakayama were named vice-chairmen. The remainder of the council's 25 members were appointed shortly thereafter, and the council held its first meeting (significantly, at the prime minister's residence) on September 5, 1984. Most of the council members are well-known men who have had outstanding careers in a wide variety of fields. They include three business leaders, two labor union representatives, a journalist-academic, and a former ambassador. Two women also serve on the council, an author and an essayist. Ages of the council members range from 39 to 78, averaging 59.6. Seventeen of the 25 members, or 68 percent, are graduates of national universities; ten are Tokyo University alumni. Underrepresented are younger people, women, and persons with specialized knowledge and experience in preuniversity education. Many Japanese, and not only left-wing critics, suspect that the council membership has been shaped to recommend to Nakasone those reforms that he has already decided are needed.

Although some observers predict educational reforms of a magnitude reminiscent of the Meiji period or the Occupation years, the results are likely to be far different. A body of this sort, particularly when in existence for a considerable period of time, tends to take on a life of its own and may weigh in with some unexpected recommendations. Regardless of the council's specific recommendations, it seems safe to predict that many of the issues to be addressed will cluster around the theme of liberalizing a system regarded by many as overly rigid. If early press reports are accurate, there will be an attempt by one faction to abolish various restrictions, such as requiring students to attend schools in their own geographic areas, but agreement on the proposed reforms seems problematic at best. More likely to be the subject of some sort of compromise is the future of the 6-3-3 system, modification of the current entrance examination system, the place of moral education in schools, the expansion of nursery schools and kindergartens, and the so-called "Mount Fuji" system of higher education, in which a handful of elite schools, led by Tokyo University, produce nearly all of the society's leaders.

In mid-November 1984, the council issued a progress report calling for an educational system that will "develop people who can be internationally trusted as citizens of an Asian nation" (*Japan Times* 1984b, p. 14) and who possess greater creativity than in the past. Such a result, the report suggests, can be accomplished through greater individualized education and a more concentrated effort to internationalize universities. According to the report, these changes will also result in far greater numbers of foreign students studying in Japanese universities and a greater utilization of foreign professors. Finally, the report suggests that the preuniversity system can be liberalized through a rethinking of both compulsory education laws and the proper role of private elementary and secondary schools. The major organizational change being contemplated is a change from the 6-3-3 to a 4-4-6 school ladder.

It is too early to predict what will finally emerge from the council's deliberations, but the first progress report does provide some insight into the council's thinking on important issues. Its final recommendations will probably reflect the Japanese preference for consensus, be based at least in part on the best the West has to offer, speak to issues broader than those of mere schooling, and shape the course of Japanese education for the next several decades. In this respect the current reform movement in Japan will be consistent with earlier reforms.

THE AMERICAN EXPERIENCE

Americans, unlike the Japanese, are often reluctant to admit to borrowing from others. Yet all of our institutions, even our most individualistic ones, owe something to other peoples in other lands. This is especially true of our educational system. To say this does not negate the idea that, in important ways, U.S. education is different from others; but it emphasizes that underlying our educational uniqueness are basic structures that can be traced to European origins. The case can be made that the history of U.S. education is the history of educational reform and that this reform borrowed extensively from European educational thought, educational practices, and institutional arrangements.

Most early European settlers in North America received a commonplace traditional education in England, the Netherlands, France, or other European countries in which they originated. When they established schools in the New World, they modeled them along lines familiar to themselves. Moreover, as Bernard Bailyn has pointed out in his classic study *Education in the Forming of Ameri-*

can Society; "The forms of education assumed by the first generation of settlers in America were a direct inheritance from the medieval past" (1960, p. 15). Although it is true that the early American settlers' schools were modified to reflect their new environment, the schools' intellectual underpinnings remained European. Not the least of these underpinnings was a strong reliance on the educational thought of such classical thinkers as Plato, Aristotle, Luther, and Calvin—all of whom had made well-known pronouncements on education. The Puritans who came to build "a city upon a hill" institutionalized their values in education. As Clarence Karier (1967, p. 2) has written, they "influenced New England's educational thought, and New England, in turn, significantly influenced the educational history of America."

Although significant differences exist between American and English educational institutions, it was initially the English who shaped American higher education. For example, the sons of Emmanuel and other colleges of Cambridge University were responsible for founding Harvard (1636), among other early colonial colleges. The English sovereigns William and Mary gave their name to another colonial institution and signed its charter. Then followed the founding of Yale and other colleges, all with English antecedents. In these institutions English traditions in curriculum, governance, and methodology dominated until the outbreak of the American Revolution.

The early British colonists also brought with them the dame school, the village reading and writing school, various types of private venture schools, the Latin grammar school, the pauper or charity school, and apprenticeship education for orphans and the poor. One of the most interesting borrowings, the so-called monitorial school based on the method of Joseph Lancaster, has contemporary reverberations in the practice of "peer teaching." In this system older pupils taught younger ones under the close supervision of a master.

This English heritage, however, must not prevent us from acknowledging the important contributions made by others—such as the Scots, Swedes, Dutch, French, and Germans—to American educational history. After the Revolutionary War and a general fall from grace of English ideas, French intellectual thought vied for influence. The great educational theorist of the era was Thomas Jefferson, whose thought reflected French educational views. It was Jefferson who in 1800 asked the French scholar and statesman Pierre Samuel Du Pont de Nemours, then living in American exile, to devise a national plan for education in the United States. The resulting plan, "the first major proposal for a national system of education in the United States prepared by a foreign educational consultant" (Fraser and Brickman 1968, p. 280), was never implemented, but it did contribute to the educational ferment of the time. With the downfall of Napoleon, however, French influence declined and was replaced by a growing interest in German, especially Prussian, educational models.

Numerous European educational theorists have played a crucial role in the development of American educational thought over the past 200 years, including Jean Jacques Rousseau (1712-78), who revealed the importance of childhood as a separate stage in life and asserted that the learning of children should be harmonious with their physical and mental development; Friedrich Froebel (1782-1852), who greatly influenced John Dewey's views of guided self-activity for children; Johann Heinrich Pestalozzi (1746-1827), who demonstrated the use of direct sense experiences in learning and developed his famous "object lessons"; Phillip Emmanuel von Fellenberg (1771-1844), whose institute at Hofwyl put Pestalozzian principles into practice; and Johann Friedrich Herbart (1776-1841), whose work laid the foundation for those advocating a science of education. The American disciples of these and other European educational theorists included such important figures as Calvin Stowe, Henry Barnard, Horace Mann, William Torrey Harris, and G. Stanley Hall, who along with many others helped to shape the contours of contemporary American education.

An interesting distinction exists between educational theories, such as those espoused by the thinkers mentioned above, and educational practices. Nevertheless, even when educational practices diverge from the details of theoretical prescription, they are still indebted to the original thought.

During much of the nineteenth century the education of an American gentleman was not complete without a period of study at a German university or at least a "grand tour" of the Old World. American travelers to Europe were favorably impressed with the work of European reformers and returned home to advocate similar reforms. Archibald Murphy, a North Carolinian, submitted a description of his observations of European education to his state legislature as early as 1817. In 1834 a report by Victor Cousin, describing Prussian education for the French government, was published in New York and enjoyed great popularity. Three years later Calvin Stowe's report to the Ohio legislature praising Prussian education gained wide currency in the United States. Perhaps the most important American reformer to advocate emulating the Prussian model of education was Horace Mann, "father of the common school." If Prussian education was superior—and Mann was convinced that it was—the United States must learn from it. He argued that if "the human faculties are substantially the same all over the world . . . the best means for their development and growth in one place, must be substantially the best for their development and growth everywhere" (Messerli 1972, p. 407).

The list of prominent Americans who studied in Germany during the nineteenth century is lengthy; and as they returned to the United States and took academic posts in strategically important American institutions, the influence of German education, especially their universities, was instrumental in reshaping American ideas about education. Indeed, the history of U.S. higher education is a textbook illustration of the interaction between European ideas and the American environment. Although the earliest American colleges, based on the English model, stressed undergraduate liberal education, the modern American university is a hybrid of this earlier structure and the German research university.

The German principles of *Lehrfreiheit* and *Lernfreiheit*—the freedom to teach and the freedom to learn—were embraced by American academics. By the latter part of the nineteenth century, research became the paramount feature of American graduate education, and increasingly the doctorate became a prerequisite for appointment to graduate faculties. New instructional methods, especially the seminar, became the hallmark of graduate-level teaching. The German university model of research and scholarship found fertile ground in nineteenth-century America.

Although German influence was preeminent during that period, other Europeans also played an important role in shaping American education. Among French contributors to American educational practice Alfred Binet is particularly noteworthy. His work on the determination of individual differences and the identification of the so-called "subnormal" child has been important in the development of both the testing movement and special education. The work of the Austrian Sigmund Freud also deserves mention for its influence on some of the important forms of alternative education during the last 60 years. Russian influence on American education should not be overlooked. Ivan Pavlov was instrumental in the development of American psychological behaviorism. American industrial arts education owes a debt of gratitude to Victor Della Vos, another Russian, whose shopwork courses inspired Calvin Woodward to open the St. Louis Manual Training School in 1890. The "Russian system" as modified by Woodward became the standard industrial arts shop course in American education for several decades. Later the Swedish *sloyd* (manual training) approach, developed by Otto Salmon in Stockholm, became popular in the United States; and the Danish folk, or people's, high schools, with their rural-oriented, liberal education for young adults, enjoyed great popularity and success in the American Midwest.

The American educational ferment of the early twentieth century that culminated in the progressive education movement was not entirely a homegrown phenomenon. The ideas of the Europeans Emile Durkheim, Herbert Spencer, Charles Darwin, Sigmund Freud, Maria Montessori, and Rudolf Steiner, among others, played an important role in helping to shape this multifaceted movement. Although American education since World War II has been a net exporter of educational ideas and practices, an important segment of the U.S. educational community has drawn intellectual sustenance from European models. Recent critics of U.S. education have advocated a return to a European style of education as a remedy for perceived excesses and failings. After the Soviets launched *Sputnik* in 1957, such books as *Why Johnny Can't Read, Ivan Can,* and *Swiss Schools and Ours* were popular among people concerned about the quality of U.S. public schools. Other critics having different ideological persuasions advocated the ideas of Jean Piaget, A. S. Neil, Basil Bernstein, Ivan Illich, and Paulo Friere. There is little doubt that the American student rebellions of the 1960s, which resulted in several reforms, were influenced at least in part by similar uprisings in Europe.

The Current Crisis in U.S. Education

Educational reform is a common phenomenon in American life. Indeed, historically it has been regarded as an appropriate response to an enormous range of problems. Whether the problem be unsafe drivers, teenage pregnancies, or drug or alcohol abuse, Americans tend to seek solutions in new curricula. This response is part of a deeply rooted faith in education that dates from colonial New England; it is reflected in reform movements that culminated in the establishment of the common school, the emergence of land-grant universities, and the philosophy of John Dewey.

Today Americans have a deep concern that somehow our educational system is responsible at least in part for our recent economic decline in relation to Japan. The current rhetoric of reform is reminiscent of that which followed *Sputnik*. At that time it was necessary to reform our schools so that we could "catch up with the Russians" and protect our national security. Now it is necessary to "catch up with the Japanese" to protect our economy. As the French say, "plus ça change, plus c'est la même chose."

Educational reform in the United States tends to occur in cycles, and a common characteristic of reform movements has been their basic optimism. No matter how bad the public schools are perceived to be at a given time, the view prevails that they can be reformed to achieve great political, economic, or social goals. In the eighteenth century, reformers and politicians viewed public education as a tool for political and social integration and the fashioning of democratic values. In the nineteenth century, public education was believed to be the institution that would "Americanize" immigrants coming to our shores while preparing them for success in a newly industrializing society. Thirty years ago schools were seen as weapons in the cold war and also as a remedy for the cancer of racism in the body politic.

Does the current reform movement have the same optimistic spirit? The answer is no. Whereas in the past the public schools and the teachers were seen as helping the young to fulfill their dreams, today they are widely perceived to be responsible for many of our national problems. The public school is now regarded as an intellectual wasteland in which both incompetent teachers and real danger lurk.

There is no longer a great social vision in our rhetoric about public education. Instead we are obsessed with the goal of academic achievement ("excellence") and the specter of two decades of declining test scores. The rhetoric emphasizes the need to compete with the Soviets militarily and the Japanese economically. On the local level we are inundated with legislation to lengthen the school year, strengthen graduation requirements, stiffen grading practices, and in general make discipline, order, mathematics, and science the centerpiece of the educational process. Little attention is paid in the current rhetoric to education's role in fostering political and social justice; to citizenship education, which prepares the young to protect their freedom; or to the utopian visions that have energized the society from the days when Thomas Jefferson spoke of "eternal hostility against every form of tyranny over the mind of man."

More than two dozen national reports on educational reform have been issued since April 1983. Of these the most influential is *A Nation at Risk: The Imperative for Educational Reform* (1983) commissioned by then Secretary of Education Terrel Bell. Since its release on April 26, 1983, well over a half-million copies have been distributed, and virtually every influential newspaper and news journal in the United States have carried extended excerpts of the report and related news stories. For example, a Department of Education review of 45 newspapers identified more than 700 articles relating to *A Nation at Risk* in the first four months after its release.

The landmark study calls for restoring traditional values, more stringent graduation requirements, more time devoted to teaching and learning, a longer school year, various drastic actions to raise the intellectual caliber of teachers, and recognition of mathematics and science as key subjects that all students need to have a rudimentary understanding of. In keeping with the Reagan administration's wish to limit the federal role in education, *A Nation at Risk* assigns primary responsibility for financing and administering the proposed reforms to local and state officials.

In May 1984, one year after *A Nation at Risk* was published, the federal government issued a second report, *A Nation Responds*, which details the various initiatives taken by state and local education agencies in response to the initial study. In April 1984 the Department of Education identified 275 state-level task forces that were working on educational reform proposals; it reported that most governors' "state of the state" messages in 1984 emphasized the theme of excellence in education and that improved textbooks, new career ladders, performance-based salary schedules, and tougher graduation requirements were under review in a majority of states. The November 1984 elections swept many candidates into office on the basis of their reform rhetoric.

At the higher education level there has been a surge of activity aimed at reforming education programs for teachers, involving schools and universities in partnership programs, raising university entrance requirements by reinstituting foreign-language prerequisites for admission, and similar measures. The business community has shown a quickening of interest in working with schools to improve educational achievement. For example, 11 major corporations have agreed to work with schools in the District of Columbia to establish a management institute for assisting principals and administrators to improve their management skills; and the California Business Roundtable commissioned its own study of how to improve that state's schools and then vigorously supported it in the political arena.

One of the most interesting and potentially useful sets of recommendations is Linda Darling-Hammond's *Beyond the Commission Reports: The Coming Crisis in Teaching*, published in July 1984 by the Rand Corporation. In the words of its author, the report "demonstrates that dramatic changes in our nation's teaching force will soon lead to serious shortages of qualified teachers unless policies that restructure the teaching force are pursued. Until teaching becomes a more attractive career alternative the problems of attracting and retaining talented teachers will undermine the success of other reforms intended to upgrade educational programs and curricula"

(p. vi). The facts uncovered by the study are that older teachers are retiring in increasing numbers through reaching normal retirement age, "burnout," or finding that early retirement is an attractive option for other reasons. At the same time many young graduates who have been educated to become teachers are finding alternative occupations more attractive and either never enter teaching or leave quickly. Another element in this equation has been the rapid opening of previously closed career opportunities for young women. Whereas in the past talented young women realistically could enter only teaching, nursing, or social work, they now have a much wider set of options. These ambitious women are increasingly entering law, medicine, business, engineering, and other more prestigious and lucrative fields.

The rhetoric of the current American reform movement has been strangely muted about the narrowness of the movement's vision. The question of whether the movement's constricted and essentially pessimistic view of the future is worthy of the American people has yet to be debated. Do we really want a society in which the values of conformity, order, discipline, and technological expertise rule?

REFORM IN JAPAN AND THE UNITED STATES

Educational systems do not exist in a vacuum. They are natural outgrowths of a nation's history, culture, economics, and politics. As a result, one must be cautious in comparing the systems or the processes through which individual systems evolved. Few countries, and none in the industrialized world, are as fundamentally different as Japan and the United States. Nevertheless, both have adopted elements of foreign educational thought and practice that, on balance, have served them well in their drive for economic development and prosperity. The details of this more or less common experience, however, occurred in very different contexts. Much of the Japanese borrowing was done under great pressure. During the Meiji period the Japanese believed that they had little choice in accepting reform from the West if they wished to protect their country from the kind of partition that China had suffered. During the Occupation they had even less choice, for Japan lay prostrate before the U.S. conqueror. Cooperation in reforming their institutions was their only alternative until Japan regained its sovereignty, and even then its national security was dependent on the American nuclear umbrella.

Other differences, however, place the two nation's reform movements in stark contrast. First, the United States is a large country, having significant regional and sectional differences. The resources available to a particular school are primarily a function of the affluence of the local community. A child fortunate enough to be born in Beverly Hills or Scarsdale will receive a better education than one born in a small town in Mississippi or on an Indian reservation in Arizona. Japan, on the other hand, is a much smaller country, with a land area approximately the size of California. The amount of resources allocated to each school in Japan depends less on local conditions than in the United States because education is a national rather than a local responsibility.

Second, the Japanese centralized system, with a Ministry of Education and a national curriculum, could not exist in the United States. Not only does our federal system preclude such an arrangement but there is also a deep-seated hostility in the American character toward federal control of education.

Third, the United States is a highly pluralistic society—racially, ethnically, linguistically, religiously, and socially—whereas Japan is one of the most homogeneous societies in the world. U.S. demographic trends suggest a "browning" of America in the twenty-first century as the proportion of Hispanics grows. In addition, the United States is enriched by increasing numbers of immigrants from South Korea, Japan, the Philippines, Indochina, Hong Kong, and elsewhere in Asia. This heterogeneity has produced linguistic and cultural problems, such as the need for bilingual and multicultural education, that are unknown in Japan. Furthermore, over the past decade there has been a religious revival in the United States; and some groups, particularly religious fundamentalists, want the public schools to promulgate their religious and cultural values. Japanese society is not divided by these kinds of conflicts.

Whatever reforms are decided upon in Japan will be implemented on a nationwide basis, through the centralized organ of the Ministry of Education. In the United States the political reality is that educational reform is a local, or at best a state, responsibility and therefore will be piecemeal and different in character, depending on the locality.

Despite these differences, however, both Japan and the United States share the common desire to prepare themselves for the challenges of the twenty-first century. Both recognize that their continued prosperity and security depend on how well they meet this challenge. In that respect these two allies of the past 40 years are rivals as well. It behooves U.S. educators and policymakers to take the Japanese seriously and to analyze their educational reform efforts. Although we can transplant few elements of reform directly from the Japanese model, we can understand our own system much more clearly if we examine it in the context of Japan's success.

NOTE

1. Six years of elementary school, three years of lower secondary school, and three years of upper secondary school.

REFERENCES

Bailyn, Bernard. 1960. *Education in the Forming of American Society*. Chapel Hill: University of North Carolina.

Beasley, William G. 1972. *The Meiji Restoration*. Stanford, Calif.: Stanford University Press.

Darling-Hammond, Linda. 1984. *Beyond the Commission Reports: The Coming Crisis in Teaching*. Santa Monica, Calif.: Rand.

Fraser, Stewart E., and William W. Brickman, eds. 1968. *A History of International and Comparative Education: Nineteenth-Century Documents*. Chicago: Scott, Foresman.

Fukuzawa, Yukichi. 1969. *An Encouragement of Learning*. Translated by David A. Dilworth and Umeyo Hirano. Tokyo: Sophia University Press.

Japan Times. 1984a. "Advisory Body Urges Diversified, Less Restrictive School System." March 23, p. 1.

____. 1984b. "Debates on Education." November 16, p. 14.

____. 1984c. "Text of the Prime Minister's Policy Speech." February 7, p. 12.

Jones, Hazel J. 1980. *Live Machines: Hired Foreigners and Meiji Japan*. Vancouver: University of British Columbia Press.

Karier, Clarence J. 1967. *Man, Society, and Education*. Chicago: Scott, Foresman.

Mainichi Daily News. 1984. "US Educ. Sec. Envies Juku." September 13, p. 1.

Messerli, Jonathan. 1972. *Horace Mann: A Biography.* New York: Knopf.

National Commission on Excellence in Education. 1983. *A Nation at Risk: The Imperative for Educational Reform.* Washington, D.C.: U.S. Government Printing Office.

National Institute for Educational Research (NIER). 1983. *National Institute for Educational Research in Japan: A Brief Outline.* Tokyo, March.

Reischauer, Edwin O., and John K. Fairbank. 1960. *East Asia: The Great Tradition.* Boston: Houghton Mifflin.

Sansom, Sir George B. 1962. *Japan: A Short Cultural History.* New York: Appleton-Century-Crofts.

United States. Department of Education. 1984. *The Nation Responds: Recent Efforts to Improve Education.* Washington, D.C.: U.S. Government Printing Office.

Vogel, Ezra. 1979. *Japan as No. 1: Lessons for America.* Cambridge, Mass.: Harvard University Press.

2
EDUCATIONAL CRISIS IN JAPAN
Ikuo Amano

During its first 100 years modern Japan experienced rapid and constant growth. The society was mobile and the system of socioeconomic stratification was open. In this rapidly changing society people could nurture their aspirations for upward social mobility. The apparently reasonable goal of "success in life" mobilized the energies of each succeeding generation. Although both the economic and educational systems had highly hierarchical structures, they were flexible and offered opportunities for all. In the process of rapid growth, as the number of newcomers to these two systems steadily increased, a fairly high level of competition was maintained among the various enterprises and between different schools and universities. Especially after World War II, Japan succeeded in creating an exceptionally egalitarian and mobile society as a result of the drastic reforms of its economic and educational systems imposed by the Occupation Forces. The rapid economic growth in the 1960s and 1970s was both a product of the Occupation's revolutionary reforms and a means for sustaining them.

THE CRISIS OF ASPIRATIONS

Recently, however, the situation has started to change. Since the middle of the 1970s, Japan's economic growth rate, like that of other industrialized countries, has stagnated. Enrollments in secondary and higher education also reached a saturation level. The age of seemingly endless rapid growth of the Japanese economy and educational system vanished (see Chapter 8). In recent years Japanese society has retained its egalitarian characteristics, but its social and economic mobility seems to be disappearing. The tightening stratification within the educational and economic systems is an important manifestation of the ongoing changes.

The tendency toward increased stratification is especially evident in the relationship between secondary and higher education. The school hierarchies within both of these educational levels are strengthening, as is the tendency for the position attained in lower high schools to determine students' place in the higher level. The opportunity for admission to the top universities is now virtually monopolized by graduates from the top high schools.

An increasingly rigid hierarchy is also developing between the educational and economic systems. Within the economic sphere each group of occupations, industries, and companies has its own hierarchy, and where individuals end up in those hierarchies is determined increasingly by the universities they attended. To secure even a clerical job in a big company of a prestigious industry, it is becoming more and more important to be admitted to a top-ranking university.

The "structuration" within and between the Japanese educational and economic systems has begun to influence the aspirations and ambitions of young people. Most children and youths still participate in the fierce competition for "success" that starts at the beginning of the educational cycle. But the number of those who are not willing to compete and who rebel against the system is also increasing. If there is any crisis in Japanese education and society, it may be the crisis of aspiration originating in their structuration (Giddens 1973). To understand the pattern of structuration in contemporary Japanese society, it is necessary to look at recent developments in the economic system and in secondary and higher education.

THE EMPLOYMENT SYSTEM

It is through the interactions of the three systems—the economic system and the secondary and higher education systems—that the tendency of mutually reinforcing structuration is emerging. It can be argued, however, that the economic system has the most influence. Young people are acutely conscious of the career implications of their educational performance and placement. Thus changes that take place in the economy, and especially in the way that major employers recruit young workers, have a profound influence on the way young people and those who advise them approach available educational opportunities.

In Chapter 10 of this book, Morikazu Ushiogi reviews postwar trends in the Japanese employment system. There he observes that young people find the large companies and the government to be the most desirable employers. Within the large companies, white-collar work is more highly esteemed than blue-collar work. Smaller companies follow in prestige.

In the immediate postwar period, high school graduates had a reasonable chance of obtaining white-collar jobs in large companies. But since then that likelihood has steadily declined, so that by 1973 only 38 percent of all high school graduates seeking jobs were able to find clerical jobs and by 1983 the proportion had decreased to 30 percent. For male graduates, the proportions were 14 and 9 percent in the respective years.

For both high school and university graduates, the difference of job opportunity is strongly influenced by the school or university from which they graduate. As for the high school graduates, now it is only those from the most selective and prestigious schools who can find clerical jobs. The job market for high school graduates is well organized and segmented by individual schools and companies. Each high school usually has a specific group of several scores of companies that are accustomed to accepting its graduates. On the other side of the market, each company makes efforts to maintain a stable relationship in recruitment with a specific group of high schools. In such a structured market situation, the status of a high school within its local hierarchy exerts a decisive influence on its graduates' job opportunities. Ironically, because commercial high schools are usually ranked toward the bottom of their local hierarchies, virtually all of their graduates are destined for blue-collar work.

In the case of the university graduates, job-market structuration is less blatant than that of high school graduates. As a formal policy the major companies open their doors to all university graduates. But in practice they give priority to graduates of the most selective universities. The bigger the company, the more likely it is to interview and hire graduates from the most selective university group (see Tables 2.1 and 2.2). Thus high school graduates who want the most desirable jobs strive to get into the most selective universities.

Table 2.1   University type of graduates who were invited to apply for employment, by size of company and type of university, Japan, 1983 (% distribution)

Type of University

Company size (number of employees)	National and public universities			Private universities			
	I	II	III	I	II	III	Total
1-99	9.1	1.5	7.6	3.0	42.4	36.4	100.0
100-499	4.4	9.0	6.4	2.9	54.7	22.6	100.0
500-999	8.9	23.2	10.3	1.8	42.0	13.8	100.0
1,000-4,999	26.9	27.6	4.7	6.3	16.9	14.3	100.0
5,000+	56.2	18.8	4.7	6.3	7.8	6.2	100.0
Total	15.8	17.9	7.7	3.9	36.7	18.0	100.0

Source: Tominaga (1984, p. 170).
Note: Type I is most selective, Type III least selective

Table 2.2   Companies where university graduates obtained employment, by type of university, Japan, 1983 (% distribution)

University type	Size of company (number of employees)						
	1-99	100-499	500-999	1000-4,999	5,000+	Civil service	Total
National and public							
I	3.1	7.0	5.6	23.9	46.4	14.0	100.0
II	5.8	13.1	8.4	24.9	33.5	14.3	100.0
III	8.6	19.6	10.9	25.4	21.5	14.0	100.0
Private							
I	3.0	7.1	7.2	34.1	43.9	4.7	100.0
II	6.5	21.2	13.8	30.8	16.5	11.2	100.0
III	15.4	28.9	12.6	18.3	8.7	16.1	100.0

Source: Amano (1984c, p. 56).
Note: Type I is most selective, Type III least selective.

Over the course of the postwar period, the economic condition of medium-sized and small enterprises has improved, and therefore the wage differential between large and small companies has declined. Because of this, young people are no longer as insistent as before on finding employment in the large companies and, it could be reasoned, have less need to seek degrees from the most prestigious universities. But, in fact, the competition for admission to the top universities has not abated. In Japanese society, where social status is so important, the university degree or credential seems to have become a symbol of personal achievement, valuable in and of itself. As the economic status of adults in different social positions has become more equal, the value ascribed to educational credentials seems to have risen. Thus the demand for entry to prestigious high schools and universities, which was once motivated primarily by economic considerations, is now strongly reinforced by other motives.

SECONDARY EDUCATION

Secondary education in pre-World War II Japan comprised three types of secondary schools: middle schools for boys, girls' high schools, and vocational schools. Those schools, most of which were five-year institutions, received the graduates of the six-year compulsory primary schools. After World War II that diversified system was drastically changed. Secondary education was divided into upper and lower stages. The lower stage consisted of *chugakko* (middle schools), which became three-year institutions and, along with the six-year primary schools, were made compulsory. The new three-year senior secondary schools, called *kotogakko* (higher schools), were created by consolidating the different types of prewar secondary schools.

The new upper secondary schools, modeled on the American high school, were created in accordance with three basic guidelines established by the Occupation Forces: coeducation; comprehensive curricula, including academic and vocational courses; and small school districts (that is, one high school in each school district). Although the original planners sought to develop a high school system in accordance with these principles, they encountered three major obstacles: the coexistence of public and private schools in the same districts; the impracticality of integrating vocational and academic courses in all high schools; and the difficulty of altering some district boundaries so as to include only one public high school.

Initially the planners tried to conform to the guidelines, with the result that more than half of the school districts had only one high school (so-called "small" districts). But the final authority for establishing school districts lay then, as now, with local governments, and over time they tended to expand their districts. By 1983 there were 542 school districts throughout Japan, and only 158 had one school in them. In contrast, 69 of the districts had ten or more academic high schools.

In organizing the school system, educational administrators also strayed from the model. Today only 28 percent of all high schools offer both vocational and academic courses, whereas 49 percent specialize exclusively in academic subjects and the remaining 23 percent emphasize vocational subjects.

The chief reason why the Occupation's plan proved impractical, however, was the imbalance between the number of upper secondary school aspirants and the number of actual places. To ensure fairness in admissions, individual schools resorted to entrance examinations. Over time, owing to the exams, a hierarchy emerged among high schools.

The greatest aberration in this selective system has been the existence of private high schools specializing in preparatory education for students planning to take college entrance examinations. Overall, the social prestige of private schools has been lower than that of the public schools. But, among the nearly 1,300 private high schools, 50 to 100 schools became well known because of their high rates of admission to the prestigious and selective universities. Many of those private schools, which resemble the American preparatory school, are six-year institutions that combine the lower and upper levels of secondary education in a common course. By combining the two levels, they are able to complete the six-year regular course within five years, leaving the remaining year for intensive preparation for the university entrance examination.

Currently 351 high schools, including 74 private schools, send graduates to the University of Tokyo, which is the most selective university in Japan. But the top 20 high schools, those sending the largest number of entrants to the University of Tokyo, are private schools. Most of these private "prep" schools are located in metropolitan areas, and in those areas the children who seek admission to them have to start preparing for the schools' entrance examinations when they are in the fourth or fifth grade of primary school. Thus these schools engender competition in the educational system at an early stage.

Another problem in the selection system for upper level secondary education is related to vocational high schools. The vocational secondary schools have existed for nearly a century and have played an important role in fostering a Japanese middle class. In recent years, however, as secondary education became nearly universal and college enrollments increased, vocational schools lost their social prestige. Today, therefore, most middle school graduates, especially those with high scholastic ability, try to get into the academic high schools. The vocational high schools are left with students who dislike study and have received low grades. Consequently, many vocational high schools have to make great effort to maintain order within their classrooms, to motivate their students to learn, and to prevent them from dropping out.

A third problem has arisen in the public general high schools, which admit the majority of middle school graduates. In many Japanese high school districts there are more than ten academic high schools. The public tends to perceive the schools as forming a hierarchy in which the position of each is based on its academic tradition, its selectivity in admitting entrants, the proportion of its graduates who are admitted to college, and the number of its graduates who are admitted to the most prestigious universities. Each high school selects entrants solely on the basis of their scholastic ability as determined by their middle school grade averages and their scores on the entrance examinations. The children are expected both to study hard every day in school and to prepare for the entrance examinations. The number of students who attend *juku* (cram schools) after formal school hours increases suddenly when they become ninth graders; in metropolitan areas the proportion exceeds 50 percent. To find where they stand, ninth graders take repeated rounds of trial examinations conducted by private examination companies. The results of the examinations give the students a clear idea of their performance in relation to other students who are aspiring to enter the same schools.

In each prefecture a single entrance examination is prepared each year for use in assigning students to public high schools. Students are permitted to choose only one public high school as their preferred school. So as not to produce *rōnin* (students who fail the entrance examination for their designated school), the middle school teachers are obliged to provide guidance to their students. To maximize placement, in providing guidance the teachers pay more attention to the scholastic ability of their students than to the students' choices or aspirations. As the result, it is rare that the ratio of applicants to entrants surpasses 1.1 even at the most desired public high schools. However, between high schools a clear division exists based on the scholastic ability of the entrants. This phenomenon, called "cutting the student population in slices," provides each high

school with a student body homogeneous in its academic ability.
"Cutting in slices" makes it easier to teach the homogeneous student
body of each school, but at high schools located at the bottom of the
scholastic hierarchy, it inevitably results in an excessive concentra-
tion of uninterested attendants.

In Table 2.3 we illustrate how slicing works in the Tokyo metropolitan area. Schools are arrayed down the table in terms of degree
of selectivity. S (superior) schools receive all of their students from
the top 10 percent of all those tested in their district. At C2 (bottom-
ranking) schools, all of the students are from the bottom quartile.
Nine of the 209 schools in the Tokyo metropolitan area are suffi-
ciently selective to justify the superior rating, and 44 schools are in
the C2 group (Table 2.3). More than half of all vocational schools
are in the bottom category. The Tokyo district is illustrative of the
national pattern.

Table 2.3   Distribution of public high schools in the Tokyo metropolitan
                area, by quality level

Percentile scores required on pretest for admission	School group	Type of school		
		General academic	Vocational	Total
70+	S	9		9
67-69	A1	14		14
62-66	A2	22		22
57-61	B1	30	4	34
52-56	B2	28	5	33
47-51	C1	33	20	53
42-46	C2	10	34	44
Total		146	63	209

Source: Tokyoto Kinken Koko Jyuken Annai (1984).

It is not surprising that such a selection system exerts strong
psychological pressure on middle school students. According to a
recent survey, more than 70 percent of all ninth graders experienced
anxiety that they might fail the entrance examination and would not
be able to find a high school to admit them (Fukaya 1983, p. 164).
In another survey 67 percent of all ninth graders indicated a strong
desire "to forget everything related to the entrance examination"

(Fukaya 1983, p. 166). Owing to the pressures of the selection system, middle school students become extremely grade-conscious, and their grades have a strong relationship to their sense of self-respect. A number of studies have shown that a greater percentage of children with lower grades than of those with higher ones feel unhappy and that many children believe their school records have a crucial effect on their future careers. The admission system of the high schools thus has a strong "cooling-out" effect on the ambitions and aspirations of Japanese children.

The high school curriculum in Japan is precisely defined by the Ministry of Education, Science, and Culture. Despite the big differences in the scholastic standards of students at different high schools, each high school teaches virtually the same content and level of curriculum. Most of the subjects are obligatory, and although there are a few elective subjects, the scope of choice permitted to the students is narrow. Not all students who study the common curriculum can attain the same level of achievement. On the one hand, students at the prep-type private secondary schools master the six-year regular curriculum in less than five years. On the other, students at the general public high schools toward the bottom of the scholastic hierarchy learn less than half of the standard curriculum. Nevertheless, Japanese custom permits even those students who master only half of the curriculum to graduate at the end of the standard three-year period.

The social pressure to keep children within the school system is extremely high in Japan. Parents make great efforts to send their children to high school and to keep them there, and teachers are expected to matriculate the pupils after three years with a minimum incidence of repetition and dropout. Japan has an exceedingly homogeneous society, and its universal upper secondary education means that virtually everyone graduates from high school. The public was surprised, therefore, when in the spring of 1984 newspapers and newscasters reported that the dropout rate among high school students had surpassed 3 percent for the first time. Those without high school diplomas suffer many social handicaps, including difficulties in employment and marriage.

HIGHER EDUCATION

In prewar Japan the higher educational system was also composed of several types of institutions: universities, higher schools (*kotogakko*), colleges (*senmongakko*), technical colleges (*jitsugyo senmongakko*), and normal schools (*shihangakko*). Among them only the universities, numbering fewer than 50, were given legal sanction for autonomy and degree granting. Among the universities, seven Imperial universities enjoyed the most privileged and distinguished status. Higher schools were public three-year institutions that admitted middle school graduates and offered a liberal arts type of education. Most of the higher school graduates entered the national universities, in particular the Imperial universities. At the private universities, special preparatory courses were offered that had the same function as the public higher schools. Colleges were also three-year institutions that admitted middle school graduates. Those that taught engineering, agriculture, and commerce were the technical colleges. The colleges accounted for more than two-thirds of the total number of higher education graduates (Amano 1979).

After World War II these diversified institutions of higher education were reorganized and integrated into new four-year universities. Some of the new universities were allowed to have five-year graduate schools (two-year master's, and three-year doctoral degree programs). After less than ten months of preparation, the drastic reform plan was implemented in April 1949. By 1950 there were 201 "new" universities, or four times the number recognized prior to the war. Most of the former higher schools, colleges, and normal schools were promoted to the status of universities without enough preparation. The accelerated launching of these new universities, at a time when Japan was suffering from economic difficulties and sociopolitical confusion, resulted in great variations in quality. The new universities inherited not only campuses and staff but also the traditions, social functions, and social prestige of the former institutions that they succeeded and were integrated into. Thus the new university system was destined to have an extremely hierarchical structure from its beginning.

The national institutions experienced the most drastic changes. Under the prewar system, various types of national institutions of higher education were spread across the nation. Only the seven former Imperial universities, which were located in metropolitan areas, had a full array of faculties. The Occupation Forces ordered the lesser institutions in each prefecture to combine with each other to form comprehensive "local" national universities. Thus in 1949 every prefecture acquired at least one multifaculty national university. It can easily be appreciated that these new national universities, composed of several institutions with their respective traditions and their separate locations, encountered many difficulties in attaining real integration as universities. The Ministry of Education was reluctant even to grant degree-granting authority to them. Even within the national sector, therefore, there emerged a clear hierarchical structure, with the former Imperial universities at the top and these new institutions arrayed below.

In contrast to the older universities of the prewar period, which offered three years of professional education to students who had finished three years of general (or liberal) education in the higher schools, the new universities provided two years of general education followed by two years of professional education. The period of both professional and general education was contracted. The basic idea of the postwar university reform was to create an American type of undergraduate educational system emphasizing liberal arts, while leaving professional training to the graduate level. The new Japanese universities, however, were not organized in conformity with the American idea. Compromising with Japanese tradition, they included both general and professional training within the undergraduate course, and thus they did not promote the graduate or professional schools. The Japanese university born after the reform had quite a different structure from its American model.

By integrating the diversified old institutions into new four-year universities and creating an egalitarian system of higher education, the reformers expected, on the basis of American experience, that free competition among the new universities would occur and that the status or rank of each within the hierarchy would be changeable. But the expected competition did not take place, for several reasons.

First, competition among the universities in raising funds was very limited. Most of the government funds supplied to each university were allocated according to a fixed standard. Only a small portion of research money was competitively distributed. As Japan did not have a strong tradition of philanthropy, competition for private donations to the universities did not develop. The majority of the private universities were obliged to depend on tuition fees paid by students as virtually their sole source of income. In 1970 the government started a subsidy system for private universities. For a while it enabled several of the private institutions to improve their situations significantly. However, the subsidy that once covered nearly one-third of the private universities' annual expenditures is currently decreasing because of the government's financial crisis. The private universities are often called "one-third universities" because their amenities, such as the teacher-student ratio and current expenditures per student, are barely one-third of those of the national universities (see Table 2.4).

Table 2.4   Educational conditions in national public universities and
             private universities, Japan (recent years)

Condition	National public universities	Private universities
Expenditures per student (1000)	220.0	87.9
Building area per student (m^2)	31.3	13.0
Campus area per student (m^2)	111.8	68.8
Students per full-time teaching staff member	8.1	25.4

Source: *Nippon Shiritsu Daigaku Renmei* (1984, p. 16).

Second, the opportunity for mobility among university professors was limited. Most of the older universities had the custom
of "in-breeding" (Shimbori 1984). Thus it was difficult for a university to improve its status within the hierarchy by recruiting high-
quality academic staff.

Moreover, the majority of universities did not have a system for
accepting transfer students. Students who wanted to move to
another university were asked to take the entrance examination
again. Only in entering a university could students enjoy free competition. Even in those graduate schools that opened their doors to
graduates of other universities, "outsiders" accounted for less than
20 percent of the student body. These conditions exist today.

In such a situation the status of each university is determined
primarily by its history and tradition as an institution of higher education, by its selection of entrants, and by the job opportunities
available to its graduates. The first of these three factors is impossible to change, and so the universities use the second and the third in
competing for improved status. How to recruit more students with
higher scholastic ability and how to place more students in the top-
ranking companies are concerns that cause the greatest competition
among Japanese universities. And as top-ranking companies tend to
recruit graduates of the more selective universities, the two aspects
of competition are interrelated.

As of 1984 there were 457 universities in Japan—95 national,
34 public, and 328 private. Twenty-four percent of university students were enrolled in national, 3 percent in public, and 73 percent
in private universities.

Entrants are usually selected on the basis of their academic ability, and most universities use scores on their own entrance examina-

tions for selection purposes. But the number of universities that admit students mainly on the basis of recommendations from high schools is increasing, especially in the private sector. Nearly 20 percent of the students admitted to private universities in 1984 were selected through this recommendation system (Kuroha 1984, p. 137). The graduation ratio of Japanese university students is very high, nearly 75 percent of entrants graduating in the usual four years and 87 percent ultimately graduating.

A critical function of Japanese universities is career placement, because employers restrict their own recruitment to new university graduates. Starting their job hunting while they are still in school, students are employed immediately after graduation. This practice makes it extremely difficult to find a job after graduation. Many students who cannot find jobs before they graduate choose to stay at the university one more year rather than to graduate and be unemployed. Competition in the job market is one important reason why high school graduates compete with each other to be admitted to the more selective universities.

Another characteristic of Japanese universities is their low quality of undergraduate education, compared with that offered by U.S. universities. Because the undergraduate curriculum is composed of both general and professional instruction, the prevailing view among university professors is that neither the general nor the professional education is complete. Professors who teach general education courses complain that general education is subordinated to professional courses. Likewise, faculty members in professional education consider the two-year professional curriculum to be inadequate. Responding to the need for more advanced professional training, the faculties of medicine and dentistry have set up four-year professional curricula, and the number of universities that have added two-year graduate programs for masters' degrees in engineering, agriculture, and natural sciences has been increasing in recent years. But, as of 1983, only 13 percent of the graduates of the three faculties entered the graduate programs (see Table 2.5).

Graduate education is thus underdeveloped in Japan. Currently nearly 60 percent of Japanese universities have graduate schools and 40 percent of them have doctoral programs. However, graduate students represent only 3 percent of total enrollment in universities. Furthermore, of the small number of graduate students, 51 percent of the masters' candidates and 66 percent of the doctoral candidates are concentrated in only 24 (5 percent of all) universities. Because the Japanese system places greater stress on professional education at the undergraduate level than does the U.S. system, graduate schools in Japan are not perceived as distinct vehicles for professional education. Their relative lack of functional specialization is one reason for the underdevelopment of Japanese graduate education.

Table 2.5   Distribution of universities and students, by university type, Japan, 1983.

Type of university	Number			Enrollment (%)		
	National and public	Private	Total	Under graduate	Master's course	Doctoral course
R	19	5	24	11.4	51.2	66.2
D1	20	101	121	43.2	22.0	23.8
D2	21	14	35	13.5	12.2	10.0
M	42	43	85	14.8	14.6	
C	23	155	178	17.1		
Total	125	318	443	100.0	100.0	100.0

Key to abbreviations: R, research; D1, doctorate granting (in all fields); D2, doctorate granting (in some fields); M, master's course only; C, undergraduate course only.
Source: Amano (1984a, pp. 71-73).

The low social demand for graduates with masters' and doctoral degrees is another. Especially for graduates in the humanities and social sciences, the only employment opportunities are as teachers and professors. Although the number of private companies that employ people with graduate degrees in engineering and natural sciences is rapidly increasing, those companies prefer masters' graduates to graduates with the Ph.D. Japanese companies attach more importance to in-service training than to graduate education in the universities. It is well known that Japanese companies recruit freshmen from the universities and train them to be researchers. Most Japanese researchers employed by those companies earn their doctorates as a result of in-service training (Miyahara and Kawamura 1984, pp. 71-74).

Another characteristic of Japanese universities is that they are extremely youth-centered and closed to adult learners. Young people who go into the labor force after high school and then later decide to seek further education find it virtually impossible to gain admission to a university. University courses, at both the undergraduate and graduate levels, are organized as day programs, and there are no specialized part-time programs for adult students. Some universities offer evening courses, but these courses also presuppose full-time enrollment and require the entrants to pass an examination.

Recently, some universities have attempted to make it easier for adults to enroll in undergraduate programs, for example, by creating a quota for adults and making special arrangements for them concerning the conditions of admission. But the number of such universities and programs is still quite limited. Unlike U.S. universities, Japanese universities do not have special divisions for adult education. Education and training programs for adults are supplied chiefly by the so-called education industry, composed of various types of profit-making institutions.

Lastly, female students have tended to be segregated into two-year junior colleges in Japan. In addition to the four-year universities there were 532 junior colleges in 1983, 84 percent of which were private, and female students accounted for nearly 90 percent of their enrollment. Only 10.7 percent of the college-age population is enrolled in junior colleges, compared with 24.4 percent who are enrolled in universities, but for young women the proportions are, respectively, 19.9 and 12.2 percent (Japan, Ministry of Education 1984). In principle the junior colleges also select their students by entrance examinations. But the number of students admitted on the basis of a recommendation from their high schools has increased rapidly in recent years, and in 1983 it exceeded 60 percent of all new entrants. The junior colleges' curricula overspecialize in such "female" subjects as home economics, teacher training, and the humanities. Rather than provide occupationally relevant education, Japanese two-year institutions tend to serve as "finishing schools." Only 3 percent of their graduates go on to universities.

Another type of short-cycle institution is the *senshu-gakko* (special training school), which provides technical and semiprofessional training. These institutions have many points of resemblance to the American preparatory schools. Their number has been expanding rapidly in recent years, and in 1983 they admitted 12 percent of the college-age population.

All of these features indicate that higher education is the weakest and most problematic part of the Japanese educational system. Although the main goal of the postwar reform of higher education was to create a new, American type of system, the reform was only half realized when the universities began to receive a flood of applications from the graduates of the newly expanded high school system. The government had failed to formulate a definite policy on how to respond to the demands of the increasing numbers of university applicants. Thus it was not the national but the private sector that accepted the great majority of new applicants. Between 1955 and 1980 the share of the private sector in total enrollment in higher education increased from 50 to 80 percent. This haphazard expansion inevitably resulted in a decline in the overall quality of education. The traditional hierarchical structure became even taller as new private universities and colleges were added to the bottom.

The declining quality, increasing tuition and fees, and increasing competition for access to the best universities intensified the dissatisfaction of young people with the higher educational system. At the end of the 1960s, Japanese universities experienced violent student revolt, which dramatized the need for a fundamental change in the university system. But the universities could not bring forth the needed reform. It might be said therefore that the postwar higher educational reform was left half done. As several Americans have suggested, higher education may become the "Achilles' heel" of Japan's further development.

ARTICULATION

Admissions to the universities and colleges continued to rise until the mid-1970s, attaining a peak of 39.2 percent of the college-age population in 1976, but since then it has steadily declined. In 1983 it was 35.6 percent (Japan, Ministry of Education 1984). The decline in the admission ratio has been most remarkable in metropolitan areas. In Tokyo, for example, it fell nearly 15 percent between 1976 and 1983. Not only the economy but also higher education has entered a phase of low growth in Japan.

The entrance examination system of Japanese universities has a history going back more than a century. But in the prewar period the entrance examination was used only in the faculties of those national institutions that attracted a large number of applicants. Most of the private institutions did not have the system. Only in the postwar period did all the universities begin to require applicants to take an entrance examination. Early in the postwar years, as part of the educational reforms, the Scholastic Aptitude Test was given a trial. It was quickly abandoned, however, and the universities decided to rely on their own exams. Very few were willing to take account of school grades or recommendations from high school teachers when evaluating entrants. But university educators became concerned that the exams did not adequately evaluate the scholastic ability of applicants. In 1979 therefore, after lengthy planning, the national and public universities introduced a common entrance examination system.

The common exam serves as the first stage in university admission; after its completion, applicants have to pass a second exam given by the university they wish to enter. In the case of the national and public universities, the second-tier exams are held on the same day, so that the applicants may apply to only one of the universities. In case of the private universities and their faculties, because the examination dates are different, the applicants can try several. On the average, applicants apply to one national and three private universities or faculties.

Because professional education starts at the undergraduate level, applicants are required to select a faculty or field of study at the time they apply for university admission. As the subjects that need to be included in the entrance examination differ from faculty to faculty, the entrance examination is actually administered by the faculty instead of the university. And within a university the selectivity differs widely by faculty. Once admitted to a university, students usually are not permitted to transfer to other faculties. For that reason it becomes most important for the applicants to select carefully the universities and faculties where they apply.

The basic qualification for university admission is a high school diploma. In 1983 about 50 percent of all male high school graduates sent applications to universities and colleges. But 58 percent of the male applicants succeeded in getting into a university or college. Of those who failed the entrance examinations about two-thirds tried again in 1984 as *rōnin*. In 1983, 24 percent of all male university applicants were one-year *rōnin* and 8 percent had been *rōnin* for two or more years (Japan, Ministry of Education 1983). As can be easily imagined, the share of *rōnin* to entrants is higher in the more selective universities and faculties. For example, 51 percent of those admitted to the entering 1984 class of Tokyo University and 48 percent of those admitted to medicine were *rōnin* (Obunsha 1984). The medical faculties are targeted by the most ambitious students of the "best" high schools. It is not surprising that the proportion from those high schools who become *rōnin* is often as high as the national average.

The most important source of this fierce competition is the hierarchical structure of the universities and faculties. Table 2.6 shows the distribution of universities and faculties based on the selectivity index calculated by a leading private testing company. Virtually all applicants prefer to apply to a high-status university. They begin preparing for the entrance examination while they are in the first year of high school, and many of them attend preparatory schools (*yobiko* or *juku*) after their classes. If they fail, they choose to be *rōnin* and spend one or more extra years attending the preparatory or cram schools. As competition for the schools and universities at the top of the educational hierarchy intensifies, the resources and time needed to prepare for entrance examinations increase. Some children are pushed to compete for admission to prep-type private secondary schools while they are still in primary school. Other children have to start preparing for the high school entrance examination at least by the time they become eighth graders, and many of them attend *juku* after school. After successfully gaining admission to their preferred school, they are required to continue preparing for the next important examination.

Table 2.6   Distribution of university faculties by applicant selectivity, for three main faculties, Japan, 1983

Selectivity	Economics and commerce			Engineering			Medicine		
	National and public	Private	Training	National and public	Private	Training	National and public	Private	Training
1 (high)	4	2	6	3		3	10	1	11
2	2	5	7	4	1	5	20	1	21
3	10	13	23	12	3	15	17	3	20
4	24	24	48	17	6	23	4	5	9
5	7	26	33	28	11	39		10	10
6		27	27	1	12	13		4	4
7 (low)		31	31		15	15		3	3

Source: Obunsha (1984).

Parents are required to spend a large amount of money to support this prolonged preparation. The system also raises the importance of "cultural capital" in the family. At the University of Tokyo (Todai), which occupies the highest status in the hierarchy, the majority of students come from the upper strata of society, and this tendency has intensified in recent years. According to the result of a study done in 1981, the average income level of the families of Todai students was nearly 30 percent higher than that of university students as a whole. As for fathers' occupations, 34 percent of the students' fathers were company administrators, 18 percent were higher civil servants, 6 percent were executives of big businesses, and 4 percent were in liberal (as opposed to scientific and technical) professions. The fathers also had above-average educational backgrounds: 51 percent of them were university graduates, compared with only 6 percent of fathers in the same age group nationwide (Todai 1981). Moreover, the ratio of the entrants from the prep-type private secondary schools has increased rapidly. In 1984 they represented about 40 percent of the total entrants.

CONCLUSION

Educational reform has become one of the most controversial political issues in Japan. Controversy about educational reform is not itself an unusual occurrence. The history of modern Japanese education reveals a recurrent pattern of political focus on education. But the latest occurrence has some special features (Amano 1984b).

In the past the focus of discussion was either on the educational system itself or on its relationship with other social systems, especially the economy. The key themes in previous reform discussion were efficiency and equality. The educational system was always asked to provide a higher level of efficiency in selecting and training the work force needed to achieve rapid growth of the economy and to progress toward equality of educational opportunity—that is, continued expansion of the educational system was the main means for developing human resources.

Today, however, after continual growth for a century, it is neither efficiency nor equality but a "crisis" in education that is the focus of the current reform debate. Such phenomena as the rising tide of school violence, student apathy, increasing numbers of dropouts, and declining scholastic ability are cited by various observers as concrete evidence of the crisis. These pathological phenomena, which have become more prominent within the past several years, indicate that the aspiration of Japanese children is changing rapidly, mainly because of increased stratification in contemporary Japanese society. The recent social changes are "cooling-out" the aspiration of young people to strive for educational and occupational mobility. If there is a real crisis of education, it must be that of the declining aspiration caused by the "overstructuration" of Japanese society.

REFERENCES

Amano, Ikuo. 1979. "Continuity and Change in the Structure of Japanese Higher Education." In *Changes in the Japanese*

University, edited by W. K. Cummings, I. Amano, and K. Kitamura, pp. 10-39. New York: Praeger.

———. 1984a. "Daigaku-gun, no Hikaku Bunseki" (A Comparison of University Groups). In *Daigaku Hyoka no Kenkyu,* edited by Keii Tominaga, pp. 70-81. Tokyo: Daigaku Shuppankai.

———. 1984b. "Education Reform in Historical Perspective." *Japan Echo* 11, no. 3: 9-16.

———. 1984c. *Gakushu Shakai eno Chosen* (Towards a Degreeocracy). Tokyo: Nihon Keizai Shinbunsha.

Fukaya, Masashi. 1983. *Koritsuka suru Kodomtachi.* Tokyo: Nihon Hoso Shuppan Kyokai.

Giddens, Anthony. 1973. *The Class Structure of the Advanced Societies.* London: Hutchinson.

Japan. Ministry of Education, Science, and Cultural (Mōmbushō). 1983. *Gakko Kihon Hokokusho* (Basic Survey of Schools). Tokyo.

———. 1984. *Monbu Tokei Yoran* (Statistical Yearbook of Education). Tokyo.

Kuroha, Ryoichi. 1984. "Senbatsu to Nyugaku." In *Daigaku Hyoka no Kenkyu,* edited by Keii Tominaga, pp. 115-38. Tokyo: Daigaku Shuppankai.

Miyahara, Shohei, and Ryo Kawamura, eds. 1984. *Gendai no Daigaku-in* (Today's Graduate Schools). Tokyo: Waseda Daigaku Shuppanbu.

Nippon Shiritsu Daigaku Renmei. 1984. *Shiritsu Daigaku—Kino, Kyo, Ashita* (Private Universities—Yesterday, Today, Tomorrow). Tokyo: Fukutake Shoten.

Obunsha. 1984. *Keisetsu Jidai, Zenkoku Daigaku Naiyo Annai Go* (Guide to the Programs of Universities). Tokyo.

Shimbori, Michiya, ed. 1984. *Daigaku Kyojushoku no Sogteki Kenkyu* (Comprehensive Study of the Japanese Professoriate). Tokyo: Taga Shuppan.

Tokyo Daigaku Kyoiku Gakuku (Todai). 1981. Kyoiku Shakai-gaku Kenkyushitsu. In *Todaisei no Seikatsu to Ishiki* (The Situation and Attitudes of University of Tokyo Students). Tokyo.

Tokyoto Kinken Koko Jyuken Annai (Guide to Performance of Tokyo High Schools in Exam Preparation). 1984. Tokyo: Shobunsha Shuppan.

Tominaga, Keii, ed. 1984. *Daigaku Hyoka no Kenkyu* (Studies in the Evaluation of Universities). Tokyo: Daigaku Shuppankai.

3
THE POLITICS OF EDUCATIONAL CRISES IN THE UNITED STATES
John W. Meyer

Even more than is generally the case in the modern world, Americans tend to interpret national successes and failures as arising from qualities belonging to individuals. This tendency leads, naturally, to a focus on the educational system as the source of many social failures and problems and to the view that the educational system requires constant and major repair. Perceptions of educational crisis are especially common in the United States.

Although U.S. society has been dominant in the world since World War II, the extent of its hegemony has been in continuous decline. The fraction of the gross world product produced in the United States, though still quite high, halved during the postwar period. Further, the attempt to maintain a worldwide pax Americana created expectations likely to generate much sense of failure. In any event, the recent period, especially the recent decade of continuous recession, led to many perceptions of national failure. And the common tendency to interpret national failure as originating in the educational system continued.

In the 1960s the countries often compared with the United States were China, Cuba, and Vietnam, which illustrated revolutionary zeal and equality. In the 1970s and early 1980s the country most often pointed to for comparison has been the one with the most conspicuous economic growth—Japan. In this general comparison, attention has tended to focus on the Japanese educational system. The subject of almost no U.S. interest a decade ago, Japanese education is now a major topic in public discussion and the press; it is discussed, without much evidence, as showing the true locus of the U.S. failure of economic competence and performance. (See Chapters 13 and 14 in this volume.)

In this chapter I review the general inclination to see national crises as rooted in education, and the way in which such crises and reforms tend to be organized in the United States.

THE PATTERN OF CRISIS

Modern public education is in itself a reform, and its changes are products of further reform. From its inception mass public education has been a rationalistic and scientific effort to reform society —to restructure the population and incorporate it into a rationalized society (and often the state organization). One can of course find precursors, but the creation of modern, nationwide systems of public education has been in each case a collective and purposive enterprise, discussed by rationalistic intellectuals and political leaders (see Ramirez and Boli-Bennett 1982).

It is important to understand why this is true, and why public education is now a worldwide institution. "Modernizing" a society involves extending an integrated system of controls and involvements down to the level of individual action. Individual membership is based ordinarily on the notion of equality. And individual action—economic, political, and cultural—is valued and regulated according to interested collective standards, such as the gross national product. Education, with its socialization, certification, and ritual properties, becomes the crucial means by which individuals are made competent members of the nation. Thus attempts to mobilize around nation building and national success always involve definitions of educational crisis and reform. This link has become tighter over time as the world system has evolved. For instance, the construction of universal mass education was on the immediate agendas of the nation-states emerging after World War II.

Historically all this has been a little more true in the United States than elsewhere. Its political system found unusual meaning in the ordinary individual. The basic U.S. economic doctrines about capital, labor, consumption, and technology placed authority in responsible (that is, educated) individual choice. Sovereignty over the state also rested there, with the social form of the election penetrating more deeply into society than elsewhere. (Even the schools are run by locally elected officials.) So, also, are cultural decisions about values, tasks, and the nature of the moral cosmos made by the individual. Education is thus highly valued in the United States, and it expanded there earlier and more completely than elsewhere. This value on education is not simply an aggregate concern of "private" individuals. It is a public matter, as almost all public goods are considered to arise from individual membership and competence. The public in question is organized at many levels, from national to local, and in many structures, from educational organizations to external social and intellectual interests. But all these components of the public, when they address education, speak of a general national public interest. Genuinely local or particularistic formulations are probably rarer in the United States than elsewhere—a phenomenon that outside observers sometimes see as reflecting high levels of hypocrisy. At the least one can note that educational discourse is legitimated by the ideology of the public interest.

It follows from the comments above that, as societies modernize and as world standards evolve over time, social and national problems tend to be seen as *educational* problems. The initial creation of systems of compulsory mass education was spurred by perceptions of national crisis (Ramirez and Boli-Bennett 1982), and modern expansion took place under the same perception in the new nations (Meyer et al. 1977). In the United States the general tendency is carried to unusual lengths, given the rooting of so much of society in conceptions of the competent and responsible individual. Thus

- The competitive concern following the Soviet *Sputnik* success was accompanied by a perception of U.S. educational failure and many attempts to reemphasize science and technology in the schools.
- The increased structural unemployment of young people is interpreted as reflecting training failures, and it produces many reforms in general education and in occupational training systems.
- An increase in unmarried teenage childbearing is seen as calling for educational change (various moral or sexual education).
- High youthful accident rates and incidences of drunken driving by youths call for driving instruction in schools.
- The national crisis provoked by the Watergate affair, which was perceived as a problem of personal ethics, led to calls for ethics lectures in law schools.
- And, most relevant to our purposes, the present world recession and competitive concerns about Japanese economic success are producing another wave of reaction to perceived U.S. failure, interpreted as a broad breakdown in educational competence and commitment.

This interpretation—a process resulting in an attempt to mobilize U.S. education to confront the international competitive arena—sees the U.S. economy as failing because American people no longer have the competence and commitment to compete effectively. In contrast, the Japanese are perceived as energetic and efficient. The process of U.S. decline is traced back to the school system. Failures of discipline and intellect in the United States are contrasted with the image of the busy Japanese students. For this reason, U.S. attention focuses on the highly disciplined and competitive secondary school system in Japan, rather than on the university system, which would provide less mobilizational advantage.

The general pattern goes far back in U.S. history, to the early years of the country. Problems are defined as requiring improvements in individual socialization through education. The crises may seem spurious to the observer, and the educational remedies farfetched. There is usually no evidence of potential effectiveness. But the general pattern is consistent.

We may conclude that modern social systems, especially the United States, tend to turn perceived national problems into educational crises and reforms. We need not consider further the conditions under which national problems or crises are defined. Common causes involve military defeat and some forms of economic failure; others involve the competitive successes that enable elites to advocate national mobilization.

ORGANIZATION OF U.S. EDUCATION

How a perception of educational crisis gets located in a society depends on the organization of the educational system. The system in the United States is highly decentralized (Meyer and Rowan 1978):

- ○ The federal government has almost no sovereign authority over public education, and it provides less than 10 percent of the funding (mostly special-purpose funding) for it. There are federal regulations and controls, such as over education for minorities and the handicapped, but no general mandate for educational action or control. The United States is one of the few nation-states without any *national* rule of compulsory education.
- The individual 50 states have general supervision of education, prescribe it, and define its general content. But they operate in a historical and political context, giving great au-

tonomy to local communities. Only one state—significantly, Hawaii—takes direct control over its schools. In all others the schools themselves are under the control of local bodies. Overall, the state governments provide more than 40 percent of the funding for public primary and secondary education. Both state funding and state regulatory power over education have expanded sharply in the last half-century.

- Below the state level are various intermediary bodies (for example, county boards of education), but power over education is really located in the school district (which is sometimes coterminous with the county, city, or other political unit, but which usually is run with considerable autonomy). These local bodies have direct control over education. They raise more than 40 percent of the funds, build and close schools, hire and fire teachers and administrators, define within broad state limits the curriculum, and set all sorts of policies—even on occasion determining the teaching methods. They are ordinarily controlled by elected boards.

- But U.S. localism does not stop here. Below the district level the schools are expected to respond to pressures from the local community. The expectation is enforced by the custom of denying tenure protection to school administrators. Organized and informal parent groups in the community commonly exercise a good deal of influence over the local school, and administrators tend to be skilled at dealing with them.

- Below the administrative level, teachers often find themselves in communication with parents and parent groups. The educational expectations of informally organized parents have considerably more legitimacy than in other countries. Teachers are well aware that the schools need parental support for both educational and financial reasons, and they tend to erect fewer professional barriers against parent communication than might occur elsewhere.

This whole decentralized system is a central feature of U.S. education. It is rarely understood by outsiders, and even more rarely copied. When elements (for example, the Parent-Teachers Association) are copied, they seldom really work. The system seems irrational to outsiders, and indeed it is a political rather than a rationalized social form. It also seems inequitable, as schools and teachers may have quite different incomes from one district to the next, and students having similar abilities may be allocated very different levels of public resources.

The element in this system that goes unnoticed is that the decentralization is only organizational, not institutional—it is in one sense a fictitious decentralization. The organizationally decentralized interests that pervade U.S. education parade under nationwide ideologies and purposes, not under localistic ones. Their purpose is not mainly to educate the community's children for the community, but rather to educate them to be successful in the national society. This characteristic of American society is closely related to homogenizing aspects of the society that have long been discussed, as, for example, by Alexis de Tocqueville (1944) in the nineteenth century.

THE CYCLE OF CRISIS AND REFORM

We thus arrive at the determining frame of educational crises in the United States. Such crises generally take the form of nationwide interpretations but have impact upon an organizational system that is highly decentralized. Their properties follow from this situation. The crises tend to produce widespread social movements rather than highly organized responses (Meyer 1983b). The movements are active at many levels and usually involve much active scientific participation and discussion. They produce organizational responses at many levels. But at the higher levels they generate limited and special-purpose legislation or changed judicial rules. The formal organizational response to the crises is usually seen as being inadequate, and public interest declines as the formal changes become routine. Often, however, sweeping changes occur in the system as a result of crises, and indeed U.S. education is so likely to change rapidly that many observers see it as faddish. The paradox is that in U.S. education, organizational failure and institutional success often go together. The rest of this chapter reviews these points in more detail.

The Prevalence of Social Movements

In most countries the cycle of educational crisis and reform seems to have a highly organized and centrist character. Cabinet ministers, elite intellectuals, and elite media are quickly at center stage. In the United States, however, central educational organization and authority are very weak; there is little authorization for national educational action, and until recently no cabinet ministry at all. And there are few strong central media or bodies of intellectuals responsible for defining such issues.

Education is everybody's business, and the process of crisis construction involves widespread participation. Faced with a national problem—for instance, the recent long recession—all sorts of groups put forward definitions of the situation as arising from educational failure. Citizens write letters to newspapers, journalists discover horror stories in the schools, business and labor groups propose educational solutions, and educators search for new meanings and resources. The intellectuals especially concerned with education offer definitions of the problem and solutions. Religious, political, and economic interest groups get involved. The purveyors of educational crisis are a chronic part of the American political scene. It is difficult to predict which national problem will be successfully turned into a major national educational crisis and which will not. But it is clear that crisis construction requires the involvement of many groups and interests (Tyack 1974; Callahan 1962).

As a result it becomes difficult to predict the ultimate form that crisis definition will take. With the evolution of multifaceted social movements, crises change their shape over time. For instance, the crisis over racial integration in education came to involve a general concern with educational equalization, reforms directed at the enhancement of female participation, and ultimately a special subcrisis concerned with improving educational conditions for the handicapped. And the subsequent current crisis in educational quality —concern about excessive permissiveness in schools and declining test scores—has come to be linked, probably because of the economic recession, with a resurgence of interest in vocational education. There is also a desire to imitate the homogeneity and discipline imagined to be characteristic of Japanese schools. Added to these are demands for religion in schools and for public support of religious education. The social movement aspects of the U.S. educational crisis mean that new groups, interests, and proponents of unrelated "solutions" can join together (March and Olsen 1976; Weick 1976).

The diffuse character of these crises means that organizational outcomes are hard to predict in detail, even given that crisis definition is achieved. The problem is that the dramaturgy of crisis construction inevitably involves the construction of some forces to be blamed for the crisis, but dispersed definitions create dispersed sources of evil. The conventional targets of reformers during the last century and a half have been slothful, inattentive, and uninterested parents; lazy, ignorant, and occasionally biased teachers; incompetent and corrupt administrators; penurious local elites filled with class and racial bias; and, more recently, do-gooders too concerned with the soft virtues to understand the need for discipline.

Targets available in other countries are not much used in the United States because of their historic weakness, though attempts to use them have been increasing in recent decades—for example, pernicious national bureaucrats and technocratic intellectuals. As these groups gain power, they will more frequently receive attributions of villainy.

Of course the dramaturgy of crisis construction also utilizes positive models of virtue and success. In the current crisis depiction, Japanese education plays this part. And it is probably true that the accidental properties of chosen models influence outcomes of crises. For instance, in the future one can expect to find odd little features of Japanese education copied in some U.S. schools or school districts.

Research in this field has been hampered by several problems. First, too many researchers are advocates on one side or another and therefore cannot have much perspective on the issue of crisis definition. Second, U.S. researchers do little comparative work in the area and are insensitive to the distinctive features of the U.S. context. And third, there is too much sampling on the dependent variable; few studies exist of the crises that do not happen or of crisis-definition attempts that do not succeed. As in other social-scientific areas of research (for example, the study of revolutions), this lopsidedness produces a literature that is somewhat teleological.

Widespread Scientific Involvement

American education is unified, not by a strong organizational tie to the national state, but by a commitment to scientific ideology analogous to earlier religious ideas. There is supposed to be an empirically and theoretically grounded "right way" (Tyack 1974). This means that educational crises are accompanied by scientific argument and evidence. Indeed, a great many U.S. educational researchers function as potential advocates of educational crises of various sorts and as promulgators of solutions to them. Such persons can be mobilized by groups trying to build social movements needed for the enactment of their ideas.

The scientific community, like the polity, is organizationally dispersed. One can therefore find scientists, like lawyers, on every side of an issue. Their involvement, however, seems crucial to the translation of generalized social movement conceptions into particular organizational policies. This ideologized role accounts for the heated way in which U.S. scholars have recently debated Japanese education and organizational practice. Assessments are important because they determine the value of alternatives.

Because of the dispersed character of the educational polity, relevant scientific activity often takes forms that might in another national context seem unusual. Scientific ideas and evidentiary studies are frequently put forward in the ordinary press. There is a tendency to use supposedly successful demonstrations, or even authoritative theories, as if they were evidence; thus observations made on casual field visits to Japan now enter public political debate. Educational scientists are frequently involved in practical demonstration programs. Research on a problem is often completed too late in the crisis cycle to enter into public discussion.

Scientific activity in this field is closely linked to cycles of reform. Given the character of U.S. educational reform, it sometimes seems to be an exercise in competition for publicity.

The Dispersed Character of Organizational Response to Crisis

Successful crises become organizational reforms, but because the organizational system is so decentralized, this process goes on at many levels simultaneously. The recent conservative trend toward more disciplined "basic education," for instance, created various effects, as the loosely coupled levels of the system responded simultaneously (Meyer and Rowan 1978). For example, teachers, whether or not required to do so, began to use more frequent, and more formally reported, grading. Schools tightened up their curricula and grading standards and probably their rules about attendance and behavior. Districts adopted policies of the same sort. Some states adopted formalized testing rules for student advancement. A national commission appointed by the secretary of education defined low educational achievement as a major national problem. It allocated blame broadly and proposed many reforms.

Earlier crisis cycles show the same pattern. Each level of the system responds independently to the same generally defined crisis. The response is organizationally uncoordinated or decoupled but displays astonishing homogeneity. For instance, one would find effects of the current "basic education" crisis in Stanford University (a highly selective institution with a reputation for excellence), where there has been a recent conservative tightening of course offerings and a concern about lax grading standards.

The Limited Central Response

In recent decades pressures have increased on the national government to respond organizationally to educational crises. The pressures date back to the early years of the republic, but they are now more intense. Yet the legitimate authority and the power to take effective action are not really there; these elements have long since been vested in other levels of the system. Results include the following:

- Peak associations—for example, national commissions and coalitions of interest groups—form and take stands at the national center in response to crises, but they are weaker and less stable than in societies having centrally organized systems.
- Legislation tends to be limited and bureaucratic rather than part of a comprehensive approach to educational policy. In classic cases it takes the form of providing funds for students or programs in special categories (the handicapped, minorities, pregnant girls, vocational training programs, foreign languages).
- Administration is also limited and bureaucratic, restricted by politics. It places much emphasis on financial accounting and formal reporting (for example, requirements for evaluation research) but little emphasis on content or the integration of reforms in the educational system. For instance, a school district may report different numbers of students in a given category to different federal programs.
- General rights are promulgated with little organizational specification. This brings the courts into action, as now-entitled parties pursue their interests judicially. The reforms that follow U.S. educational crises often generate large waves of court action (the school consolidation wars earlier in this century, the racial integration conflicts, the reforms affecting the treatment of the handicapped). One can foresee such a response to the recent emphasis on basic education (litigation over the rights of students who fail minimum competency tests, for example).

Organizational Failure

To an astonishing extent, there is agreement that reform fails. The wave of enthusiasm passes, the national agenda changes, and advocates recede from public attention. Several reasons can be offered for why this happens especially often to organizational aspects of reform.

First, a system with decentralized organization has little room for organizational heroes (Tyack and Hansot 1982; Meyer 1983a). The celebrated figures in the history of U.S. education tend to be people outside the main chain of national education authority. (Most professors of education could name few U.S. commissioners of education or state superintendents of the past.) Thus even successful reforms tend to be absorbed in organizational routine.

Second, the U.S. system is one in which the top-down organizational aspects of reform and innovation tend to fail. Serious research literature on the topic is quite pessimistic (see, for example, Berman and McLaughlin 1975-78; Bardach 1977; Wildavsky and Pressman 1979). For reasons outlined above, reforms adopted organizationally are often merely procedural and out of tune with the inspiring imagery. Implementation is often missing, there being no real enforcing impulse from the center. Cynics in the field sometimes see organizational reform as a symbolic alternative to real reform (Baldridge and Deal 1983). Even when attempted, implementation often fails. Reform is met by much resistance, or only procedural conformity, from levels below. Competing interests dominate. When implementation occasionally occurs, reforms nevertheless fail because the context is unsupportive. Teachers and administrators do not provide the requisite support and the reforms remain peripheral to the main programs of the system.

The admission that top-down organizational reform is usually only symbolic does not explain why so much American effort goes into it or why generations of researchers in the field have given these reforms their full attention. One explanation would be that U.S. education is held together by institutional agreements. But these are *indicated*, not really managed, by central organizational rules, and it is over them that the great symbolic battles are fought. The point is to make the rules, even if they will not be applied; the rules signal a changed game to all the dispersed constituencies.

Reform processes, in short, have dramatic properties. The drama has heroes, villains, and fools (Klapp 1962). In different organizational systems different actors will play these parts. In the decentralized U.S. system the central organizational bureaucrats are the villains, and the literature, as it were, places their severed heads on the walls to signal social change. The heroes are the common citizens and their societal, not organizational, elites: the good people of society accepting change as if it were their own. In a more centralized system the heroes might be the central organizers, and the walls would be topped with the heads of dissident citizens and their revolutionary leaders (all now seen as yokels).

Institutional Success

The literature on the failures of reform reads strangely when set beside the voluminous literature on the changeability and faddishness of U.S. education. The system is well known to adapt quickly to changed fashions in education, down to the details of curriculum and instruction. The liberalizing reforms of the 1960s penetrated quickly into the schools. So have the basic education ideas of the past decade.

The explanation for the paradox is that change in U.S. education occurs through institutional channels. Changed fashions pass through all sorts of media, affecting teachers, parents, and local school boards and administrators, as well as the august functionaries at the top of the system. Thus changes occur where they are mandated and also where they are not. The changes may not be precisely what were organizationally specified but are likely to be akin in spirit. We find probabilistically enacted but sweeping changes in recent decades in all the issues brought up in educational crisis formation: the treatment of minorities, equalization of schools, expanded access for female students, expanded special programs for the handicapped, and now tightened standards of achievement. We find them throughout the system, not merely where they were planned and enforced by centrist authorities. The same institutional integration that blocks organizational change becomes the main medium for enforcing educational change.

CONCLUSION

Education in the United States is organizationally decentralized but institutionally integrated. It is also a central institution in an individualistic society. Crises in education occur frequently and gather momentum in decentralized social movements. These movements generate formal organizational changes and institutional changes, the two being somewhat disconnected. The resultant equilibrium continues the pattern of organizationally decoupled but institutionally integrated control. Americans (and their researchers) tend to be pessimistic about organizational centralism but highly optimistic about education. Their chronic crises are part of the process that maintains the centrality and the decoupled character of the educational system.

American crises are accompanied by dramatic depictions of successes and failures—given realities and wonderful possibilities. The recent wave of concerns about U.S. economic and, by inference, educational failure has involved a great increase in attention paid to Japanese education as a model of educational success. People have shown less interest in real research on the subject than in depicting Japanese education as a mythological device to portray a desirable future.

The U. S. educational crises, and the definitions that arise around them, have tended to become worldwide perceptions and to cause changes in other countries. Such crises are often ideological in content and spread easily. One wonders whether the crises that are announced by peripheral countries reflect local reality or emulation (Boli-Bennett and Meyer 1978). Certainly liberal U.S. issues of the 1960s (such as the emphasis on individualized education and ethnic integration) went quickly onto the world agenda. Perhaps, with the conservative crisis now occurring in the United States, we will begin to see a worldwide process of discovering illiteracy. And there may be a corresponding inclination to use Japanese education as the ideological model, replacing the earlier American one.

NOTE

This chapter builds on research conducted at the Institute for Research on Educational Finance and Governance, supported by funds from the National Institute of Education. The views expressed here are the author's. The general research was conducted jointly with W. Richard Scott and several other research collaborators, and the general research background for the present chapter is reported in Meyer and Scott (1983). I am indebted to Professor Scott for his comments on the issues involved here.

REFERENCES

Baldridge, Victor J., and Terrence Deal, eds. 1983. *The Dynamics of Organizational Change in Education.* Berkeley: McCutchan.

Bardach, Eugene. 1977. *The Implementation Game.* Cambridge, Mass.: MIT Press.

Berman, Paul, and Milbrey McLaughlin. 1975-78. *Federal Programs Supporting Educational Change.* Vols. 1-8. Santa Monica, Calif.: Rand.

Boli-Bennett, John, and John Meyer. 1978. "The Ideology of Childhood and the State." *American Sociological Review* 43 (December): 797-812.

Callahan, Raymond. 1962. *Education and the Cult of Efficiency.* Chicago: University of Chicago Press.

Klapp, Orrin. 1962. *Heroes, Villains, and Fools.* Englewood Cliffs, N.J.: Prentice-Hall.

March, James, and Johan Olsen. 1976. *Ambiguity and Choice in Organizations.* Bergen, Norway: Universitetsforlage.

Meyer, John. 1983a. "Centralization of Funding and Control in Educational Governance." In *Organizational Environments,* edited by John Meyer and W. Richard Scott, pp. 179-97. Beverly Hills, Calif.: Sage.

_____. 1983b. "Innovation and Knowledge Use in American Public Education." In *Organizational Environments,* edited by John Meyer and W. Richard Scott, pp. 233-60. Beverly Hills, Calif.: Sage.

Meyer, John, Francisco Ramirez, Richard Rubinson, and John Boli-Bennett. 1977. "The World Educational Revolution, 1950-70." *Sociology of Education* 50 (October): 242-58.

Meyer, John, and Brian Rowan. 1978. "The Structure of Educational Organization." In *Environments and Organizations,* edited by Marshall Meyer et al., pp. 78-109. San Francisco: Jossey-Bass.

Ramirez, Francisco, and John Boli-Bennett. 1982. "Global Patterns of Educational Institutionalization." In *Comparative Education,* edited by P. Altbach, R. Arnove, and G. Kelley. New York: Macmillan.

Tocqueville, Alexis de. 1944. *Democracy in America.* New York: Vintage Books.

Tyack, David. 1974. *The One Best System.* Cambridge, Mass.: Harvard University Press.

Tyack, David, and Elisabeth Hansot. 1982. *Managers of Virtue: Public School Leadership in America.* New York: Basic Books.

Weick, Karl. 1976. "Educational Organizations as Loosely Coupled Systems." *Administrative Science Quarterly* 21 (March): 1-19.

Wildavsky, Aaron B., and Jeffrey L. Pressman. 1979. *Implementation: How Great Expectations in Washington Are Dashed in Oakland: Or, Why It's Amazing That Federal Programs Work at All, This Being a Saga of the Economic Development Administration as Told by Two Sympathetic Observers Who Seek to Build Morals on a Foundation of Ruined Hopes.* Berkeley: University of California Press.

PART II
STRUCTURE

4
JAPANESE AND U.S. CURRICULA COMPARED
Victor N. Kobayashi

Japan and the United States share similar general features that allow for a fruitful comparison of their school curricula. Both nations are economically and industrially advanced and committed to the ideals of formal education, so as to have an informed citizenry, and equality of educational opportunity. Both countries have a wide network of public and private schools that reach almost all youths from early childhood through high school. They are among the few nations in the world that offer to almost all who complete secondary schooling the opportunity to enter postsecondary institutions of education. These general similarities provide a basis for investigating differences between Japanese and U.S. education. This chapter examines the difference between the two nations' elementary and secondary curricula, focusing especially on the latter.

GENERAL FEATURES OF THE SCHOOL SYSTEM

To understand the Japanese and U.S. school curricula, it is first necessary to know something about the general features of schools in Japan and America.

Unlike the U.S. school year, which begins in early September and ends at the beginning of summer, the Japanese school year starts in April, goes through the summer months, and ends in March of the following year. The first term begins on or about April 6 and ends about July 19, for the summer vacation; the second term begins in early September and ends about December 24, for the New Year's vacation. The final term begins the second week of January, and the academic year closes about March 25. Schools are in session Mondays through Fridays, but, unlike U.S. students, Japanese children also attend school for a half day on Saturdays. Japanese youths, therefore, spend more hours in school than their American counterparts, averaging the equivalent of 225 full weekdays in school, compared with U.S. students' average of about 180 days.

Automatic advancement from grade to grade is the general rule in Japanese schools. There are no school-leaving examinations, so that all students tend to graduate once they have entered a school or college. Japan has national compulsory school attendance for all children from grades 1 through 9, and virtually all children attend school. Children who have reached six years of age enter the first grade of elementary school (grades 1 through 6) and after completing grade 6 advance to lower secondary school (grades 7 through 9). Fewer than 1 percent of the children attend private schools during the compulsory years.

Kindergarten enrollment is growing rapidly in the United States and is expected to become almost universal in a few years. About 64 percent of Japanese primary school entrants in 1984 had completed the noncompulsory kindergarten. The majority of kindergartens in Japan are privately operated.

Most Japanese youths (more than 90 percent) attend the noncompulsory upper secondary school (grades 10 through 12). School programs at this level are differentiated into general courses, offering academic and general education subjects, and specialized vocational courses, including agriculture, fishery, home economics, technical and commercial subjects, and health and physical education. In 1976 about one-third of the upper secondary schools offered only general courses, while another third offered a comprehensive program that included both general and specialized vocational courses. Fewer than one-third of the schools offered only specialized vocational courses. In 1978 about two-thirds of all upper secondary school students studied in general academic programs, while most of the remainder were in some kind of specialized vocational course (Japan, Ministry of Education 1979, pp. 50-51).

As in many countries, vocational schools in Japan are considered less prestigious than the academic high schools. Night high schools also have low status. Entrance examinations determine who enter the noncompulsory schools that follow graduation from the lower secondary schools.

About 28 percent of the students in upper secondary schools attended private schools in 1979 (Japan, Ministry of Education 1979, p. 49). Most of the public upper secondary high schools were operated by prefectures. National high schools were also attached to national universities.

Since 1962 Japan has established five-year technical colleges that, like upper secondary schools, admit students after grade 9 who have completed their compulsory school requirements. Most of these colleges are operated by the national government.

The U.S. system has emphasized the public comprehensive high school, which provides general education for all while including an academic stream for students who plan to continue on to college and a vocational stream for other students. American educators tend to view the typical high school as a place where students can explore their interests freely in a relaxed setting, and college as a place for serious study. In contrast, the Japanese consider the high school as a place for intense, demanding studies, while their colleges in general are much less demanding, allowing students much free time. Although the majority of U.S. public high schools are comprehensive, there are also many private schools that prepare students exclusively for college and a few public schools that are academically or technically specialized.

The American school system varies from state to state and sometimes from locality to locality. More than half of U.S. high schools are four-year schools (grades 9 through 12), but there are many exceptions (Boyer 1983, p. 20).

Both nations are among those having the highest percentage of college-age youth attending institutions of higher education. In 1980 about 37 percent of Japanese high school graduates attended postsecondary schools, including two-year junior colleges and four-year universities, while about 42 percent found employment. Many of the other students were unemployed or studied in nonformal schools, such as the *yobiko*, to prepare for the next annual cycle of university entrance examinations. Unlike most other countries, both Japan and the United States have enough spaces in their colleges and universities for almost all high school graduates who apply. Some colleges in Japan are relatively easy to enter, whereas others have highly competitive entrance examinations. In the United States, about 50 percent of high school graduates enter higher education, and about 70 percent of them eventually graduate. Almost all students who enter institutions of higher education in Japan receive their diplomas.

In both nations it is difficult to gain admittance to the most prestigious universities. As many Americans know from their newspapers and newsmagazines, entrance examinations in Japan generate much anxiety among youths seeking to enter the few top-ranked universities, which offer the greatest opportunity upon graduation for high-level employment in government and business. The U.S. system is more diffuse, in that there is less focus on specific prestigious institutions and less emphasis on entrance examinations held at a critical time. A comparison of these patterns suggests that whereas the Japanese punctuate certain decisive turning points in the life cycle, Americans prefer greater flexibility in the timing of crucial choices, so that choices can be reversed, delayed, and made less critical. Americans can more readily enter and reenter universities throughout their lives, for example, and transfer from one college to another, or interrupt and postpone studies for various reasons, whereas the Japanese view college education as taking place only at a certain time in one's life.

_ Many upper secondary school students in Japan attend *yobiko*, nonformal schools that help them to prepare for college entrance examinations. Some high schools, however, have large numbers of students who have no intention of going to college. High school grades are not so important for college entrance as they are in the United States; scores on the college entrance examinations in Japan are the major criterion.

In both nations preparation for college entry affects what is offered in the secondary school curriculum and what proportion of students will study certain elective courses. Practically all students in Japanese schools, starting from the seventh grade in the lower secondary school and continuing into the upper secondary school, study English. Although English is an elective, knowledge of written English is tested in college entrance examinations in Japan. In the United States, high school subjects required for college entrance, especially credits in foreign languages, vary widely from school to school. Only about 15 percent of U.S. high school students study a foreign language, usually for only one or two years (Boyer 1983, p. 99). Almost all U.S. universities and colleges dropped their foreign-language requirement for entering students in the 1960s, but such requirements are being reinstated (Boyer 1983, pp. 98-100; U.S. Department of Education 1984, pp. 180-81). The percentage of students studying foreign languages in American high schools most likely will increase therefore in the near future. California and Illinois, in 1983, included the study of a foreign language as a choice among several subjects required for high school graduation, and several states require foreign-language courses for secondary students in the college preparatory program (see Table 4.1).

Table 4.1 Minimum requirements (in credit units) for high school graduation, United States, 1984
(1 credit = 1 year)

State	Total	E	SS	M	S	Other
Alabama	22	4	3	2	2	1 PE; 0.5 each CP, personal management, H (E1984)
Alaska	21	4	3	2	2	1 PE or H (1984, E1985)
Arizona	18	4		2	2	(1983, E1987)
Arkansas	20	4	3			5 M&S; 0.5 each PE, H, FA (1984)
California	23	3	2	2	1	FA or FL (1983, E1986)
Colorado	18					Local
Connecticut	20	4	3	3	2	PE and arts or VE (1984, E1986)
Delaware	18			2	2	(1983, E1987)
Washington, D.C.	20.5					(E1984)
Florida	24	4	3	3	3	0.5 each PE, H, FA, VE (E1987)
Georgia	20	4	3	2	2	1 PE-H, CP, FA, or VE (E1988)
Hawaii	20	4	4	2	2	1 PE; 0.5 H; 0.5 guidance/career (E1983)
Idaho	20	4		2		Additional courses in S, speech, reading, history (E1984)
Illinois	16	3	2	2	1	1 art, music, VE or FL (1983)
Indiana	19	4		2	2	1983
Iowa						Local
Kansas	21		3	2	2	(1983; E1989)
Kentucky	20	4	2	3	2	1 H, PE (1983, E1984)
Louisiana	23			3	3	1 world history; 0.5 CP (E1989)
Maine	16		2	2	2	1 FA, CP (1984, E1989)
Maryland	20			2	2	
Massachusetts						Local
Michigan						Local
Minnesota	15					Local
Mississippi	16			1	1	
Missouri	22	3	2	2	2	1 FA, practical arts, PE (E1987)
Montana	20					(1984, E1989)
Nebraska	16					
Nevada	20	3		2	2	(1982)
New Hampshire	19.75	4	2.5	2	2	1 PE, 0.5 each arts, CP; 0.25 H (1984, E1989)

Table 4.1, cont.

New Jersey	20	4	2	2	1	4 PE; 1 FA, performing or practical arts; 0.5 career exploration (1983)
New Mexico	20	4	2	2	2	1 FA; 1 PE (1983; E1987)
New York	18.5	4	4	2	2	1 art or music; 0.5 H (1984, E1989)
North Carolina	20	4	2	2	2	1 PE, H (1983)
North Dakota						Local
Ohio	18			2	1	(1982)
Oklahoma	22	4	2	2	2	(1983, E1987)
Oregon	21			2	2	(1984)
Pennsylvania		4	3	3	3	2 art, humanities (1983, E1985)
Rhode Island		4	2	2	2	(1985)
South Carolina	20	4	3	3	2	1 PE (1984)
South Dakota	20	4	3	2	2	0.5 CP; 0.5 FA (1983, E1988)
Tennessee	18			2	2	(1983, E1987)
Texas	21	4	2.5	3	2	0.5 economics, 1.5 PE, 0.5 H (E1986)
Utah	15			1	1	All graduates must be CP literate (1983)
Vermont	15.5	4	3	3	3	1 art; 1.5 PE & CP (E1985)
Virginia	20	4	2	2	2	1 more in M or S; 1 PE (1983, E1984)
Washington	29	3		2	2	1 history & U.S. government; 0.5 state history & government; 1 contemporary world history; 1 occupational education; 2 PE
West Virginia	20	4	3	2	1	(1981)
Wisconsin		4	3	2	2	1.5 PE, 0.5 CP, H (E1989)
Wyoming	18					

Sources: *Education Week* (1983, pp. 6-17; 1984a, pp. 8, 14; 1985, pp. 11-29); U.S. Department of Education (1984, pp. 173-77); data for New York: *Livonia Gazette* (1984, p. 4); data for Washington State: *Your Public Schools* (1984, p. 17).

Notes: Year of enactment and year requirements become effective (E) are in parentheses. Blank cell may indicate locally set requirements ("local"), no requirement, or no data available.

Key to abbreviations: CP = computer science or literacy; E = English or language arts; FA = fine arts; FL = foreign language; H = health; M = mathematics; PE = physical education; S = science; SS = social studies.

A large proportion of Japanese youths attend nonformal schools held after school. In 1976 the Ministry of Education found that 20 percent of all elementary school children attended *juku*, which may offer lessons in academic subjects (including remedial studies and lessons for school entrance-examination preparation) or in piano, violin, calligraphy, and other arts. About 38 percent of all lower secondary school students also attended *juku* after school. The large number of students, especially those entering the higher grades of secondary schools, who spend much time outside of formal school hours studying for entrance examinations in *yobiko* or *juku*, or with a tutor or on their own, helps to explain why the Japanese need to require many hours of physical education in the compulsory schools as well as in upper secondary schools.

CONTROL OF THE CURRICULUM

In any study of American school curricula, it is important to emphasize that the curricula not only change continually with time but also vary widely from school to school throughout the country. Curriculum standards are defined differently from state to state, and many states leave the establishment of all or some of the standards to local school authorities. Furthermore, the curricula used by teachers may deviate widely from the official curricula. Thus it is very difficult to generalize about the school curriculum in the United States.

Recently, many efforts to reform the curriculum have been taking place in most of the states as a reaction to the flood of generally unfavorable reports on the condition of American schools, most notably the report of the National Commission on Excellence in Education, *A Nation at Risk* (1983), which received much attention by the media. Many legislatures, boards of education, and departments of education, all at the state level, have begun using their legal powers to mandate curriculum standards, textbook-selection requirements, graduation requirements, and school exit examinations. For example, California's legislature has recently established competency testing and more stringent high school graduation and teacher certification requirements for all schools in the state. As a result of this trend of state-level involvement, local school districts have been losing some of their delegated powers, much to the dismay of proponents of local control over the curriculum (see, for example, Olson 1984).

The trend toward greater state control and lessened local autonomy has produced controversy because many U.S. communities have traditionally resented direction from a government located outside their immediate jurisdiction. The trend is related also to the states having become the principal funding source for public schools, the traditional sources of local funding (especially the property tax) not having kept up with the rise in the cost of living. State legislatures, therefore, have been able to initiate directives pressuring state boards of education to exert greater control over local units of educational administration on many matters, including school curricula.

The details of curriculum control vary from state to state. For example, the Minnesota Board of Education set curriculum standards for high schools in 1984; but they specify only that schools must offer a minimum set of courses, and this minimum curriculum does not constitute graduation requirements (*Education Week* 1984b, p. 3). Several states, on the one hand, do not set statewide curricular requirements, leaving them to local districts; Hawaii, on the other, has no autonomous local school districts and is therefore the most centralized state in its curriculum development. It prescribes statewide minimum requirements for high school graduation. A study by Wirt (1977) shows the wide variety of school control practiced in the different states in the 1970s.

Table 4.1 not only shows the variety of state requirements for high school graduation in 1984 but also indicates that some of the states still permit local districts to determine the requirements. If a similar table were made for 1950, the number of states having local determination of requirements would be much larger.

Although local control has been traditional in many states, schooling in America has been primarily the legal responsibility of the states. The federal government plays only an indirect role, although it has been at times a significant force in shaping the curricula of U.S. schools. For example, vocational education was given great impetus by the Smith-Hughes Act of 1917, and the passage in 1975 of Public Law 94-142, the Education for All Handicapped Act, has greatly influenced both the development of special education programs and the nature of regular classroom teaching because the law has been interpreted to mean "mainstreaming" handicapped youth, whenever possible, with the other students.

Important to Americans though the federal government may be as an influence on school curricula, its role fades when one compares it to that of the central government in Japan. Japan's elementary and secondary school curricula are established nationwide for both private and public schools by the central government's Mōmbushō, the Ministry of Education, Science, and Culture. Although the U.S. Occupation Forces attempted to institute a more decentralized system of administrative control after World War II, the Japanese returned to a system of greater national control. Thus the Japanese curriculum, in comparison with that of the United States, is easier to delineate; furthermore, my observations suggest that most Japanese teachers follow the official curricula more closely than their American counterparts. Nevertheless, the most recent cycle of curricular revisions, announced in the late 1970s and enacted in the early 1980s, shows an attempt by the central government to give local authorities greater discretion in some of the details of the curriculum.

IMPLICIT PHILOSOPHY OF THE CURRICULUM

Differences in the philosophical perspectives of those who study Japanese or U.S. education color the description of the curricula and school systems of both countries. Recent books of two major American scholars of Japanese education are a case in point: William K. Cummings in his *Education and Equality in Japan* (1980) tends to emphasize the advantages of the demanding Japanese curriculum, which conforms to an official standard and assures that "children throughout the nation are exposed to a common body of knowledge in an identical sequence" (p. 10). Thomas P. Rohlen's *Japan's High Schools* (1983), on the other hand, is more critical of the Japanese curriculum and more favorable to America's greater tendency to value the spontaneous and the informal. He employs military metaphors in his description of Japanese high schools as "Spartan" (p. 167), a "social boot camp" (p. 168), and the purveyors of "a buttoned-down sense of time and space not unlike what one finds in the military" (p. 316). Both views reflect the differences in educational philosophy one finds among Americans: the conservative, essentialist philosophy of education represented by Cummings and the progressivist sympathies expressed by Rohlen. It is important, therefore, in any cross-cultural study of schools and their curricula to be aware of the philosophical and ideological lenses used to describe the curricula and teaching approaches.

If American researchers represent a range of value orientations in their views of education, so too do the Japanese. Yet distinct differences between the U.S. and Japanese approaches to the curriculum emerge because the curricular policies and practices result from various influences peculiar to the respective societies and cultures in which they are embedded. An attempt is made here to delineate these differences.

STABILITY AND CHANGE IN THE CURRICULUM

The American perspective on the curriculum, compared with that of the Japanese, seems more dynamic and pupil-centered. Although

Americans vary widely in their views of the curriculum, the recent record indicates that they are generally more experimental than the Japanese; new subjects can, and do, enter quickly into the classroom. The impetus stems from a variety of changes within local communities: new needs (the influx of Southeast Asian refugees, for instance) or the formation of political interest groups (the Moral Majority, environmental activists). There is also the American value of basing the curriculum on needs of individual pupils as perceived by the educators. In some schools, teachers can introduce a new elective course without much difficulty, whereas in Japan such an opportunity is less available to the teacher. What are permissible as elective courses in Japan are generally spelled out by the national courses of study, which change only about every ten years, after lengthy deliberations by the Ministry of Education and its advisory Curriculum Council, composed of teachers, professors, and others.

The phenomena of the "new mathematics," "open schools," and the recent emphasis on computer literacy are examples of the American receptiveness to change, a characteristic that can be described either in positive ("flexible," "innovative," and "progressive") or derogatory ("trendy," "faddish," and "directionless") terms, depending on one's point of view.

Rohlen (1983, p. 157) found that high schools in Japan offered only 25 to 30 courses in a year, whereas "a typical suburban American high school offers about two hundred courses over two semesters." Many high schools in Hawaii, with about 1,500 to 2,000 students in grades 9 through 12, offered more than 250 different courses in the 1984-85 academic year. In my visits in 1976 and 1978 to several general high schools in the Tokyo area that had about 800 to 1,200 students in grades 10 through 12, I found the number of different courses to range from about 40 to 55. The difference between my count of Japanese courses and that of Rohlen may be due to different criteria for determining what constitutes a course, but both counts are of similar magnitude when compared with the count for a moderate to large U.S. high school. The larger number of courses offered in U.S. schools is due partly to the larger size of many high schools, which affords a greater variety of teachers. The recent study of American high schools conducted by the Carnegie Foundation for the Advancement of Teaching found that some of the schools had more than 5,000 students, but half of them had fewer than 600 students (Boyer 1983, p. 20). Nevertheless, American high schools appear to have more latitude than the Japanese in deciding what are appropriate credit courses for meeting graduation requirements.

The following courses, which are often found in the course catalogues of U.S. high schools, normally would not be offered in Japanese high schools as separate credit courses, although some might be topics included in other courses:

- Driver education. Some states and local districts require that it be offered (Boyer 1983, p. 75). (In Japan, private entrepreneurs offer classes in their own schools.)
- Environmental studies
- Newswriting
- Yearbook production
- Science fiction
- Psychology
- Photography
- Weight lifting
- Ethnic studies
- Work experience
- Guitar

The Carnegie Foundation's study also found that in U.S. high schools about 55 percent of the courses offered during the four-year program were required, and the remainder were elective; and in many of the high schools most of the electives that students chose were in nonacademic fields (Boyer 1983, p. 77). In comparison, the Japanese specify only substantive courses (courses in academic subjects, arts, and industrial arts) as electives, while providing time in the school day for noncredit special activities. The U.S. National Commission on Excellence in Education (1983, pp. 18-19) found fault with the American "curricular smorgasbord," reporting that substantive elective courses were low in enrollments or were not even offered.

Japan is a leading manufacturer of computers, and computers have rapidly entered everyday Japanese life. Although many Japanese advocate the use of computers in schools, Japanese schools have not yet added computer instruction to the list of official courses in elementary and lower secondary schools or general upper secondary schools. But Japanese elementary schools still teach the use of the abacus in arithmetic calculations.

This example underscores the Japanese tendency to view the basic curriculum as unchanging and to regard new course material as rearranging the place of older material rather than replacing it: Use of the computer, the pocket calculator, and the slide rule is as important to learn as the abacus (Japan, Ministry of Education 1983a, p. 55; 1983b, p. 43). This tendency for rearrangement (rather than replacement) in the school curriculum is found in the inclusion of *rōmaji* (romanized Japanese writing using the English alphabet), along with *kanji* (Japanese written with Chinese characters) and two forms of *kana* (syllabary Japanese).

American educators, in contrast, tend to think of new material as replacing the old. During the Occupation many U.S. educational reformers (and also some Japanese educators) advocated substituting *rōmaji* for what they considered the cumbersome use of Chinese characters and *kana* in their unsuccessful attempt to have the Japanese simplify the process of attaining full literacy. Instead, the Japanese merely included *rōmaji* along with the three traditional scripts in their required course of study.

Japan also seems to have retained some elements of its oral tradition, despite having attained a high degree of literacy. Rote learning and memorization of certain material continue to be emphasized in the prescribed national courses of study, along with the development of creative and imaginative thinking. For example, rote is used in teaching the multiplication table and calligraphy. In music classes, students learn not only how to read and write music but also how to sing or play musical instruments by imitation and rote, thus maintaining both the chirographic and oral traditions in music. The use of rote is an especially important approach to teaching in nonformal schools that offer instruction in the Japanese traditional arts, such as the *Noh* dance, the tea ceremony, and flower arrangement (Kobayashi 1984).

Americans tend to discourage rote learning of material, perhaps because in the recent past rote learning was used as a form of punishment and the material to be memorized was often trivial. Thus the Japanese have moved toward more complex curricula, adding new elements to older ones and incorporating both Eastern and Western knowledge, whereas Americans prefer to substitute the obsolete with the new, their approach stemming perhaps from a more pragmatic mind-set.

In principle the Japanese are open to changes in their curriculum. Radical changes occurred during the Meiji period, when Japan began to modernize and Westernize and also during the U.S. Occupation. The changes in the last 20 years, however, have been more moderate, the official cycle of change occurring about every ten years.

THE CURRICULUM AS A REPRESENTATION OF NATIONAL CULTURE

Related to the greater variety of school courses and topics in the United States than in Japan are the cultural differences between the two countries, specifically the existence in Japan, but not in the United States, of a body of learning common to all youths undergoing formal education. Many U.S. educators yearn for a "common core" that Americans can learn in their schools. The Paideia proposal, advanced by Mortimer Adler (1982), is a sweeping "educational manifesto" that calls for a basic body of knowledge and learning through a common course of study. Although the Carnegie Foundation's report on U.S. high schools does not recommend "a national great books curriculum" (Boyer 1983, p. 96), it does view the attainment of common shared experiences as a desirable goal for high schools and seems nostalgic for the days when all students read such works as Shakespeare's *Julius Caesar* or Lowell's *Vision of Sir Launfal* in their literature classes. The authors of the report found only a few high schools today that require any of the great works of English literature (Boyer 1983, pp. 95-97). But even where there is support for a common core, educational policymakers disagree about what it should be. (For a recent discussion, see Ranbom 1984.)

The philosopher Harry Broudy (1981) asserts that until recently Americans had a consensus on the values and the culture that a public school should promote, but today they have "a public school without a public" because single-interest political groups all claim a place for their concerns in the curriculum. Even the middle class, he argues, no longer shares a common view of the values that schools should promote.

In Japan, on the other hand, the importance of learning a common body of material is continually emphasized by schools, to a degree unimaginable in the United States today. The following examples of this tendency to emphasize familiarity with common material are only a few of those found in Japan's compulsory lower secondary schools. It is noteworthy that the Japanese include both Japanese and Western classics in their core curriculum.

- In music, all eighth graders can be expected to have studied Beethoven's *Fifth Symphony*, Bach's *Little Fugue in G Minor*, and Debussy's *Clair de lune* along with *Etenraku* from the traditional *gagaku* repertoire and a song from the famous Kabuki play *Kanjincho*. All ninth graders have studied Smetana's *Die Moldau*, Grieg's *Piano Concerto in A Minor*, and the *shakuhachi* (Japanese traditional flute) masterpiece *Shika no Tohne* (Japan, Ministry of Education 1983b, pp. 65, 67). The curriculum for elementary school (grades 1 through 6) specifies works of Bach, Mozart, Beethoven, and other Western composers, as well as such Japanese traditional songs as *Sakura* and *Furusato* (Japan, Ministry of Education 1983a, pp. 71-84).

- All students learn to read and write music in standard Western notation and also learn music through rote (Japan, Ministry of Education 1983a, p. 77).
- In physical education, all students in the compulsory lower secondary school learn to swim, using the crawl, breaststroke, and backstroke, and all learn to play basketball, soccer, and volleyball, as well as the traditional *sumo*, *judo*, and *kendo* (Japan, Ministry of Education 1983b, p. 78).
- All boys learn how to read electrical circuit diagrams of electrical devices (Japan, Ministry of Education 1983b, p. 91).

Because the curriculum is specified at the national level and the courses of study prepared by the Ministry of Education set the standards for all schools, the Japanese curriculum permits little opportunity for unnecessary repetition of subject matter. For example, the courses of study specify which Chinese and other writing characters must be learned at each grade level in the courses of Japanese languages, so that by the end of elementary school, students should have learned both *kana* syllabaries used and a minimum of 996 *kanji* Chinese characters (Japan, Ministry of Education 1983a, pp. 24-26). By the end of ninth grade, which is the last grade of compulsory school, students should have learned to read most of the 1,945 standard *kanji* in use in Japanese newspapers, magazines, and popular books and to write at least 1,000 of them (Japan, Ministry of Education Culture 1983b, p. 12). From kindergarten through upper secondary school, topics in all courses—from literature, history, science, and mathematics to physical education—are spelled out in the national courses of study. (See Exhibit 4.1 for the *kanji* required of children in grades 1 through 9.)

Exhibit 4.1. *Kanji* to be learned by grade level, Japan, 1983

Grade 1 (76 characters)

一 古 雨 円 王 音 下 火 花 学 気 九 休 金 空 月 犬 見 五 口
校 左 三 山 子 四 糸 字 耳 七 車 手 十 出 女 小 上 森 人 水
正 生 青 夕 石 赤 千 川 先 早 足 村 大 男 中 虫 町 天 田 土
二 日 入 年 白 八 百 文 木 本 名 目 立 力 林 六

Grade 2 (145 characters)

引 雲 遠 何 科 夏 家 歌 画 回 会 海 絵 貝 外 間 顔 汽 記 帰
牛 魚 京 教 強 玉 近 形 計 元 原 戸 古 午 後 語 工 広 交 光
行 考 高 黄 合 谷 国 黒 今 才 作 算 止 市 思 紙 寺 自 時 室
社 弱 首 秋 春 書 少 場 色 食 心 新 親 図 数 西 声 星 晴 切
雪 船 前 組 走 草 多 太 体 台 池 地 知 竹 茶 昼 長 鳥 朝 通
弟 店 点 電 冬 刀 当 東 答 頭 同 道 読 南 馬 買 売 麦 半 番
父 風 分 聞 米 歩 母 方 北 毎 妹 明 鳴 毛 門 夜 野 友 用 曜
来 楽 里 理 話

Grade 3 (195 characters)

悪 安 暗 医 意 育 員 院 飲 運 泳 駅 園 横 屋 温 化 荷 界 開
階 角 活 寒 感 館 岸 岩 起 期 客 究 急 級 宮 球 去 橋 業 曲
局 銀 苦 具 君 兄 係 軽 血 決 県 研 言 庫 湖 公 向 幸 港 号
根 祭 細 仕 死 使 始 指 歯 詩 次 事 持 式 実 写 者 主 守 取
酒 受 州 拾 終 習 週 集 住 重 所 暑 助 昭 消 商 章 勝 乗 植
申 身 神 深 進 世 整 線 全 送 息 族 他 打 対 待 代 第 題 炭
短 着 注 柱 帳 調 直 追 丁 定 庭 鉄 転 都 度 投 島 湯 登 等
動 童 内 肉 農 波 配 畑 発 反 坂 板 皮 悲 美 鼻 氷 表 秒 病
品 負 部 服 福 物 平 返 勉 放 万 味 命 面 問 役 薬 由 油 有
遊 予 洋 葉 陽 様 落 流 旅 両 緑 礼 列 路 和

Exhibit 4.1, cont.

Grade 4 (195 characters)
愛 案 衣 以 囲 位 委 胃 印 英 栄 塩 央 億 加 貨 課 芽 改 械
害 各 覚 完 官 漢 管 関 観 願 希 季 紀 喜 旗 器 機 議 求 救
給 挙 漁 共 協 鏡 競 極 区 軍 郡 型 景 芸 欠 結 建 健 験 固
功 候 航 康 告 差 菜 最 材 昨 刷 殺 察 参 散 産 残 士 氏 史
司 姉 試 辞 失 借 種 周 宿 順 初 省 唱 照 賞 焼 臣 信 真 成
清 勢 静 席 積 折 節 説 浅 戦 選 然 争 相 倉 想 象 速 側 続
辛 孫 帯 隊 達 単 談 治 置 貯 腸 低 底 停 的 典 伝 徒 努 燈
堂 働 毒 熱 念 敗 倍 博 飯 飛 費 必 筆 票 標 不 夫 付 府 副
粉 兵 別 辺 変 便 包 法 望 牧 末 満 脈 民 約 勇 要 養 浴 利
陸 良 料 量 輪 類 令 冷 例 歴 連 練 老 労 録

Grade 5 (195 characters)
圧 易 移 因 永 営 衛 益 液 演 往 応 恩 仮 果 河 過 価 賀 快
解 格 確 額 刊 幹 慣 歓 眼 基 寄 規 技 義 逆 久 旧 居 許 境
興 均 禁 句 訓 群 経 潔 件 券 険 検 絹 限 現 減 故 個 護 効
厚 耕 構 講 鉱 混 査 再 災 妻 採 際 在 財 罪 雑 蚕 酸 賛 支
示 志 師 資 似 児 識 質 舎 謝 授 収 修 衆 祝 述 術 準 序 除
招 承 称 証 条 状 常 情 織 職 制 性 政 精 製 税 責 績 接 設
舌 絶 銭 善 祖 素 総 造 像 増 則 測 属 損 退 貸 態 団 断 築
張 提 程 敵 適 統 銅 導 特 得 徳 独 任 燃 能 破 犯 判 版 比
非 肥 備 俵 評 貧 布 婦 富 武 復 複 仏 編 弁 保 墓 報 豊 防
貿 暴 未 務 無 迷 綿 輸 余 預 容 率 略 留 領

Exhibit 4.1, cont.

Grade 6 (190 characters)
異 道 城 壱 宇 羽 映 延 沿 可 我 灰 街 革 拡 閣 割 株 干 巻
看 勧 簡 丸 危 机 揮 貴 疑 弓 吸 泣 供 胸 郷 勤 筋 系 径 敬
警 劇 穴 兼 憲 権 源 厳 己 呼 誤 后 好 孝 皇 紅 降 鋼 刻 穀
骨 困 砂 座 済 裁 策 冊 至 私 姿 視 詞 誌 磁 射 捨 尺 釈 若
需 樹 宗 就 従 縦 縮 熟 純 処 署 諸 将 笑 傷 障 城 蒸 針 仁
垂 推 寸 是 聖 誠 宣 専 染 泉 洗 奏 窓 創 層 操 蔵 臓 俗 存
尊 宅 担 探 段 暖 値 仲 宙 忠 著 庁 兆 頂 潮 賃 痛 展 党 討
糖 届 難 弐 乳 認 納 脳 派 拝 肺 背 俳 班 晩 否 批 秘 腹 奮
陛 閉 片 補 宝 訪 亡 忘 棒 枚 幕 密 盟 模 矢 訳 郵 優 幼 羊
欲 翌 乱 卵 覧 裏 律 臨 朗 論

Source: Japan, Ministry of Education, Science, and Culture (1983a, pp. 24-26).

THE CURRICULUM: NATIONAL UNIFORMITY OR DIVERSITY?

The uniformity of subject matter considered so important by the Japanese would be disturbing to many Americans, who would regard it as incompatible with American individualism and freedom of choice. Although the rhetoric might not match the reality, Americans like to emphasize the development of creative thinking, problem solving, "learning to learn," and the respect for individual differences—thus preferring a flexible curriculum suited to the interests and aptitudes of individual students. The U.S. school is thus the scene of continual debate about what should be the orientation and content of the school curriculum. As a result, the curriculum is often eclectic, based on a compromise between groups having different values. It also varies from school to school, depending on the outcome of local educational politics, as influenced by national and international events, such as the publication of a Coleman Report or *A Nation at Risk* or the orbiting of the Soviet satellite *Sputnik* in 1957. The wide variety and ephemeral character of the American curriculum may have negative effects on its credibility to children and the general population by conveying the message that what is taught is arbitrary and therefore insignificant.

The U.S. curriculum is influenced by special interest groups advocating the teaching of such topics as "creationism" in science classes, sex education, driver education,[1] law-related education, global education, career education, peace education, consumer education, and ethnic studies--all of which compete for the limited time frame of the curriculum. Because of the decentralized control of the curriculum in the United States, what might be agreed upon as a common curriculum for all students in one state or school district would not necessarily be acceptable in another. Many states require all students to learn about their state or region. Hawaii, for example, includes in its statewide public school curriculum the study of Polynesian culture and the history of modern Hawaii.

Although the Japanese do have disagreements about curriculum content, their differences are not so basic among the population as a whole nor among the dominant groups that determine national curriculum standards. It is not that Japanese devalue the freedom of young people to pursue subjects that interest them but that the official school is the one place where children have an opportunity to acquire fundamental knowledge and values and to achieve physical development. Special activities, including hobbies and student government, are offered during schooltime, and minimum hours for them are mandated in the more recent courses of study; but they do not have the same importance as credit courses required for completion of schoolwork. The Japanese view these activities as important primarily in their contribution to all-around development. The objectives for special activities in the course of study for lower secondary schools are stated in the following way:

> Through desirable group activities, to promote harmonious development of mind and body, to develop the individuality, to enhance the self-awareness of being a member of a group, and to cultivate self-reliant, independent, and practical attitude[s] to enrich the school life in co-operation with others. (Japan, Ministry of Education 1983b, p. 126)

RELATIVE STABILITY OF CURRICULUM IN JAPAN

The Japanese approach to curriculum reform is also more stable because it has been determined at the national level by a government run continuously by the Conservative party since the end of the Occupation. Thus the curriculum has been less susceptible than it otherwise might have been to pressures from political groups that might be dominant at the local level. Although shifting coalitions within the Conservative party might affect the national leadership, including the appointment of the minister of education, the ministry itself is a fairly stable bureaucracy. The ten-year cycles of curriculum reform worked out by the educational bureaucracy contribute to the stability of the curriculum. In comparison, American curriculum reform tends to occur in an ad hoc, less predictable manner. The stability of the Japanese curriculum is also related to the relative homogeneity of Japanese society, so different from the multiethnic society of the United States.

The Japanese Curriculum Since World War II

The U.S. Occupation (1945-52) initiated radical changes in the Japanese curriculum, as well as in other aspects of Japanese education. Pupil-centered, problem-solving approaches emphasizing student initiative and direction, with attempts to correlate different subjects, were tried out by the Japanese. There was even a "Dewey boom" in Japan, whereby educators became fascinated by the ideas of John Dewey, America's patron saint of liberalism and progressive education, whose pragmatic philosophy was considered the underlying basis for American education (Kobayashi 1964; Nagai and Nishijima 1975, p. 179).

Since the 1950s, however, the curriculum has again become more subject-centered, with key subjects dominating the curriculum that would please more conservative American educators but would disappoint those who prefer a more Deweyan, experimentalist, problem-centered, activities approach to schooling. Although the Japanese approach recognizes the validity of Dewey's ideas, it embodies the view that for most students and teachers a conservative, systematic, essentialistic approach to curriculum is necessary and desirable because the strict application of Dewey's ideas to the curriculum would be difficult for ordinary pupils and teachers to handle effectively. Ordinary teachers require greater structure in order for the curriculum to have direction and content. The system of entrance examinations that figures so importantly for students interested in entering prestigious universities also reinforces the view of the curriculum as composed of fixed bodies of essential knowledge rather than as a series of experiences organized around "felt needs" and social problems.

The present curriculum for Japanese elementary and secondary schools was enacted in 1977-78 and went into effect in 1981. It is the third of a series of revisions that have taken place since the sweeping curricular reforms of the Occupation period, under the principles established in two laws passed by the government in 1947: the Fundamental Law of Education, which sets the goals of the educational system, and the School Education Law, which provides the direction for the organization of schools and for the curriculum. In 1947 the Ministry of Education drafted the first school course guidelines, which were greatly influenced by American models. The first post-Occupation revision was made in 1958. The second came in 1968-70 and was enforced in 1971-73. The recent revisions came in 1977-78.

School course guidelines primarily establish national standards for the content of what is to be taught and the minimum standards required of all students, whether they are in private or public elementary and secondary schools. Although each prefecture and each school establishes its own curriculum, the curriculum must be based on these national guidelines and standards. The latest revision provides for schools to have greater flexibility in organizing their curricula, but because of the national standards, Japanese schools have much less flexibility than U.S. schools, with their decentralized and looser system of curriculum standards. Exhibit 4.2 shows the shifts in emphases made in the Japanese curriculum during the periodic revisions since the end of the U.S. Occupation.

Today's Curriculum Content in Japan

In the present curriculum for grades 1 through 12, the list of "basics" for the Japanese includes not only Japanese language and literature, social studies (civics, geography, history, and contemporary society), mathematics, and science but also the arts, physical education, and homemaking and industrial arts. Moral education, based on democratic and humanistic ethics, has also been in the list of required courses for the compulsory school levels, grades 1 through 9, since it was introduced in the early 1960s, amid great controversy. With a solid content, with a variety of key subjects in the sciences and the arts, and with an eye to the moral and physical development of youth, the Japanese curriculum should be considered by American educators who favor "essentialism" as a philosophy of education. From such a perspective the Japanese curriculum seems quite balanced and impressive.

Tables 4.2 and 4.3 show the most recently enacted standard requirements for all students in the elementary grades (1 through 6) and lower secondary grades (7 through 9), which are compulsory. Table 4.4 shows the number of credits and their clock-hour equivalents required to complete upper secondary school, which is noncompulsory. The standards apply to both public and private schools.

Exhibit 4.2   Summary of curriculum revisions since the U.S. Occupation,
Japan, 1958-78

1958

Effective in 1961 for elementary schools, in 1962 for lower secondary schools,
and in 1963 for upper secondary schools. The Ministry of Education, Science,
and Culture, through the 1956 revision of the School Board Law, was given
more authority to determine curriculum and course content, reducing degree of
freedom previously held by teachers. A minimum number of hours was established. A course in moral education, one hour weekly, was introduced and
required in schools at the compulsory level (grades 1 through 9).

1968-70

Effective in 1971 for elementary schools, in 1972 for lower secondary schools,
and in 1973 for upper secondary schools. Standard hours were set. With more
than three-fourths of graduates of compulsory school going to upper secondary
school, the lower secondary school curriculum needed to be articulated with that
of upper secondary school. No changes were made in hours for subjects for elementary school. Standard hours in lower secondary schools increased for Japanese language, mathematics, fine arts, health and physical education, industrial
arts (for boys), homemaking (for girls), and special activities.

1977-78

Effective in 1980 for elementary schools, in 1981 for lower secondary schools,
and in 1982 for upper secondary schools. The revisions permit greater flexibility
to schools in organizing the curriculum, although national standards must be
followed. Minimum requirements for academic and other subjects have been reduced, allowing local levels and individual schools to have more discretion in
utilizing schooltime. The number of classroom hours required in elementary and
lower secondary school have been reduced for Japanese language, social studies,
mathematics, and science. Hours have been reduced in music and arts/handicrafts
in elementary school; lower secondary school electives and industrial arts hours
for boys and homemaking hours for girls have been reduced; more school hours
have been specified for special activities; total hours required for lower secondary
school children have been reduced. For upper secondary school, minimum credit
requirements have been reduced for Japanese language, social studies, mathematics, and science, and the minimum total number of credits required to graduate reduced from 85 to 80 credits (1 credit = 35, 50-minute periods).

The requirements that became effective in 1980 reduced the number of hours for required courses in language, mathematics and science, and social studies. The academic content of previous courses of study was found to be too advanced for the average pupil, and the revisions therefore reduced the amount of material to be covered. More time was provided for special activities, including extracurricular activities. The intent was to provide more time for the teachers to attend to the development of students' character and personalities (Ichikawa 1984, p. 106). In the words of the Curriculum Council, which advises the Ministry of Education on the general policies to be followed in curriculum revision, the new revisions had a goal of enabling students "to lead a relaxed and full school life" (Japan, Ministry of Education 1976c, pp. 81-82). There was also, perhaps, the recognition that many students in upper secondary schools that had low rates of continuation into college were unable to keep up with the demands of the previous standards. Table 4.5 shows the changes in required hours for all of the major subjects for elementary, lower secondary, and upper secondary school.

Table 4.2   Standard curriculum for elementary schools, Japan, 1980

Subject	Grade					
	1	2	3	4	5	6
Japanese language	272	280	280	280	210	210
Social studies	68	70	105	105	105	105
Arithmetic	136	175	175	175	175	175
Science	68	70	105	105	105	105
Music	68	70	70	70	70	70
Arts and crafts	68	70	70	70	70	70
Physical education	102	105	105	105	105	105
Homemaking	0	0	0	0	70	70
Moral education	34	35	35	35	35	35
Activities[a]	34	35	35	70	70	70
Total	850	910	980	1,015	1,015	1,015
Total clock hours	637.5	682.5	735	913.5	913.5	913.5

Note: 1 school hour = 1 45-minute class period.

[a]Activities include both after-school activities and those held during school hours, such as class assemblies, field trips, library-use training, traffic safety training, and guidance, for which time is allotted within the school curriculum.

Source: Japan, Ministry of Education (1983a, p. 122).

Table 4.3   Standard curriculum for middle schools, Japan, 1980

Subject	Grade 7	Grade 8	Grade 9
Japanese language	175 (146)	140 (117)	140 (117)
Social studies	140 (117)	140 (117)	105 (88)
Mathematics	105 (88)	140 (117)	140 (117)
Science	105 (88)	105 (88)	140 (117)
Music	70 (58)	70 (58)	35 (29)
Fine arts	70 (58)	70 (58)	35 (29)
Health and physical education	105 (88)	105 (88)	105 (88)
Industrial arts (boys)/homemaking (girls)	70 (58)	70 (58)	105 (88)
Foreign language or other subject[a]	105 (88)	105 (88)	105 (88)
Other subjects[b]	0	0	35 (29)
Moral education	35 (29)	35 (29)	35 (29)
Activities[c]	70 (58)	70 (58)	70 (58)
Total	1,050 (875)	1,050 (875)	1,050 (875)

Notes: 1 school hour = 1 50-minute class period. Numbers in parentheses represent clock-hour equivalents.

[a]Almost all students study English to meet this requirement.

[b]Students are required to take one of the following subjects: music, fine arts, health and physical education, industrial arts, or homemaking.

[c]Activities include both after-school activities and those held during allotted school hours.

Source: Japan, Ministry of Education (1983b, p. 131).

Table 4.4   Number of credits and hours required to complete upper secondary school (grades 10-12), Japan, 1980

Subject	Credits[a]	Classroom hours
Japanese	4	117
Social studies	4	117
Mathematics	4	117
Science	4	117
Physical education[b]	7-9	204-262
Health[b]	2	58
Art	3	87
Other courses, including electives	52	1,604
Total required to graduate	80	2,333

[a]1 credit = 35 unit hours. Each unit hour = 50 minutes of teaching. Therefore, clock-hour equivalents are obtained by multiplying the number of credits by 35 and also by 50 minutes and then dividing the product by 60 minutes.

[b]For physical education and health combined, 11 credits, or 320.8 clock hours, are required for most males. The figure given here is the minimum of 9, which applies to all females and to males in vocational programs.

Source of credit hour requirements: Japan, Ministry of Education (1983c, pp. 2-3).

Table 4.5   Changes in minimum clock hours required for various
                 subjects, Japan, 1971-80

Subject and year	Hours		
	Elementary (grades 1-6)	Lower secondary (grades 7-9)	Upper secondary (grades 10-12)
Japanese			
1971	1,202	437	262
1980	1,149	379	117
Change	-53	-58	-145
Social studies			
1971	497	379	292
1980	418	321	117
Change	-79	-58	-175
Mathematics			
1971	785	350	175
1980	758	321	117
Change	-27	-29	-58
Science			
1971	471	350	175
1980	418	292	116
Change	-53	-58	-59
Health and physical education			
1971	470	312	262-321[a]
1980	470	262	262-321[a]
Change	0	-50	0
Music			
1971	339	146	117[b]
1980	313	146	117[b]
Change	-26	0	0
Arts and crafts			
1971	339	146	117[b]
1980	313	146	117[b]
Change	-26	0	0
Homemaking/industrial arts			
1971	105	279	117[c]
1980	105	204	117[c]
Change	0	-75	0
Moral education			
1971	157	87	none
1980	157	87	none
Change	0	0	
Electives			
1971	none	350	ns
1980	none	292	ns
Change		-58	

Table 4.5, cont.

Special subjects			
1971	ns	125	ns
1980	235	175	ns
Change		+50	
Total			
1971	4,366	2,946	2,479[d]
1980	4,365	2,625	2,334[d]
Change	-1	-321	-145

ns = not specified

[a]Health and physical education requirement varies, depending on sex and whether one is enrolled in vocational courses.

[b]For upper secondary school a total of three credits was required for art *or* music, but because courses came in modules of two credits, the actual minimum became four credits. The four-credit equivalent is used in this table.

[c]In upper secondary school, industrial arts are required only of boys and home economics is required only of girls. At the elementary level both are required for boys and girls.

[d]The minimum number of hours required for upper secondary schools.

JAPANESE AND U.S. REQUIREMENTS COMPARED

If minimum requirements for graduation from the twelfth grade are considered, American schools require, on the average, more clock hours of classroom instruction in language arts and social studies than do Japanese schools. (A clock hour, 60 minutes, is used as the unit of comparison, because U.S. class periods vary in length, whereas the Japanese use a 50-minute class hour as the basic unit.) Japanese schools, on the other hand, require more hours of instruction in mathematics, science, and physical education and health (see Tables 4.5 and 4.6).

Table 4.7 shows the U.S. minimum requirements for graduation from twelfth grade in 1980 compared with those of Japan under the newly revised curriculum in effect since 1981, in terms of classroom-hour equivalents. The U.S. data are averages of minimum requirements specified by different states (some states require more classroom hours in some subjects, others fewer). The minimum requirements for the Japanese case hold for all students in both academic and vocational courses throughout the nation, and were calculated by combining the requirements for the last year of lower secondary school (ninth grade) and for the nearly universally attended noncompulsory upper secondary school (grades 10 through 12).

Table 4.6   Average number of academic units (years) mandated for graduation from four-year high schools, United States, 1980

Subject	Units[a]	Clock hours[b]
English	3.53	424
Social studies	2.05	246
Mathematics	1.28	154
Science	1.24	149
Physical education and health	1.38	166
Other electives	8.02	962
Total	17.5	2,100

[a]Average number of academic units required by states.

[b]Clock hours were calculated by multiplying number of academic units by 120 hours, based on the conversion formula of 1 Carnegie unit = 120 hours in a year.

Source of average number of academic units required by the states: NASSP (1980).

This comparison is only suggestive because the hours listed indicate merely what is *minimally* required in both countries. In actual practice the average numbers of clock hours in classrooms spent by students in various subjects in both Japan and the United States will be above the minimum because many of the students will be completing more classes than are required in those subjects.

Table 4.8 illustrates this for U.S. high school students in 1982 and for college-bound high school students in 1983. It indicates that the *average* number of units earned by U.S. high school graduates in 1982 was 2,616 clock hours, as compared with the 3,150 classroom hours that are *minimally* required of all Japanese high school students (Table 4.7): a difference of 534 clock hours. (The average number of units earned in Japan would be even higher.)

Table 4.7   Minimum amount of class time (in clock hours) required in several key subjects for graduation from high school, Japan and the United States, recent years

Subject	Japan[a] (since 1982)	United States[b]	
		Average (1980)	State X (1984)
Language arts	233	424	480 (at least 26 states)
Social studies	204	246	480 (Hawaii, New York)
Mathematics	233	154	360 (8 states)
Science	233	149	360 (Florida, Louisiana, Pennsylvania, Vermont)
Physical education and health	233	166	480 (New Jersey)
Arts/music[c]	175		120 (5 states)
Electives	1,825		
Total required	3,150	2,100	2,880 (Florida)[d]

[a]Clock hours for the Japanese case were calculated by combining clock-hour equivalents for the minimum requirements for ninth grade (grade 3 of lower secondary school) requirements with the clock-hour equivalents for the minimum credits required to complete upper secondary school (grades 10 through 12). Hours are for the standard curriculum in effect since 1982.

[b]The U.S. classroom time in clock hours was derived by multiplying number of credits by 120 hours, a formula that may not be exactly applicable to all U.S. states. Hours in the first column are the average required among states in 1980. Since then many states have raised their requirements, a fact reflected in the data for "State X," which represents a composite of the highest minimum requirements among the 50 states listed in Table 4.1. Some of these requirements are being phased in and may not yet be required.

[c]Although only three Japanese credits in art or music are required in the general course of the upper secondary school level (grades 10-12), students take four credits because the courses come in modules of two credits each. This calculation is based on the four-credit figure. The figure would be 116 hours for students in the vocational course. Students take 70 hours (56 clock hours) of art or music in the eighth grade.

[d]The next highest numbers of minimum credits required to graduate are 2,760 hours (Louisiana, with 23 units) and 2,640 hours (Alabama, Missouri, and Oklahoma, with 22 units). See Table 4.1 for complete list.

Source: Derived from data presented in other tables of this chapter.

Table 4.8 Average number of units earned by high school graduates in selected
subjects, United States, 1982 and 1983

Subject	1982		1983 (college-bound only)	
English	3.8	(456)	3.99	(479)
Social studies	3.1	(372)	3.23	(388)
Mathematics	2.6	(312)	3.62	(434)
Science	2.1	(252)	3.25	(390)
Computer science	0.1	(12)	ns	
Foreign language	1.1	(132)	2.23	(268)
Average total earned in all subjects	21.8	(2,616)		

Notes: Units are Carnegie units. Numbers in parentheses represent clock-hour equivalents. 1 Carnegie unit = 120 clock hours.
ns = not specified
Source: Adapted from U.S. Department of Education (1984, p. 170).
Figures for 1983 are from Educational Research Service (1984, p. 1).

Other considerations suggest that, compared with the American high school curriculum, the Japanese curriculum for grades 9 through 12 is even more demanding than the classroom-hour figures in Tables 4.7 and 4.8 indicate. The U.S. figures were calculated by converting each Carnegie unit into 120 classroom hours, but one unit represents 120 teaching hours that may be anywhere from 45 to 60 minutes long per hour (that is, one Carnegie unit could represent as few as 90 classroom hours, if the teaching hour is 45 minutes). Because the topics to be covered are spelled out nationally, Japanese schools also generally cover more material in their classroom hours than does the average high school in the United States. U.S. high school teachers generally have more latitude in how they use class time and what subjects they may cover.

Moreover, in Japan the minimum number of required credits applies only to specific courses and does not include activities that would be given credit in some U.S. high schools. Required and standard courses cover topics incrementally so as to avoid repeating the same material. Remedial lessons are left to nonformal private schools and tutors. Standard courses offered in upper secondary school are shown in Table 4.9.

Table 4.9　　　　Standard upper secondary school curriculum, Japan, 1983

Subject and course	Credits
Japanese language	
Japanese Language I*	4
Japanese Language II	4
Japanese Language Expression	2
Contemporary Japanese Language	3
Classics	4
Social studies	
Contemporary Society*	4
Japanese History	4
World History	4
Geography	4
Ethics	2
Politics and Economy	2
Mathematics	
Mathematics I*	4
Mathematics II	3
Algebra and Geometry	3
Basic analysis	3
Differential and Integer Calculus	3
Probability and Statistics	3
Science	
Science I*	4
Science II	2
Physics	4
Chemistry	4
Biology	4
Earth Science	4
Health and physical education	
Physical Education*	7-9
Health*	2
Arts[a]	
Music I, II, III	2 each
Fine Arts I, II, III	2 each
Crafts Production I, II, III	2 each
Calligraphy I, II, III	2 each

(continued on next page)

Table 4.9, cont.

Subject and course	Credits
Foreign languages[b]	
English I	4
English II	5
English IIA, IIB, IIC	3 each
Home economics	
General Home Economics*	4

Notes: An asterisk(*) indicates a required course. One credit = 35 school hours of 50 minutes each (29 clock hours). Individual schools may increase the number of credits over the standard number. Only girls are required to take home economics. Boys, except those in vocational courses, and all girls are required to take seven to nine credits of physical education. Students in general courses are required to take at least three credits in the arts.

[a]One arts course is required.
[b]French or German may be substituted for English.
Source: Japan, Ministry of Education (1983b, pp. 2-8).

Another indication that the typical Japanese secondary school student receives more intense exposure to course subjects than the typical American student has to do with the way class time is utilized. My own observations of Japanese schools in 1976 and 1978 confirm previous suggestions that Japanese teachers use class time more efficiently for instruction than do American teachers, who seem to spend more time getting the class settled and dealing with disturbances and interruptions (Cummings 1980, pp. 111, 153). The much higher dropout rates in U.S. high schools also suggest that student absentee rates may be substantially higher in the United States than in Japan.

I have observed, moreover, that American teachers spend more classroom time than Japanese teachers in discussions with students, who have a greater say in determining the direction of the discussions. Americans have much more tolerance for this tendency, considering it an asset. Other observers have noticed similar tendencies (Rohlen 1983, pp. 241-47; Bereday and Masui 1973, pp. 110-14). The Japanese curriculum can be described, then, in two ways, depending on one's orientation: as more uniform, more demanding, more efficient, more focused, than the U.S. curriculum; or as overly standardized, oppressive, and rigid.

Another difference between the U.S. and Japanese curricula is the lack of required courses in art and music and in domestic and industrial arts in U.S. secondary schools. The Japanese require these subjects from kindergarten through secondary school. The U.S. study by the National Commission on Excellence in Education, *A Nation at Risk* (1983), did not include these subjects in its list of "new basics" recommended as prerequisites for a high school diploma. The report by the U.S. Department of Education, *The Condition of Education* (1984), provides no data on the number of courses taken by U.S. high school students in art or music, although it provides data on English, mathematics, science, social studies, foreign languages, and computer sciences. The Carnegie Foundation report considered the arts "shamefully neglected" in most of the high schools its researchers visited (Boyer 1983, p. 98). The Gallup polls over the last few years have consistently indicated that only about one-fourth or less of the American public support art and music requirements in public high schools (Gallup 1984, p. 30). To my knowledge only Missouri, New Jersey, New Mexico, New York, Pennsylvania, and Vermont among the 50 states have instituted a one-year arts requirement for high school graduation, although a few states now include it as one of several options in meeting a one-unit requirement for high school (see Table 4.1).

CONCLUSIONS

The Japanese have been relaxing their standards, allowing for more time in nonacademic activities and decreasing the number of minimum hours in such subjects as language, mathematics and science, and social studies, at a time when Americans have been attempting to increase both the hourly and content requirements of academic subjects. Nonetheless, both the required Japanese curriculum and the standard Japanese curriculum continue to have greater intensity of subject matter than the typical U.S. curriculum up to 1981.

The Japanese have been decreasing the degree of uniformity in their national curriculum by reducing the standard requirements for lower secondary and upper secondary schools, while encouraging local authorities to use more discretion in determining the curriculum. In contrast, U.S. states are moving toward more uniformity of minimum standards for high school graduation. Japan, nevertheless, continues to have a very high degree of uniformity, with a national course of studies, unlike the United States.

Japanese children spend more hours in the classroom than do American students, and the minimum requirements of their curriculum include more subjects. Schools in the United States tend to focus on mathematics and science, reading, and "basic survival skills," whereas the Japanese have a broader conception of "the basics" that includes classics, foreign languages, art and music, industrial arts and homemaking, and physical education, as well as the native language, social studies, science, and mathematics.

The Japanese approach to the curriculum is to set high standards for all at each grade level and to encourage teachers and students to meet those standards. As a result, the Japanese may actually promote greater achievement rates among the average pupils and perhaps raise levels of those below. However, students in the lower percentile ranks of academic achievement may still not be able to meet the standards set. The Japanese, nevertheless, automatically pass such students on through secondary schools. Their rationale is that doing one's best is as important as meeting the standards set. Most of those students do not intend to take college entrance examinations or enter a college that might accept them. They seem able to find a place in society. In contrast, U.S. schools seem to prefer less demanding curricula that almost all students can handle successfully, leaving room for students to choose electives appropriate for their different abilities. They have also begun adopting minimum competency exit tests and are deeply ambivalent about the issues of automatic promotion from grade to grade and of automatic graduation.

In the early 1980s many states in the U.S. raised minimum high school graduation requirements, but even after those new standards go into effect the *overall* Japanese class time requirements will be higher than for any of the states. However, the minimum number of classroom hours in language arts, social studies (including history and civics), mathematics, and science needed for graduation from high school will exceed Japanese requirements in many states as new requirements go into effect. The new U.S. classroom hour requirements in the late 1980s for most of the states will continue to be less than Japan's in art and in physical education and health. Japan will allow more electives to be applied toward its graduation requirements than will the United States; but because its range of electives offered will be narrower, the actual classroom time spent by most students in various academic subjects may continue to be as high as, if not higher than, by most U.S. students. Therefore, the two countries' curricular requirements seem to be growing more similar, except in the arts.

NOTE

1. Gallup (1984) reports that almost three-fourths of the American public support driver education as a high school requirement.

REFERENCES

Adler, Mortimer J. 1982. *The Paideia Proposal: An Educational Manifesto*. New York: Macmillan.

Anderson, Ronald S. 1975. *Education in Japan: A Century of Modern Development*. Publication No. (OE)74-19110, Department of Health, Education, and Welfare. Washington, D.C.: U.S. Government Printing Office.

Bereday, George Z. F., and Shigeo Masui, eds. 1973. *American Education Through Japanese Eyes*. Honolulu: University Press of Hawaii.

Boyer, Ernest L. 1983. *High School: A Report on Secondary Education in America by the Carnegie Foundation for the Advancement of Teaching*. New York: Harper & Row.

Broudy, Harry S. 1981. "A Public School Without a Public." *Occasional Papers in Social Foundations of Education*, No. 5. Honolulu: Department of Educational Foundations, University of Hawaii.

Cummings, William K. 1980. *Education and Equality in Japan*. Princeton, N.J.: Princeton University Press.

Educational Research Service. 1984. "Profiles of College-Bound Seniors." 11, no. 10: 1.

Education Week. 1983. December 7, pp. 5-17.

_____. 1984a. April 11.

_____. 1984b. "Minnesota Board Sets Requirements for High Schools." September 26, p.3.

_____. 1985. February 6.

Gallup, George H. 1984. "The 16th Annual Gallup Poll of the Public's Attitudes Toward the Public Schools." *Phi Delta Kappan* (September): 23-38.

Ichikawa, Shogo. 1984. "Japan." In *Educational Policy: An International Survey*, edited by J. R. Hough, pp. 100-35. New York: St. Martin's.

Japan. Ministry of Education, Science, and Culture (Mōmbushō). 1960. *Revised Curriculum in Japan for Elementary and Lower Secondary Schools.* Tokyo.

_____. 1971. *Educational Standards in Japan, 1970.* Tokyo.

_____. 1976a. *Course of Study for Elementary Schools in Japan.* Tokyo.

_____. 1976b. *Course of Study for Lower Secondary Schools in Japan.* Tokyo.

_____. 1976c. *Educational Standards in Japan, 1975.* Tokyo.

_____. 1976d. *Course of Study for Upper Secondary Schools in Japan.* Tokyo.

_____. 1979. *Statistical Abstract of Education, Science, and Culture.* Tokyo.

_____. 1983a. *Course of Study for Elementary Schools in Japan.* Tokyo.

_____. 1983b. *Course of Study for Lower Secondary Schools in Japan.* Tokyo.

_____. 1983c. *Course of Study for Upper Secondary Schools in Japan.* Tokyo.

Kobayashi, Victor. 1964 *John Dewey in Japanese Education Thought.* Ann Arbor: School of Education, University of Michigan.

_____. 1984. "Tradition, Modernization, Education: The Case of Japan." *Journal of Ethnic Studies* 12, no. 3: 95-118.

Livonia Gazette. 1984. December 27. Livonia, Wash.

Nagai, Michio, and Takeo Nishijima. 1975. "Postwar Japanese Education and the United States." In *Mutual Images: Essays in American-Japanese Relations*, edited by Akira Iriye, pp. 169-87. Cambridge, Mass.: Harvard University Press.

National Association of Secondary School Principals (NASSP). 1980. *State Mandated Graduation Programs, 1980.* Washington, D.C.

Olson, Lynn. 1984. "Opinions Clash at Conference to Define History Curriculum." *Education Week*, September 5, pp. 10-11.

Ranbom, Sheppard. 1984. "Realms of Knowledge: Is There a Common Core?" *Education Week*, Special Report, "Cracking the Code: Language, Schooling, Literacy," September 5, pp. 1 L24-L25, L68.

Rohlen, Thomas P. 1983. *Japan's High Schools*. Berkeley: University of California Press.

United States. Department of Education, National Center for Education Statistics. 1984. *The Condition of Education*, edited by Valena White Plisko. Washington, D.C.: U.S. Government Printing Office.

____. National Center for Educational Statistics. 1984. "Science and Mathematics Education in American High Schools: Results from the High School and Beyond Study." *NCES Bulletin*, May.

____. National Commission on Excellence in Education. 1983. *A Nation at Risk: The Imperative for Educational Reform.* Washington, D.C.

Your Public Schools. 1984. "High School Graduation Requirements." June, pp. 16-18.

Wirt, Frederick M. 1977. "School Policy, Culture, and State Decentralization." In *The Politics of Education*, edited by Jay Scribner, 76th Yearbook of the National Society of Education, P. II, pp. 164-87. Chicago: National Society of Education.

5
A FACTUAL OVERVIEW OF JAPANESE AND AMERICAN EDUCATION
Mamoru Tsukada

Meaningful cross-national comparisons of educational statistics are rare (Ramirez and Meyer 1982, p. 216), for, among other reasons, nations tend to collect dissimilar statistics. Therefore the first part of this chapter examines three aspects of Japanese and American education that can be statistically described; the second part discusses some of the difficulties of comparing cross-national statistics, pointing out the problems of collecting and interpreting the statistics.

In examining the aspects of Japanese and U.S. education that can be statistically described, the chapter first compares several general characteristics of education in the two countries, noting differences in the enrollment of students, the enrollment rate for all levels of education, and the number of institutions of higher education, controlled for sector. Sex differences in the enrollment rate for higher education are also considered. Next, two comparisons of national expenditure on education are made. Third, two social problems in Japan and the United States, juvenile suicides and juvenile delinquency, are examined. Those problems are often discussed in connection with the success and failure of public education.

HISTORICAL TRENDS IN EDUCATION

Enrollment Rates in Japan and the United States

Table 5.1 and Figure 5.1 show historical trends in the enrollment of students for elementary, secondary, and higher education in

Japan between 1950 and 1982. Because elementary education (which in Japan includes primary and junior high school) is compulsory, the enrollment level of Japanese elementary students has remained virtually unchanged. Changes in enrollment depend on the population size of age group 8-15; thus more than 99 percent of that age group have attended school (Japan, Ministry of Education, Science, and Culture 1982, pp. 18-19).

Table 5.1 Historical trends in school enrollment, Japan, 1950-82

Year	Elementary	Secondary	Higher education
1950	16,523,916	1,935,118	240,021
1955	12,855,344	2,592,001	601,240
1960	18,490,653	3,239,416	709,878
1965	15,732,162	5,073,882	1,085,119
1970	14,210,318	4,231,542	1,669,740
1975	15,127,288	4,333,079	2,087,864
1980	15,920,975	4,621,930	2,206,436
1981	17,223,935	4,682,827	2,194,523
1982	17,525,495	4,600,551	2,191,923

Source: Nihonkyoiku Nenkan Kankōiinkai (1983, appendix).

In contrast, enrollment in secondary and higher education increased rapidly between 1950 and 1965. Enrollment in secondary education increased by about 30 percent every five years during the period, so that by 1965 it was 2.6 times greater than in 1950. The corresponding increase in the number of schools, however, was only 657, or 15 percent, during the same period. This means that the number of students per school grew substantially.

The same tendency is even more apparent in the statistics on higher education. In 1965 enrollment in higher education (including enrollment in junior colleges and universities) was 4.5 times greater than in 1950. In contrast to enrollment in secondary education, which stabilized after 1965, higher education enrollment continued to increase until 1975.

Figure 5.1 indicates historical trends in the percentages of Japanese and U.S. students enrolled in secondary and higher education for each age cohort. In 1975 the percentages stabilized in both countries, and they have not increased since. The period from 1950 through 1975 can be regarded as an era of expansion in secondary and higher education in Japan.

Figure 5.1   Historical trends in school enrollment rates, Japan and the United
States, 1950-82

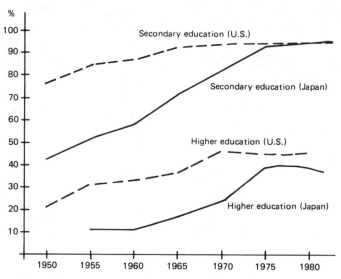

Source: Nihon Kyoiku Shinbunsha (1983).

In the United States enrollment increases since 1950 in secondary and higher education have been much lower overall than those of
Japan (see Figure 5.1 and Table 5.2). The unusually high elementary enrollments in 1960 and 1970 were probably due to the matur-
ing of the "baby boom" cohort born after World War II.

Table 5.2   Historical trends in school enrollment, United States, 1950-81

Year	Elementary	Secondary	Higher education
1950	21,031,929	6,453,009	2,659,021
1960	30,118,744	9,599,810	3,215,544
1970	34,190,177	14,418,301	7,136,075
1980	28,725,209	15,301,233	11,569,899
1981	27,978,927	14,304,254	12,371,672

Source: U.S. Department of Education, *Digest of Education Statistics*
(1951-82).

One way to compare enrollment trends in Japan and the United States is to compare the number of students enrolled per 100 persons 14-17 years of age in each country. In 1950, 76 percent of this age group were enrolled in high school in the United States, and as early as 1965 the proportion had risen to 92 percent. Enrollment in secondary education thus stabilized ten years earlier in the United States than in Japan. In higher education 30 percent of the appropriate age group were enrolled in the United States in 1950. That proportion increased gradually, reaching a peak level of 46 percent in 1970, and it has remained almost unchanged since then. In contrast, in Japan only 10 percent of the comparable age group were enrolled in 1950. By 1975 the proportion had reached 38 percent and stopped increasing (Figure 5.1).

Enrollment and Number of Institutions by Sector

Another way to compare educational trends in the two countries is to consider the proportions of students enrolled at each educational level by public and private sector. Since 1950 more than 98 percent of primary students in Japan have been enrolled in public schools, compared with only about 90 percent of American elementary students. However, in its secondary education, Japan depends more upon the private sector than does the United States. About 30 percent of all secondary students are enrolled in private schools, compared with only about 10 percent of U.S. secondary students. Japanese higher education depends mainly on the private sector, whereas historically in the United States the public sector has accommodated more students than the private sector. In Japan, in 1950, 62 percent of students in institutions of higher education attended private junior colleges and universities, and by 1975 the proportion had risen to 78 percent (see Figure 5.2). In contrast, although half of the students in U.S. institutions of higher education were enrolled in private institutions in 1950, by 1982 the proportion had decreased to 22 percent. Thus the expansion of total enrollment in higher education can be attributed to differences in the private and public sectors' efforts in each country: Japan's expansion was brought about by the private sector, whereas America's expansion resulted from an increase in public institutions (see Figure 5.3).

Figure 5.2   Percentages of total enrollment in private schools, Japan and the United States, 1950-82

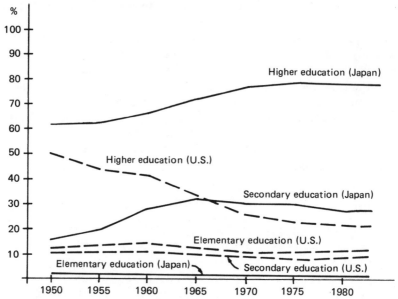

Source: Nihon Kyoiku Nenkan Kankoiinkai (1983); United States: U.S. Department of Education, *Digest of Education Statistics* (1983).

Likewise, the number of private universities grew from 140 to 305 during the same period. The growth in total number of junior colleges and universities in Japan was achieved overwhelmingly through the creation of private institutions.

The United States has employed a slightly different strategy for expanding the number of institutions of higher education. As in Japan, private four-year institutions have increased in number, beginning in 1965. However, most of the growth has occurred in two-year institutions (public community colleges and junior colleges), which increased from 420 in 1965 to 767 in 1975, whereas the number of private universities increased by only 46. This development reflects a governmental move to provide at least some form of higher education for more high school graduates while "cooling out" those who lacked sufficient motivation or mobility for a full four-year program.

Figure 5.3   Number of institutions of higher education by type and sector, Japan and the United States, 1950-82

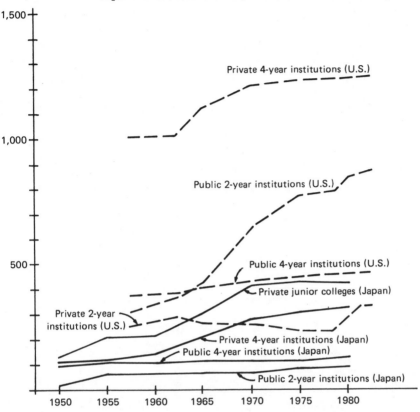

Sources: Japan: Nihon Kyoiku Nenkan Kankoiinkai (1983); United States: U.S. Department of Education, *Digest of Education Statistics* (1983).

Women's Position in Higher Education

The situation for women in higher education differs between Japan and the United States. In Japan the overall difference between male and female enrollment rates in higher education in 1981 was only 7.5 percent. This difference probably will diminish in the future (Sōrihu 1983, p. 139). But controlling for type of institution reveals a significant sexual difference in the Japanese enrollment rate. As Figure 5.4 shows, females accounted for 39 percent of total enrollment in junior colleges in 1950, but by 1981 they represented nearly 90 percent of enrolled students in junior colleges. Over the same period, however, their representation at four-year colleges and universities increased from about 6 percent to only 22 percent. This indicates that the substantial increase in overall female enrollment in higher education stemmed mainly from increased enrollment in junior colleges. Thus, in Japan, a distinctive sexual segregation exists in higher education, with females far more likely to go to junior colleges than males.

Figure 5.4   Females as a percentage of total enrollment in institutions of higher education, Japan and the United States, 1950-82

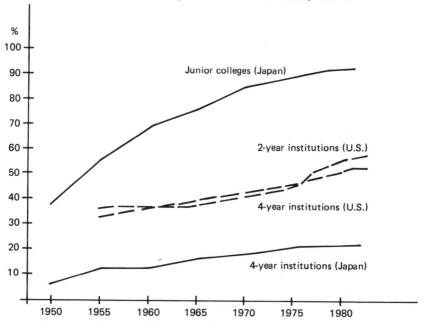

Sources: Japan: Nihon Kyoiku Nenkan Kankoiinkai (1983); United States: U.S. Department of Education (The Condition of Education, 1983, 1984; Projections of Education Statistics, various years).

In the United States chances for higher education have become equal between males and females, and females have started to exceed males in enrollment rates for higher education. In 1955 the female enrollment rate in both two-year and four-year institutions was about 35 percent. In 1979 the percentage of females enrolled in four-year institutions exceeded that of males by 3 percent. This indicates that females have had progressively improved opportunities for higher education.

Financial Situation of Education

In Japan public expenditure on education was about 4 percent of the gross national product (GNP) before 1970, but it has increased steadily since 1970. By 1980 it was 6 percent of GNP (see Figure 5.5). In contrast, U.S. public expenditure on education began to increase earlier, reached a peak of nearly 7 percent of GNP in 1975, and has declined since. By 1980 it was at about the same level as in Japan.

Figure 5.5   Public expenditure on education as a percentage of gross national product; Japan and the United States, 1955-80

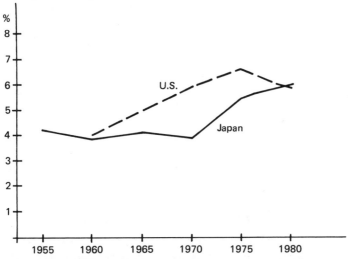

Sources: Mombushō (1980); United States: U.S. Department of Education (*Digest of Education Statistics* 1983, table 165).

Another way of looking at expenditure for education is to examine the ratio of public expenditure for education to governmental expenditures for all purposes. Table 5.3 presents the ratio for selected countries and years from 1960 through 1980. In comparison with almost all the other countries in the table, Japan and the United States allocated the largest percentages of governmental expenditure to education. Both countries consistently spent about 20 percent of governmental expenditure on education.

Table 5.3 Expenditure on education as a percentage of governmental expenditure for all purposes, selected countries, 1960-80

Country	1960	1970	1970	1978	1979	1980
Japan		20.4	22.4	20.6	20.1	19.7
United States	15.1	20.3	22.0	21.0	20.5	19.9
Australia		13.3	14.8	16.0	15.0	
Canada	14.3[a]	24.1	17.8	18.5	18.3	17.3
Chile	12.6	22.0	12.0			11.9
France					17.8[b]	
Germany, Federal Republic of		9.4	10.6	9.9	13.6	
Hungary	8.4	6.9	4.2	4.2	4.2	5.2
Italy		11.9	9.4	9.8	11.1	
Mexico		8.5	11.9	10.9		
Netherlands					24.1	
Nigeria			16.5[c]	13.9	16.2	
Norway		15.5	14.7	14.4		16.3
Sweden			13.4	13.1	13.7	14.1
Thailand		17.3	21.0	19.9	18.8	20.6
United Kingdom		14.1	14.3	13.8		
USSR	11.7	12.8	12.9	12.0	11.6	11.2

[a]1961 data.
[b]Percentage based on central government expenditures only.
[c]1976 data.
Source: U.S. Department of Education, *Digest of Education Statistics* (1983).

Juvenile Suicide and Juvenile Delinquency

Critics and the general public tend to think that social problems, especially those affecting youths, are closely related to the condition of public education. This section examines the relationship between education and two social problems in Japan and the United States, juvenile suicide and juvenile delinquency.

Contrary to the popular belief that there is a causal relationship between the intensification of Japan's "examination hell" since World War II and the increased incidence of juvenile suicide during the postwar period, the historical trend in the juvenile suicide rate does not show a consistent relationship between them (see Figure 5.6). The suicide rates for both 15- to 19-year-olds and 15- to 24-year-olds rose sharply between 1947 and 1955, then declined almost as sharply between 1955 and 1965, becoming rather stable thereafter.

Figure 5.6   Juvenile suicide rates by age group, Japan and the United States, 1947-81 (Suicides per 10,000 persons)

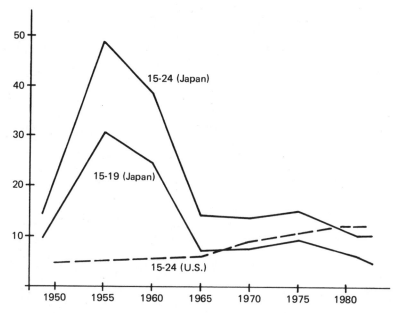

Sources: Sorihu (various years); U.S. Department of Health and Human Services (1983).

A closer examination of the statistics on suicide reveals the characteristics of juvenile suicide in Japan (Rohlen 1983, appendix). Table 5.4 shows that, among youths under 20 years old who committed suicide between 1977 and 1982, those in school composed about 60 percent. Because compulsory education causes virtually all youths in Japan to be enrolled in school through junior high school, few are employed or unemployed. Thus suicide rates among those not in school were disproportionately high. Likewise, Table 5.5 shows that for 16- to 18-year-olds (the age group for senior high school students in Japan), there were more suicides among those in school than among those not in school. But because the school enrollment rate for that age group has been more than 93 percent since 1977 and only 7 percent of 16- to 18-year-olds have not been in school, the suicide rate among those not in school has been about six times higher than that of students. This finding may indicate that the examination-oriented school system does not affect students *directly* by increasing their probability of committing suicide. It suggests, instead, that those who cannot be in school tend to commit suicide because they are outside the normative school situation.

Table 5.4   Suicides among persons under age 20 by employment status, Japan, 1977-82 (percent distribution)

	Year and number				
Status	1977 (N = 784)	1978 (N = 866)	1979 (N = 919)	1980 (N = 678)	1982 (N = 599)
Students	58	58	61	57	60
Employed	22	26	22	24	18
Unemployed	20	16	17	19	22
All suicides	100	100	100	100	100

Source: Sōrihu (1978-83).

Table 5.5   Suicides among 16- to 18-year-olds, by whether in school, Japan, 1977-82 (percent distribution)

	Year and number				
Status	1977 (N = 421)	1978 (N = 461)	1979 (N = 502)	1980 (N = 354)	1982 (N = 305)
In school	57	59	64	57	65
Not in school	43	41	36	43	35
All suicides	100	100	100	100	100

Source: Sōrihu (1978-83).

Among students under 20 years of age "school-related reasons" were an important contributing factor in suicide. About 45 percent of all suicides committed by Japanese students between 1977 and 1982 were attributed to such reasons (calculated from Sōrihu, various years).

Anxiety about academic achievement and entrance examinations "caused" 64 percent of suicides in the category of "school-related reasons" in 1977, but by 1982 that percentage had increased to 75 percent (Sorihu 1978, 1983). These "school-related reasons" tended to affect male and female students differently. About 10 percent more male students than female students committed suicide for those reasons. For female students "opposite-sex-related reasons" were as crucial as "school-related reasons" (Sorihu 1978, 1983).

To summarize, Japanese juvenile suicides have been occurring more among those not in school than among those in school; and among students, particularly male students, school-related problems have been identified as the most common cause of suicide.

To compare juvenile suicide rates in Japan and the United States, respective suicide rates among 15- to 24-year-olds were examined. In 1950 the suicide rate for that age group in the United States was as low as 4.5 suicides per 100,000 persons. It gradually increased, however, and by 1980 exceeded that of the Japanese. During the ten-year period between 1965 and 1975 the U.S. juvenile suicide rate more than doubled (Figure 5.6).

Substantial differences in male and female suicide rates exist between blacks and whites in the United States as well as between Japan and the United States. Among six groups (males and females in Japan and white males, white females, black males, and black females in the United States) the suicide rate has risen most rapidly since 1965 among white males. By 1980 their rate was the highest, at 22 per 100,000 persons (see Figure 5.7). The suicide rates of white and black U.S. females, which were lowest of all six groups at the beginning of the period, increased only slightly.

Another social problem discussed in connection with public education is juvenile delinquency. To achieve comparability between Japan and the United States, I examined the crime rates for Japanese and U.S. juveniles over the period from 1960 to 1982 (see Figure 5.8). In Japan the number of delinquencies per 1,000 persons in the 10- to 19-year-old age group was low (about 9.4) until 1977, but within the four-year period from 1977 to 1981 it increased 1.5 times.

A recent phenomenon is the emergence of age-group differences in the increase of the Japanese juvenile delinquency rate. Compared with the crime rate of the 18- and 19-year-olds, that of 14- and 15-year-olds increased rapidly between 1973 and 1982. The number of 14-year-olds arrested in 1982 was about 2.5 times that of 1973, whereas there was almost no change in the number of 19-year-olds arrested.

Japan's juvenile crime rate has been lower than that of the United States. In 1960 the number of juvenile cases per 1,000 persons in the 10- to 17-year-old age group in the United States was more than twice as high as in Japan. By 1980 the American juvenile crime rate was three times that of the Japanese.

Figure 5.7   Juvenile suicides by sex and ethnicity, Japan and the United States, 1950-82 (suicides per 100,000 persons)

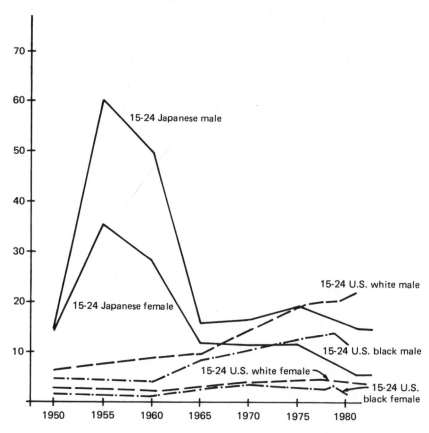

Sources: Sōrihu (various years); U.S. Department of Health and Human Services (1983).

The ratio of juvenile crime to adult crime in Japan and the United States was compared. In Japan the ratio declined rapidly between 1965 and 1970 as the postwar "baby boom" generation passed through the juvenile period (Figure 5.8). Then it began to rise again, gradually at first and after 1977 more rapidly. In the United States, although the juvenile crime rate increased every year between 1960 and 1982, the juvenile crime ratio declined after 1975. Recently adult crime problems have appeared to be much more severe than juvenile crimes in the United States.

Figure 5.8   Juvenile crime rates and ratios, Japan and the United States, 1960-82

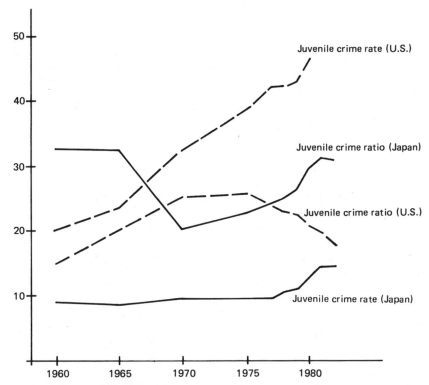

Sources: Hōmushō Hōmu Sōgōgkenjyusho (1983); U.S. Department of Commerce (various years).

Notes: Juvenile crime rate = number of juvenile arrests/juvenile population x 1,000. (Juvenile population comprises ages 10-19 in Japan and ages 10-17 in the United States.) Juvenile ratio = (number of juvenile crimes/[number of juvenile + adult crimes]) x 100.

As for types of juvenile offenses, Table 5.6 reveals that property crime accounted for three-quarters of all juvenile offenses in Japan in 1982 compared with one-third in the United States. Although levels of "intellectual" offenses were low in both countries, they were five times higher in Japan than in the United States.

Table 5.6   Juvenile crime by type, Japan and the United States, 1982
             (percent distribution)

Type	Japan	United States
Property crime	74.8	32.6
Intellectual crime	7.5	1.5
Violent crime	14.4	8.4
Severe violent crime	1.0	2.4
Other	2.3	55.1
All types	100.0	100.0

Notes: Property crime includes burglary, larceny-theft, and motor vehicle theft. Intellectual crime includes forgery, counterfeiting, fraud, and embezzlement. Violent crime includes aggravated assault and other types of assault. Severe violent crime includes murder, arson, and robbery. "Other" crime in the United States includes liquor law violations, disorderly conduct, runaways, vandalism, and drug abuse violations.

Sources: Hōmushō Hōmu Sōgōkenkyusho (1983); U.S. Department of Justice (1983).

THE QUESTION OF COMPARABILITY

In his presidential address to the comparative and International Education Society (CIES), Farrell (1979) pointed out two problems regarding data comparability: the problem of data equivalence and the problem of uncontrolled variables. I discuss only the former problem in this chapter because here I am dealing with comparative statistics of only two countries. The problem of data equivalence involves the difficulty of adequate measurement in a comparative framework.

In this part of the chapter I address the problem of data comparability by discussing some of the difficulties in collecting and analyzing U.S. and Japanese statistics on education. The difficulties arise because of cultural and social differences between the two countries that lead to different conceptualizations of the statistics.

One problem is assessing the enrollment rate in higher education in Japan and the United States. With Japan's statistics the enrollment rate for higher education is calculated by dividing the number of all entrants to higher educational institutions by the number of junior high school graduates of three years before. Using U.S. statistics, I assume the rate to be equal to the retention rates for the fifth through twelfth grades of public schools, adjusted to include estimates for nonpublic schools. Rates for first-time college enrollment include enrollment of full-time and part-time students in programs creditable toward a bachelor's degree.

Here two problems arise in comparing enrollment rates for Japan and the United States. First, the enrollment rates collected in the above way for the United States do not include returnees to school. Given the large percentage of enrolled students over 25 years of age in the United States, this enrollment rate underestimates the substantial enrollment of returnees. In Japan virtually all students enrolled in higher education are under age 25. Second, in Japan all students must be enrolled in higher education on a full-time basis. The enrollment rate in Japan is therefore that of full-time students, whereas 42 percent of all U.S. students enrolled in institutions of higher education are part time.

These two problems of statistical interpretation can be understood by considering social and cultural differences between Japan and the United States. For example, Japanese and U.S. universities have different admission policies. Japanese admissions are based almost exclusively on the results of entrance examinations, which most high school students take just before graduation. The system discourages those over 25 years old from entering universities. In contrast, U.S. universities, especially community colleges, employ an "open admission" policy.

A degree earned after a certain age does not benefit the Japanese because of the seniority and lifelong employment system in companies. Japanese organizations are inclined to ". . . recruit pliable youth without too much concern for their specialized skills and then to socialize them intensively" (Krauss, Rohlen, and Steinhoff 1984, p. 382). Thus, obtaining a degree after a certain age does not help to improve one's social or economic status because of the Japanese employment system of low social mobility between employers.

In the United States, however, academic degrees and varied career experiences are important factors in promotion. Graduate degrees are evaluated as indicating the possession of specialized skills. People are motivated to return to school as part-time or full-time students in order to improve their earning potential. Because changing one's company is a common practice, it is relatively easy to move up by obtaining a higher position in a different company.

These differences indicate that Japanese and U.S. enrollment rates in higher education cannot be accepted at face value. Not only are the statistics collected by different methods, but also, because of differences in their systems of admission to universities, the age composition of enrolled students in Japan and the United States is not the same. Moreover, owing to a difference in the importance attached to earned degrees, substantial numbers of Americans are enrolled as part-time students, whereas virtually no students in Japanese universities are part-time students. Thus, even though we may describe Japanese and American higher education as "mass education" because the two countries have the highest enrollment rates in the world, the nature of mass education is different in the two educational systems. Japanese four-year universities are open only to young adults and primarily to males, whereas U.S. institutions of higher education are open to older people and females as well as to youths and males.

In comparing Japanese and U.S. expenditures on education, I have not considered private expenditures such as the substantial amounts that Japanese parents spend on tutoring, or *juku* (cram courses after school), for their children. Thus my comparison of public expenditures may underestimate the level of actual expenditure on education in Japan.

Statistics on suicide in Japan and the United States are basically comparable because both countries collect them by age group 15-24 and suicide rates are expressed as the number of suicides per 100,000 persons. But there are two possible difficulties in interpreting the statistics on suicides. The first is determining whether suicide has occurred from a forensic medical standpoint. In the Japanese culture many suicides tend to be hidden by the victims and their families because suicide is regarded as shameful (Kato 1974, p. 379). Japanese suicide statistics based on official records tend to be underestimated. The second difficulty is that the ratio between attempted suicides and completed suicides is different in Japan and the United States. Estimates of the ratio of attempted suicides to actual suicides range from only .15:1 to .40:1 in Japan (Kato 1974, p. 361). By contrast, estimates of this ratio for the U.S. range from 5:1 to 50:1 (Jacobs 1982, p. 94). Obviously there are far more failed attempts in the U.S. than in Japan. In light of the high ratio of attempted suicides to completed suicides in the United States, juvenile suicide may be a more severe problem in the United States than in Japan.

By converting the U.S. statistics on detailed categories of juvenile offenses into the major categories of juvenile offenses used in Japanese statistics, I was able to compare the types and prevalence of juvenile delinquency in the two countries. For this comparison I used the crime rate as defined in Figure 5.8 rather than the number of arrested juveniles. The total number of arrested juveniles cannot be compared directly for Japan and the United States because the population size of the appropriate age groups is different and the number of agencies reporting arrested juveniles in the United States is different depending upon the year of investigation (U.S. Department of Justice, 1980-83). The Japanese police records, in contrast, seem comprehensive because of Japan's nationally centralized system. Therefore, the best comparison of juvenile delinquencies in Japan and the United States is one based on the crime rate.

Nevertheless, the comparative statistics on juvenile delinquencies presented earlier in the chapter may include some biases. The Japanese define juveniles as youths 10 to 20 years old, whereas the U.S. equivalent is youths under age 18. Since the respective categories have meaning in each country's context, I have not adjusted for the age-group difference in reporting the statistics. Use of the existing categories may cause some bias in the comparison of juvenile delinquencies in Japan and the United States.

Another difficulty results from cultural differences in official crime statistics in Japan and the United States. In Japan arrests may be underreported because Japanese parents make more efforts than American parents to prevent their children from being arrested.

SUMMARY AND CONCLUSION

This chapter has attempted to draw a comparison between Japanese and U.S. education, in particular three aspects of the two countries' educational systems.

First, it has described several general characteristics of their educational systems. At the primary education level the public sector has a monopoly on enrollment in Japan, whereas in the United States about 10 percent of primary enrollment is in the private sector. Although Japan started expanding its secondary and higher levels of education about ten years later than did the United States, after 1975 enrollment levels for secondary and higher education became similar in the two countries. One difference that persists is that in the United States more people over age 25 are enrolled in institutions of higher education than in Japan. Another difference is that Japan has relied upon the private sector to build new junior colleges and universities. Although the United States has also turned to the private sector to establish new four-year institutions, historically its public sector has tried to build new two-year institutions. The position of females in higher education is another point of difference. In Japan females tend to be enrolled in junior colleges, whereas in the United States female enrollment in four-year institutions is equal to or even slightly higher than the male enrollment rate.

The second area of comparison has been governmental expenditure on education. Both countries historically have increased their expenditures on education, except for a recent decline in U.S. outlays. The proportion of total governmental expenditures on education in both countries has been higher than in other countries.

The last area of comparison has been juvenile suicides and juvenile delinquency. With respect to juvenile suicide in Japan, since reaching a peak in 1955 the suicide rate has decreased continuously. In the United States the suicide rate started low but has continuously increased and by 1980 exceeded the Japanese suicide rate. Male suicide rates are higher than female suicide rates in both countries and across ethnic groups in the United States. The juvenile delinquency rate in the United States has always been higher than the Japanese rate and has consistently risen. In contrast, the Japanese juvenile delinquency rate, historically low, has increased rapidly in recent years. The most serious problem now is with the younger teenage juveniles.

What do these differences add up to? Japan and the United States have become similar to each other in their school enrollment rates, expenditures on education, and juvenile suicide rates but not in the position of females in higher education, the role of the private sector in education, or juvenile delinquency. Females' more limited access to higher education, the private sector's important role in higher education, and a low delinquency rate distinguish Japan from the United States.

Using national statistics to make cross-national comparisons always raises the question of data comparability. Because statistics collected by different countries tend not to be strictly comparable, it is necessary to convert them into a comparable scale by using a standard scale or changing one data set to conform to the other. Such arbitrary standardization of statistics necessitates interpretation with reference to each country's cultural and social background. Otherwise, comparison is not very meaningful. Use of governmental statistics also requires cautious consideration of the possible political manipulation of statistics.

One question remains, to which we seek an answer: Are the differences in Japanese and American education going to disappear? One point of view argues that they will not disappear because they are deeply rooted in each country's cultural and social structure. Another argues that they will disappear because Japan and the United States are becoming the same kind of highly industrial society, in which all institutions will be similar in the long run.

REFERENCES

Farrell, Joseph P. 1979. "The Necessity of Comparison in the Study of Education: The Salience of Science and the Problem of Comparability." *Comparative Education Review* 23 (1): 3-16.

Hōmushō Hōmu Sōgōkenkyusho, ed. _1950- . *Hanzai Hakusho* (White Paper of Crimes). Tokyo: Ōkurasho. Annual.

Jacobs, Jerry. 1982. *The Moral Justification of Suicide.* Springfield, Ill.: Charles C. Thomas.

Kato, Masaaki. 1974. "Self-Destruction in Japan: A Cross-cultural Epidemiological Analysis of Suicide." In *Japanese Culture and Behavior*, edited by Takie S. Lebra and William P. Lebra, pp. 359-82. Honolulu: University of Hawaii Press.

Krauss, Ellis S., Thomas P. Rohlen, and Patricia G. Steinhoff. 1984. *Conflict in Japan.* Honolulu: University of Hawaii Press.

Japan. Ministry of Education, Science, and Culture (Mombusho). 1980. *Wagakuni no kyoiku Suijun* (The Standard of Education in Japan). Tokyo: Okurasho.

____. 1982. *Education in Japan: A Graphic Presentation.* Tokyo.

Nihonkyoiku Nenkan Kankōiinkai. 1983. *Nihonkyoiku Nenkan* (Statistical Yearbook). Tokyo: Gyosei. Annual.

Pempel, T. J. 1973. "The Politics of Enrollment Expansion in Japanese Universities." *Journal of Asian Studies* 33 (1): 67-86.

Ramirez, Francisco, and John W. Meyer. 1982. "Comparative Education: Synthesis and Agenda." In *The State of Sociology: Problems and Prospects*, edited by James Short, pp. 215-37. Beverly Hills, Calif.: Sage Publications.

Rohlen, Thomas P. 1983. *Japan's High Schools.* Berkeley: University of California Press.

Sōrihu, ed. 1960- . *Seishonen Hakusho* (White Paper of Juveniles). Tokyo: Ōkurasho. Annual.

United States. Department of Commerce, Bureau of the Census. 1980-83. *Statistical Abstract of the United States: National Data Book and Guide to Sources*. Washington, D.C.

United States. Department of Education, National Center for Education Statistics. 1983-84. *The Condition of Education*. Washington, D.C.

____. 1950- . *Digest of Education Statistics*. Washington, D.C. Annual.

____. 1950- . *Projection of Education Statistics*. Washington, D.C. Annual.

United States. Department of Health and Human Services, Public Health Service. 1980-83. *Health United States*. Washington, D.C.

United States. Department of Justice, Federal Bureau of Investigation. 1950- . *Uniform Crime Reports*. Washington, D.C. Annual.

6
PATTERNS OF ACADEMIC ACHIEVEMENT IN JAPAN AND THE UNITED STATES
William K. Cummings

The decline in academic achievement of high school students is the most consistently mentioned theme in the recent indictments of American education. For example, the National Commission on Excellence in Education observed that "average achievement of high school students on most standardized tests is now lower than 26 years ago when Sputnik was launched" and "the College Board's Scholastic Aptitude Tests (SAT) demonstrate a virtually unbroken decline from 1963 to 1980. Average verbal scores fell over 50 points and average mathematics scores dropped nearly 40 points" (1983, pp. 8-9). The commission also noted that "international comparisons of student achievement, completed a decade ago, reveal that on 19 academic tests American students were never first or second and, in comparison with other industrialized nations, were last seven times" (1983, p. 8).

In all the international tests in which Japanese students participated, they scored at or near the top. Their superior achievement was once again manifest in the Second International Survey of Mathematics Achievement, conducted during the 1981-82 school year in 24 countries. For both 13-year-olds and students in the final high school year, in virtually every subarea of mathematical skills examined, the average achievement for Japanese students was either first or second (Crosswhite et al. 1984, pp. 53, 66). In contrast, the average scores for American students were usually well below the international mean.

As many of the questions of the second survey had also been used in the First International Mathematics Survey of 1964, those countries that had participated in both had a unique opportunity to examine national trends in mathematics achievement. Looking at the results for the 13-year-old group, few were surprised to find that U.S. scores for 1981 were lower than for 1964. Unexpected, however, was the parallel finding of a modest decline in the average achievement of Japanese 13-year-olds. Figure 6.1 illustrates the subareas of relative decline and improvement for the two groups. In contrast to the declining scores for the 13-year-olds, the scores for the final-year groups of both countries rose, by 5 percent in the U.S. case and 12 percent in the case of Japan.[1]

Figure 6.1   Changes in mean scores, Population A, 1964-82

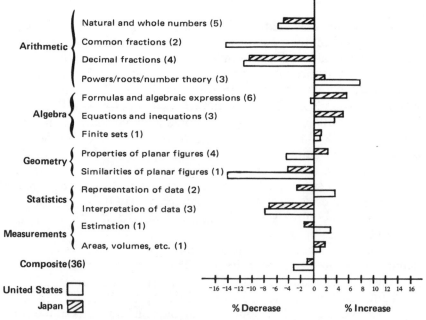

Source: Crosswhite et al. (1984, p. 82).

Thus the latest survey does not fully support the current belief that U.S. and Japanese education is in decline. Although Americans are more likely to be pleased with the parcel of good news concerning the high schoolers, Japanese educators are more likely to focus on the bad news about the declining achievement of their 13-year-olds. Despite major improvements in Japan's educational facilities

and technology over the past two decades, the survey did not provide a clear sign of improved student performance.

The latest survey suggests the value of looking both at the patterns of academic achievement in the two societies and the way those
patterns are perceived. These two phenomena are addressed below.

THE INTERNATIONAL SURVEYS

Before advancing into the interpretation of country differences, it
will be helpful to take a more careful look at the relevant sources of
information.

IEA Surveys

The most extensive available comparative information comes
from the series of international surveys coordinated by the International Association for the Evaluation Achievement (IEA). Draw-
ing on the budgets of foundations and governments of participating
nations, the association conducted its first multinational survey of
mathematics achievement in 1964 (Husen 1967). The format for the
sample design and content of the first mathematics survey is summarized here because it has been followed in most of the subsequent
surveys.

The sample design and the questions for the achievement tests
and related questions on student and teacher characteristics were
drawn up by several international expert committees. The initial
study focused on two subgroups: Population A, consisting of students who had completed basic education and were approximately
13 years old, and Population B, consisting of students who were in
the final year of precollege schooling. Sample designs were drawn
up in each country to approximate these conceptual parameters. In
developing the achievement tests, the international committee
sought, through repeated reviews and meetings, to identify the universal expectations of math achievement for the respective population. The international tests were then designed to measure student
competence relative to those commonly shared expectations.

Essentially the same procedure was followed in developing the
Second International Mathematics Survey and other surveys covering such areas as science, reading, civics, foreign language, and
classroom environment. The extent of international participation in
the surveys has varied, the Japanese restricting their participation to
the surveys testing science and math achievement. In those, Japanese students have manifested exceptionally high scores for both
average achievement and motivation. Moreover, the variation in

Japanese scores as measured by the coefficient of variation has been exceptionally low. The Japanese scores have usually assumed the pattern illustrated in Figure 6.2, which is based on the actual results from the First International Survey of Science Achievement.

Figure 6.2   Performance of school children on the International Test of Science Achievement, Japan and all economically advanced societies, 1974

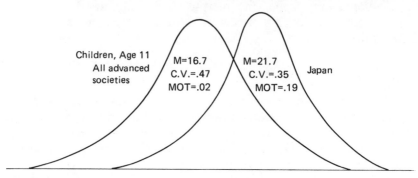

Children, Age 11
All advanced societies

M=16.7
C.V.=.47
MOT=.02

M=21.7
C.V.=.35
MOT=.19

Japan

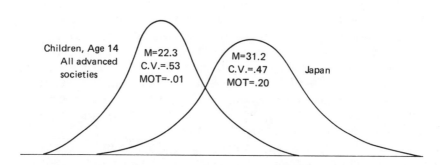

Children, Age 14
All advanced societies

M=22.3
C.V.=.53
MOT=-.01

M=31.2
C.V.=.47
MOT=.20

Japan

Source: Comber and Keeves (1973, pp. 108, 159).
Note: M = mean scores on the respective tests; C.V. = coefficient of variation on tests; MOT = average standard score (average of all students in IEA surveys is 0) on a scale that indicates attitude to school.

Ethnographic Studies

In contrast to the precise information obtained from the international surveys of educational achievement are a handful of comparative ethnographic studies that provide rich detail on methods of classroom teaching, school management, and the relation of school activities to the broader environment. My own study (Cummings 1980) focused on the egalitarian spirit and educational processes in the primary and lower secondary level, and that of Rohlen (1984) focused on high schools.

Intensive Comparative Surveys

Combining the strengths of the above studies, an international group of researchers has recently completed intensive surveys of classroom processes for 20 first-grade and 20 fifth-grade classes in each of the "representative" cities of Sendai (Japan), Minneapolis (Minnesota), and Taipei (Taiwan) (Stigler et al. 1982; Stevenson et al. 1985, pp. 7, 12). Tests of student achievement were also carried out and the results correlated with the measures of classroom activity.

STRUCTURE OF THE TWO EDUCATIONAL SYSTEMS

As discussed elsewhere in this volume, the basic structures of the Japanese and U.S. educational systems have many common features. Similar subjects are taught in both systems, although Japan provides more time for the arts. In both systems six years of primary education are followed by six years of secondary education, and in both systems postsecondary education is provided primarily in two-year junior colleges and four-year colleges and universities for those who qualify. The Japanese system is more centralized, though there are national norms in the administratively decentralized U.S. system.

Because of the U.S. Occupation of Japan after World War II the Japanese system was subject to extensive American influence, and thus many of its formal elements have an American imprint. But the Japanese system has always had a more explicit concern with moral education and a closer relation to the labor market than the U.S. system. At least until very recently, Japan was much less affluent than the United States and hence the public sector tended to allocate less money for education. After World War II free compulsory education in Japan was extended through the ninth grade, whereas in most U.S. states education was, and still is, required through age 16 but is available for virtually no fee through the final year of high school. Japan's relative scarcity of educational funds was reflected in higher student-teacher ratios, less space per student in schools, and a more efficient use of facilities.

These and other differences in structure to be detailed below are related to the differences in the two countries' patterns of education achievement—that is, Japan's higher mean and low variation around this mean and America's lower mean and greater variation.

FACTORS SUPPORTING EQUALITY OF EDUCATIONAL ACHIEVEMENT IN JAPAN

The effectiveness of the Japanese system in enabling the great majority of entering primary students to get off to a good start is possibly the most important reason for the exceptional performance of Japanese middle and high school students in the international tests. Japanese educators evidence a strong commitment to providing all young people with a solid basic education, both because they see this as a means of creating a national citizenry who share a common culture and because they believe basic educational skills are essential for effective performance in the labor force. This conviction is reflected in a variety of educational practices that we will review shortly.

Parental Concern and Student Motivation

Parents' concern for the educational success of their children has tended to reinforce the educators' efforts. Far more than in the United States, parents believe that their children must do well in school in order to do well in society, especially to obtain a promising first job. Anticipating the challenges of formal schooling, virtually all parents send their children to kindergarten. Although only 75 percent of four-year-olds attend kindergarten or nursery school, 85 percent of five-year-olds and nearly 100 percent of six-year-olds are enrolled in kindergarten. In preschool most children learn how to write the basic *hiragana* (the key phonetic alphabet used in writing Japanese) and numbers, along with other school-related skills. Stevenson et al. (1985, p. 2) found that because of their early start, 85.6 percent of Japanese first graders read above their grade level, compared with 56.6 percent for American first graders.

The combination of parental interest and kindergarten exposure seems to cultivate a positive regard for school. Several studies, including the above-mentioned IEA surveys, have noted the high motivational level of Japanese schoolchildren. By the time Japanese children enter school, a greater proportion of them have already acquired what Bloom (1976) describes as the necessary cognitive and affective entry characteristics.

Social Homogeneity

Easing the early years of schooling in Japan is the relative homogeneity of the Japanese population. Japan's two principal minority groups, the *burakumin* and Koreans, are numerically small and tend to live in specific areas. Moreover, in their physical characteristics most members of these groups closely resemble the Japanese majority group. Thus the racial cleavages that disturb many U.S. schools are not common in Japan.

It is also likely that Japanese schools are less affected by class differences than are U.S. schools. According to recent surveys, nearly nine out of every ten Japanese consider themselves members of the middle class. School practices and policies, such as the stress on uniform pronunciation of the Japanese language, field trips paid out of the school budget rather than family contributions, the insistence that all children either walk or use public transportation between home and school, and the use of uniforms by secondary students, tend to obscure the class origins of individual Japanese students. In contrast, the wardrobes and the cars of American students symbolize their relative affluence.

Uniformity in Facilities and Curriculum

The facilities and curricular provisions of Japanese schools are far more standardized than those in the United States. National minimal standards are prescribed for all schools, whether public or private. In the American case, in contrast, standards for public schools are set by more than 30,000 decentralized school boards, and private schools are usually allowed to set independent standards. Whereas nearly one-quarter of U.S. primary students attend private schools, fewer than 1 percent do so in Japan. Only beginning with the upper secondary level does a substantial proportion of Japanese young people attend private schools.

Equality of School Finance

In the United States wide variations exist among public school districts in the level of support for education. Per capita student expenditures in many areas of the Northeast are more than double those in certain areas of the South. In contrast, the per capita variation in expenditures for Japanese students attending ordinary public schools is less than 25 percent, although certain public schools in isolated mountainous and island locales or with large proportions of minority group students receive public subsidies that may increase their per capita student expenditures to more than twice the national norm (Cummings 1980, p. 9). Thus, whereas favorably located schools in the United States tend to have higher per capita expenditures, such is not the case in Japan, at least through the junior high school level.

Uniformity in Curriculum Implementation

To ensure compliance with the official Course of Study, Japan's Ministry of Education reviews all textbooks intended for use in public schools. This process ensures that the texts for all fourth-grade students throughout the nation cover essentially the same material. The principle of exposure to common material is maintained in most school districts through the third year of junior high school, after which students are allowed a narrow range or electives. The American system of textbook review and selection is more decentralized. Moreover, from as early as the first grade some U.S. schools practice ability grouping, and beginning in junior high school a relatively wide range of curricular choices is available to students. These differences in the development of curriculum and student assignment mean that Japanese young people of any given age and grade level experience a greater communality of cognitive exposure than do their American counterparts.

Rotation of Teachers

Also contributing to the communality of Japanese experience is a centrally prescribed personnel system that sets a uniform salary schedule for teachers throughout the nation; the major determinant of pay differentials is seniority. In local school districts, of which there are fewer than 5,000 in Japan, schoolteachers are expected to stay at a particular school for between four and seven years. This system of rotating assignments enables personnel offices to achieve consistency in the qualifications and skills of teachers at each school under their authority. In contrast, salary differentials among American school districts are often substantial, and in most local systems personnel offices lack the authority to move teachers from one school to another without the consent of the teachers. Thus, compared with the between-school equality in qualifications and experience that obtains in most Japanese school districts, there is greater inequality in U.S. districts, the more qualified and experienced teachers gravitating to the schools with the best reputations. The greater between-school inequality in teacher attributes contributes to the greater inequality in student achievement in the United States.

Management and Student Grouping

Within schools several differences in classroom and school management practices work to amplify the differences in degree of cognitive equality. Perhaps the most fundamental difference concerns the procedures for assigning children to classes and subgroups within classes. In Japan, at the beginning of primary school, children are randomly assigned to one of the available classes in such a manner as to approximate mixed ability levels within each class and overall parity in ability among the classes. Children stay with the same class (and often the same teacher) until the end of second grade, when they are reassigned in such a way as to create a mixed ability classroom. The process is again repeated at the end of fourth grade.

Similarly, in junior high schools assignments are made in such a way as to equalize the average ability level among homerooms of the same grade level. Weekly meetings are routinely held among teachers of the same grade level to ensure that their classes are proceeding at a similar pace in all subject areas. The practice of forming equivalent classes allows for meaningful between-class competition. American primary schools also tend to strive for parity among classes, at least at the lower grade levels. Some U.S. schools, however, have accelerated classes, usually beginning in the third or fourth grade. By the junior high level the practice of stratifying classes is common.

The most marked differences between Japanese and U.S. schools, however, are related to within-class grouping. In the American case, ability grouping is common to enable slow and fast learners to progress at their own pace. Even though ability grouping is practiced, children tend to be automatically promoted at the end of each year. Thus by the sixth grade the fast learners may be performing eighth-grade work while others are still struggling to read and solve basic arithmetic problems. In contrast, ability grouping in Japan is never allowed. Rather, teachers form mixed ability groups and depend on the fast learners of a group to coach the slower members.

In handling classes and groups, Japanese teachers prefer to address the whole unit and spend relatively little class time on working with individual students (Stevenson et al. 1985, p. 23). To avoid bias, Japanese teachers think of themselves as addressing the average student; empirical data suggest that they spend the least amount of time with the top students in their classes. In contrast, U.S. teachers are more inclined to teach individual students while having other students work quietly on their own. A number of reports (for example, Rist 1973; Rosenbaum 1976) suggest that American teachers tend to favor their best students.

Because of the common curriculum and the uniform pacing that takes place among classes, Japanese teachers find it relatively easy to use tests and other evaluative instruments prepared by commercial firms. The greater complexity of American pedagogy, combined with the more individualistic tendency of U.S. teachers, results in a stronger preference for teacher-designed tests. However, as the teacher-designed tests require more of the teachers' time, American schoolchildren are less frequently evaluated than their Japanese counterparts. The more frequent evaluation in the Japanese case enables a faster identification of learning difficulties and a quicker supply of remedial materials.

Despite the concern of both systems to facilitate all children's mastery of their subjects, inevitably some children fall behind. In Japan teachers may communicate this situation to parents, who in turn may send their children to after-school *juku* (cram courses) or review schools, paying the tuition out of their own pockets. Approximately one-quarter of Japanese sixth graders and two-fifths of the ninth graders attend *juku*. In most areas of the United States there is no equivalent institution, and therefore children who fall considerably behind are likely to stay there unless they can obtain remedial help from their parents. Many receive automatic promotion without mastering the necessary material, although a few are required to repeat their grade level. In Japan, repetition of a grade is rare.

AVERAGE ACHIEVEMENT

The relative success of the Japanese system in realizing cognitive equality at the primary level—that is, in conveying the intended primary-level curriculum to the majority of primary students—is a key factor in accounting for the higher average achievement of Japanese students in junior high and high school work. More Japanese than American children do well at those advanced levels simply because they have the necessary background. Conversely, fewer Japanese children do poorly; thus, when the average scores on achievement tests are computed, there are fewer low scores to pull the Japanese average down.

Genes

Distinct from the statistical explanations for the high achievement level of Japanese students are some others. Least convincing is Lynn's (1982) suggestion that the Japanese are endowed with superior "math genes." His report of significant differences in mean intelligence quotient scores of Japanese and Western populations does not seriously address the question of instrument comparability. Besides, the Japanese samples he relied on, being disproportionately composed of children from the schools attached to national universities in metropolitan areas, had an elite bias (Stevenson and Azuma 1983).

Abacus Socialization

Intriguing is Stigler's recent suggestion that Japanese children may do better in mathematics because abacus training makes them more skilled in mental arithmetic (1984). According to Stigler, the abacus, once it is internalized in an individual's memory, provides a convenient framework for working out arithmetic problems ranging from simple addition and multiplication problems to lengthy serial computations. Stigler's research, actually carried out in Taiwan, indicates the impressive skill of Chinese children in mental arithmetic and their tendency to rely on the abacus framework in doing their mental computations. Although the abacus is not as common in Japan, most Japanese schools devote several weeks to teaching the abacus, and many schoolchildren obtain additional instruction in *juku* for this purpose. The role of abacus training in Japanese math achievement therefore deserves further investigation.

Labor Market and Motivation

Earlier I noted that Japanese children usually score higher than American children on measures of such variables as eagerness to learn and liking school. Strengthening their motivation is parental support, which is, in turn, shaped by the widespread belief that a solid educational performance is the key to career success. Because moving from firm to firm is discouraged in the Japanese employment system, the employer that an individual starts with is critical to his future. The larger Japanese employers recruit new employees from the annual crop of university and school graduates, focusing initially on graduates from the most prestigious schools. Young people become aware of these employment practices at an early age and thus set their sights on getting into the most prestigious universities. But to do so they must pass the universities' entrance examinations. As the exams consist of factual questions related to the content of the official school curriculum, young people soon recognize the importance of taking school seriously. The looser connection between schools and the labor market in the United States and the emphasis on aptitude rather than on mastery of subjects taught in school enable American students to take a more casual approach to their schooling. And this casualness is reflected in their mediocre scores on the international tests of educational achievement.

The Challenge of the Curriculum

The Japanese curriculum itself helps to account for the higher achievement of Japanese children—it is more challenging than the American curriculum. As illustrated in Table 6.1, Japanese fourth graders encounter more difficult problems than their American counterparts. Japanese textbooks contain larger numbers, especially for multiplication and division problems, and Japanese texts devote more attention to geometry. Mental computations are expected of the Japanese children, but not of the Americans.

In the seventh grade the Japanese Course of Study moves from arithmetic to algebra. In contrast, most American seventh graders grapple only with advanced arithmetic. Although exceptional students are introduced to algebra in the eighth grade, the majority do not encounter algebra until the ninth grade.

Calculus is introduced to all Japanese students in the eleventh grade, and the more talented continue with advanced calculus in the twelfth grade. In contrast, the vast majority of U.S. high school students do not encounter calculus in high school; according to the IEA survey, 12 percent study precalculus and only 2 percent study calculus prior to graduation. The more challenging Japanese curriculum provides Japanese schoolchildren with the opportunity to learn more of the material included on the international tests than their American counterparts.

There are also important differences in the way the two curricula are structured. The American curriculum is said to be organized in a spiral so that new material is briefly introduced and then periodically returned to at increasingly advanced levels over a period of several years. The approach is designed to minimize boredom and discouragement when pupils are confronted with new and difficult material. In contrast, the Japanese curriculum tends to advance from one set of basic principles to the next. Each new set of principles is given extended treatment before students move on to the next. Once a topic has been completed, it figures in subsequent instruction only to the extent that it is essential for the subsequent material. Thus the Japanese curriculum places greater reliance on one-time mastery and less on explicit review.

Table 6.1   Characteristics of typical fourth-grade arithmetic texts, Japan and the United States

| Characteristic | Japan | | A current American commercial text |
	1958 Course of study	1970 Course of study	
Number of teaching units (chapters)	17	25	13
Pages in text	260	254	410
Pages devoted to multiplication	52	8	64
Typical multiplication problem	64 x 58	3,547 x 4,398	807 x 98
Typical division problem	8,742 ÷ 6	24,702 ÷ 537	4,192 ÷ 90
Largest number explained	10,000	100,000,000	10,000,000
Largest number in a problem	34,567 + 17,506	5,000 million + 10,000 (to do in one's head without pencil or paper)	8,424,826 + 2,937,939
Fractions	Which is larger, 1/2 or 1/3?	Addition and subtraction of fractions	Addition and subtraction of fractions
Geometry	Draw triangles, quadrilaterals	Draw, compute perimeter, diagonal, surface of triangles, quadrilaterals	Same as Japan, 1970

Source: Cummings (1980, p. 213).

Both curricular principles have a coherent rationale, but their success is dependent on the way in which they are applied in the classroom. Observational studies of math education point out that many American math teachers spend a disproportionate amount of time on the early sections of their texts and fail to get to the final chapters, where many new principles are introduced. Thus American math education often takes the form of a collapsed spiral or, more precisely, a circle. In contrast, the Japanese system of monitoring within school ensures that most teachers make it through their texts. Although the Japanese texts themselves include less review than U.S. texts, the children often engage in self-reviews or tutor-guided reviews as they prepare for critical exams. Thus the Japanese curricular principles may have a closer correspondence with curricular implementation than do the American.

One manifestation of differential success in curricular implementation is the higher average gain scores for 13-year-old Japanese students in the IEA Second Study of Mathematics: Over the full range of questions the average gain scores (the difference in the percentage of students who can answer a question at the beginning and at the end of the school year) was only 7 percent for American students, compared with 16 percent for Japanese students (see Table 6.2). The Japanese children already had extensive exposure to measurement and statistics before grade 7 and thus scored high on the pretest, leaving less for them to gain. On the other hand, they first received intensive exposure to algebra in the testing year and their gain score was 38 percent. Algebra was also the area of highest gain for American students, but the difference from pretest to posttest was only 11 percent.

Time on Task

The greater number of hours that Japanese children spend in school is often cited as a reason for their higher achievement in various subjects. However, this explanation fails to take account of the broader range of subjects covered by the Japanese curriculum. Through the ninth grade the actual number of hours allocated for mathematics during the Japanese school year is no greater than the number allocated in most U.S. schools. There are some differences, however, in the use made of those hours. Primary teachers in the United States are more likely than their Japanese counterparts to utilize math time to teach other subjects; in this way the time devoted to mathematics in U.S. schools is cut considerably (Stevenson et al. 1985, p. 20). American teachers make less effective use of their time in the classroom than do Japanese teachers. In the above study the American teachers were found to spend about 35 percent of class time on "transitional" matters, such as getting out texts and arranging desks; Japanese teachers spent only 17 percent of class time in such activities. And once the American teachers began teaching, they had to devote a greater proportion of their time to controlling inappropriate behavior and hence had less time for instruction. In sum, while the time allocated for mathematics in the two systems is essentially similar, the actual time spent on mathematics tasks differs considerably. The greater in-school exposure of Japanese children to mathematics tasks is certainly related to their higher average achievement.

Table 6.2   American and Japanese gain scores in mathematics, Population A (13-year-olds), 1980

Subarea	United States			Japan		
	Mean pretest score	Mean posttest score	Gain score mean	Mean pretest score	Mean posttest score	Gain score mean
Arithmetic (62 items)	42	51	9	44	59	15
Algebra (32 items)	32	43	11	36	68	32
Geometry (42 items)	31	38	7	51	70	19
Measurement (26 items)	35	42	7	64	69	5
Statistics	53	57	4	77	80	3
Overall	38	46	8	50	67	17

Sources: Computed from statistics in Crosswhite et al. (1984, p. 18), and Kokuritsu Kyoiku Kenkyusho (1981, p. 12).

A DECLINE IN EDUCATIONAL ACHIEVEMENT

As noted, the Second International Survey of Mathematics Achievement suggests a slight decline between 1964 and 1981 in mathematics achievement for the 13-year-olds of both nations. But average scores were higher in 1981 than in 1964 for the twelfth-grade samples of both countries—5 percent higher for U.S. students and 12 percent higher for the Japanese.

The decline in the educational achievement of American high schoolers has been richly documented in other studies (see, for instance, Austin and Garber 1982). Demographic shifts in the high school population related to improved opportunities for minority group members are an important factor. The changing structure of the American family and decreased academic encouragement to young people may have contributed to the decline. The quality of the teaching force and the rigor of the courses required for graduation have declined. Although these developments have usually been cited to account for the decline in high school scores, they also may have implications for the lower levels. The lowered standards for high school performance may have trickled down, resulting in a lowered level of learning aspirations for 13-year-olds.

In Japan, until recently the question of educational decline did not arise. Most Japanese educators were concerned with the opposite trend, of intensified competition for academic success, which had resulted in a proliferation of informal institutions such as *juku*, tutors, and *yobiko* (proprietary schools for university exam preparation)—all available to bolster the academic performance of young people. Educators urged means to control this competition so that young people could have a richer youth, freed from the burden of excessive study. In response to their pleas the academic goals of the official Course of Study were somewhat reduced in the late 1970s. But still the competition seemed to accelerate.

Over the past several years, however, with the increased information, mock testing, and counseling involved in educational competition, many young people have been opting out of serious participation in this competition. Most of those who opt out do so because they realize from their grades and their performance on mock ability tests that they are far back in the race. Moreover, with the "baby boom" past and the number of universities stable, they believe that some institution will be happy to receive them. Thus those who opt out of the competition, estimated by Amano in this volume to be as many as 70 percent of a given cohort, stay in school but do not try as hard as the front-runners. This decline in average motivation is possibly the most important reason for the decline in educational achievement among Japan's 13-year-olds.[2] However, the senior-year group, involving students in the advanced math course, is composed largely of the most highly motivated of their cohort. Thus it is not surprising that they do ever better than their counterparts of 15 years ago.

CONCLUSION

This discussion has focused on academic decline in the United States and Japan as measured primarily by a test of educational achievement developed by Western mathematicians. The low performance of American students has contributed to the crisis psychology in American education, which may ultimately lead to some improvements. Some hints about new ways to conduct mathematics education may come from Japan, whose young people appear to be the world leaders.

Whereas the results of the second mathematics survey received considerable attention in the United States, in Japan they provoked less interest. The Japanese were already familiar with the results of earlier surveys and had little reason to believe that educational achievement had declined. For the Japanese, the problem was that the pursuit of educational achievement might be getting out of hand. An elite subgroup continued to believe in the value of pursuing high levels of academic achievement, no matter what the cost in family resources or personal happiness. But increasing numbers of young people were opting out of the competition. Although most stayed in school and lived a sober life, a new and growing minority was dropping out of school and engaging in a variety of antisocial acts, such as hot-rodding on motor bikes, that deeply disturbed society. In thinking of how to alleviate this problem, Japan's leaders were considering ways to reduce the pressure of high educational achievement at the very time that U.S. leaders were considering ways to heat up their system. Whereas a decline in academic achievement disturbs American educators, it is not altogether objectionable in the contemporary Japanese context.

NOTES

1. In contrast to the decline for the 13-year-olds, the final-year high school samples of both countries experienced modest gains. The complexities of sampling for this level are considerable and lead me to have far less confidence in the appropriateness of comparisons over time or between countries.

2. For Japan's Population A, other possible reasons for decline include a modest easing of curriculum standards since 1979, when the revised Course of Study was implemented, and a declining level of family support, which may be related to increasing proportions of children from broken families and families with both parents in the labor force.

REFERENCES

Austin, G., and H. Garber. 1982. *The Rise and Fall of National Test Scores*. Catonsville, Md.: Academic Press.

Bloom, Benjamin. 1976. *Human Characteristics and School Learning*. New York: Wiley.

Comber, L. C., and John P. Keeves. 1973. *Science Achievement in Nineteen Countries*. New York: Wiley.

Crosswhite, F. Joe, et al. 1984. *Second Study of Mathematics: Summary Report, United States*. Champaign-Urbana, Ill.: U.S. National Coordinating Center. Mimeographed.

Cummings, Williams K. 1980. *Education and Equality in Japan*. Princeton, N.J.: Princeton University Press.

Husen, Torsten, ed. 1967. *International Study of Achievement in Mathematics: A Comparison of Twelve Countries*, 2 vols. New York: Wiley.

Kokuritsu Kyoiku Kenkyusho. 1981. *Chugaku-Kokosei no Sugaku Gyosei: Dai-Nikai Kokusai Sugaku Kyoiku Chosa Chukan Hokokusho* (The Mathematics Achievement of Middle School and High School Students: Interim Report of the Second International Mathematics Survey). Tokyo: Daichi Hooki.

Lynn, R. 1982. "IQ in Japan and the United States Shows a Growing Disparity." *Nature* 297: 222-23.

National Commission on Excellence in Education. 1983. *A Nation at Risk: The Imperative for Educational Reform*. Washington, D.C.: U.S. Government Printing Office.

Rist, Ray. 1973. *The Urban School: A Factory for Failure*. Cambridge, Mass.: MIT Press.

Rohlen, Thomas P. 1984. *Japan's High Schools*. Berkeley: University of California Press.

Rosenbaum, James. 1976. *Making Inequality: The Hidden Curriculum of High School Tracking*. New York: Wiley.

Stevenson, Harold, and Hiroshi Azuma. 1983. "IQ in Japan and the United States: Methodological Problems in Lynn's Analysis." *Nature* 306: 291-92.

Stevenson, Harold, et al. 1985. "Classroom Behavior and Achievement of Japanese, Chinese and American Children." Ann Arbor: Department of Psychology, University of Michigan. Unpublished.

Stigler, James W. 1984. "'Mental Abacus': The Effect of Abacus Training on Chinese Children's Mental Calculation." *Cognitive Psychology* 16: 145-76.

Stigler, James W., et al. 1982. "Curriculum and Achievement in Mathematics: A Study of Elementary School Children in Japan, Taiwan, and the United States." *Journal of Educational Psychology* 74: 315-22.

7
COMPARING YOUTH CULTURES: PRECONCEPTIONS IN DATA
Carol Bowman Stocking

When we seek models for improving an education system by finding strengths in the system of another country, we are at great risk of incomplete understanding. We tend to know our (or another) educational system in only the most general way. We know how aspects of the system are intended to work. Some aspects we know from the way they are described by dedicated practitioners or other advocates. Others we know from the efforts of critics. Both of these, of course, are quite unbalanced views.

When we attempt to compare perceptions of the Japanese and American educational systems, of schools, or of students in the two settings, we find that we have many ideas but that some of those ideas are based on insufficient information. It is important that researchers exploit available data about both the U.S. and the Japanese educational systems in trying to understand where our preconceptions and the data support each other and where they may collide.

Using data from parallel studies, we can find confirmation of some of our preconceptions about differences between Japanese and U.S. high school students. We can also find data that perhaps will surprise us. Such surprises must be explored and understood if we contemplate policy reforms based on estimates of the educational system of either country.

136

THE HIGH SCHOOL & BEYOND DATA SETS

In the U.S. study High School & Beyond (HS&B), sponsored by the National Center for Education Statistics (NCES), data were collected from a sample of seniors (and of sophomores not reported on here) enrolled in a probability sample of about 1,000 public and private high schools. The data include the results of cognitive tests and transcript information. Base-year data were collected in 1980, and about 12,000 members of each cohort were followed up in 1982 and 1984. (They will be tested again in 1986.) Questionnaires were also collected from the principals (or their designates) of the sample schools, from a subsample of parents, and from classroom teachers. (Data tapes and documentation are available from the NCES, U.S. Department of Education.)

In Japan, Tamotsu Sengoku, director of the Japan Youth Research Institute, anticipated the importance of United States-Japan comparative research and designed a project to parallel the U.S. study. The Japanese and American base-year instruments therefore contain about 50 identical questions. In the Japanese study, questionnaires were collected in 1980 from about 7,000 seniors at 46 high schools. Data were also collected from principals and teachers. Follow-up data from the students were collected in 1982.

Most numbers mentioned in this chapter are from the base-year data. Only the 1980 senior cohort was studied in Japan, and only data from the U.S. 1980 senior cohort are reported here. Because follow-up procedures were quite different, a lower response rate was obtained in the Japanese follow-up survey, making comparison of the follow-up data in the two countries difficult. For detailed analyses of the base-year data, weights must be applied to the U.S. data and may also be indicated for the Japanese data. In this chapter, however, I discuss simple unweighted frequency distributions of responses in the two settings. It is my hope to stimulate comparative analyses.

FINDINGS

Student Behavior and Attitudes

Many of the notions we have about Japanese and U.S. high schools and high school students are supported by HS&B data. For example, we find as expected that Japanese students spend more time on homework than their American counterparts. More than a third (36 percent) of Japanese students but only 6 percent of U.S. students surveyed reported spending ten or more hours a week on homework. The data also confirm that more Japanese than American students study advanced secondary school mathematics. About a quarter (24 percent) of Japanese students took Math III (usually including advanced calculus), whereas only 9 percent of American students studied calculus. This smaller U.S. figure is somewhat anomalous, given that a larger proportion of American (43 percent) than of Japanese (20 percent) students reported getting good grades in math and more U.S. students expected math to be useful to them in the future (62 percent as compared with 47 percent).

Although many of the studies' findings confirm our knowledge, others do not. Because Japanese students have longer school days and spend more out-of-school time doing homework, it may surprise us to learn that about half of those surveyed (51 percent) spent two or more hours a day watching television. (About two-thirds of U.S. students reported spending that much TV time daily.) Our predisposition may be to imagine that American students are much more involved than Japanese students in extracurricular activities, but the proportions of students in both cultures who stated that they had *not* participated in sports, hobby clubs, student government, or similar activities were quite close: Approximately four-fifths to three-quarters of students in each culture reported having no involvement in specific activities (see Table 7.1).

Table 7.1   High school seniors who reported *not* participating in selected extracurricular activities, Japan and the United States, 1980 (percent)

Activity	Japan (activity in school in the past 3 years)	United States (activity in or out of school in the past year)
Athletic teams	44	59
Hobby Clubs	75	76
School newspaper/magazine	94	80
Subject-matter clubs	89	76
Student government	81	82
Vocational clubs	90	76

Another aspect of adolescent life—life outside of school—differs in some ways that we might predict. Many fewer Japanese students reported dating; about 9 percent of them as compared with 57 percent of American students reported having weekly dates with members of the opposite sex. About half (52 percent) of American students but only 7 percent of Japanese students reported chatting with friends on the telephone almost daily. In contrast, nearly half (48 percent) of Japanese students reported visiting with their friends almost every day, whereas about a quarter (26 percent) of American students did so.

Similar proportions of students in the United States and Japan considered success at work, marriage and family life, living close to parents, and having leisure time to be very important (see Table 7.2). (In both countries about 15 percent fewer girls than boys valued having lots of money, perhaps for similar reasons.) In Japan having children was rated as very important by 55 percent of both boys and girls. In the United States 44 percent of girls give it that rating, but only 34 percent of boys did so. This finding is one of the few in which a sex difference emerged in the U.S. data and not in the Japanese.

Table 7.2   High school seniors who rated selected values as very important, Japan and the United States, 1980 (percent)

Value	Japan	United States
Success in work	84	88
Marriage and happy family life	81	81
Having lots of money	28	31
Strong friendships	92	81
Finding steady work	69	84
Correcting social and economic inequities	22	13
Having children	55	39
Living close to parents and relatives	13	14
Having leisure time	67	70

Other authors in this volume have pointed out the inadequacy of the American stereotype of Japanese students' "examination hell." The HS&B data indicate that about one-third of Japanese seniors "often" feel that school life is pleasant and another 45 percent feel that way at least occasionally. Perhaps the 17 percent of seniors who plan to go to college and also intend to become *rōnin* if they are not admitted to the college of their choice is one indication of the extent of the supposed hell. (*Rōnin* are high school graduates who spend an extra year or more studying to gain admission to a prestigious university.)

Another stereotype, the "education mama" (*kyōiku mama*), has had some currency in the U.S. press. Although the HS&B data sets contain only indirect evidence about this issue, it is noteworthy that 86 percent of U.S. seniors reported that their mothers monitored their schoolwork but only 47 percent of Japanese seniors did so. Forty-three percent of U.S. seniors and 13 percent of Japanese seniors reported that their mothers influenced their post-high school plans a great deal. (The same percentage was reported for Japanese fathers; I mention mothers because of the stereotype.) In the United States more girls than boys (47 percent compared with 30 percent) gave this response; in Japan the percentages reporting a great deal of maternal influence were reversed, 19 percent of boys and 6 percent of girls. These data suggest that most Japanese students are not aware of being pressured by "education mamas."

Another aspect of the lives of Japanese students' mothers may jolt our preconceptions. A higher percentage of them are or have been employed than we might have expected. Approximately one-third (32 percent) of the Japanese students reported that their mothers had worked while the students were in elementary school, and stated that 38 percent of their mothers had worked while the students were in lower secondary school. In comparison, 54 percent of U.S. students reported having working mothers while the students were in elementary school, and 69 percent reported their mothers had worked while the students were in high school.

We might have expected that American students would wax more enthusiastic than Japanese students about aspects of their schools, such as the condition of buildings and library facilities, but we might not have expected high ratings of the quality of academic instruction. On the one hand it may be heartening to know that two-thirds of American students consider that their schools have a good reputation in the community; on the other it may cause us to reassess their enthusiastic rating of their schools' characteristics. In each category listed, about two-thirds of American students and roughly a quarter of Japanese students rated their schools as good or excellent (see Table 7.3). It would be a mistake simply to compare such responses between the two cultures. This information is less factual than the other items I have mentioned, and it allows more room for culturally determined styles of expression. However, within each culture it would be interesting to study the responses of students in different types of schools.

Table 7.3   High school seniors who rated aspects of their schools as good or excellent, Japan and the United States, 1980 (percent)

Aspect	Japan	United States
Condition of buildings and classrooms	22	62
Library facilities	26	67
Quality of academic instruction	20	61
Reputation in the community	36	66

Attitude Scales

Although the Japanese and U.S. questionnaires included some identical scale items, cross-cultural comparison of such measures would require an understanding of the norms of the scales in both contexts and extensive analysis. One aspect of the scales, however, is so interesting that I will briefly report it in hopes of stimulating a full analysis.

In general, American high school students' responses were much more positive than those of their Japanese peers. To give some examples, about 80 percent of U.S. students reported being satisfied with themselves; in Japan the figure was 32 percent for boys and 24 percent for girls. In both cultures more girls than boys agreed that "at times I think I'm no good" (51 percent of girls and 41 percent of boys in the United States and 71 percent of girls and 49 percent of boys in Japan).

I cannot estimate the bias that the low response rate on the Japanese survey's first follow-up may introduce. However, when the same students again answered those question two years later, the responses of the Japanese almost precisely duplicated those of the Americans. I have already pointed out that, in 1980, 30 percent of Japanese seniors reported being satisfied with themselves, as compared with 80 percent of American seniors. When these students responded again in 1982, 80 percent of each group reported being satisfied with themselves. In 1980 about half of the American seniors and three-quarters of the Japanese seniors agreed that they sometimes felt they were no good at all. Two years after high school, 60 percent of each group were prepared to *disagree* with that statement. Six such scale items were repeated in the Japanese first follow-up, and five of them moved substantially toward the upper end of the scale (see Table 7.4).

Table 7.4   U.S. and Japanese respondents giving optimistic responses to
                  scale items as seniors and two years after high school (percent)

	United States		Japan	
		Two years after high		Two years after high
	As		As	
Item	seniors	school	seniors	school
Good luck is more important than hard work for success (disagree)	83	86	45	80
Planning only makes a person unhappy, since plans hardly ever work out anyway (disagree)	77	75	79	75
On the whole, I am satisfied with myself (agree)	80	79	30	79
People who accept their condition in life are happier than those who try to change things (disagree)	54	61	50	75
At times I think I am no good at all (disagree)	48	61	26	61
When I make plans, I am almost certain I can make them work (agree)	78	77	39	79

The change in responses to these scale items leads me to specu-
late that being a student in Japan fosters feelings of powerlessness
and low self-esteem. Leaving secondary school seems to have had a
remarkable effect on the Japanese students' psychological scale
scores but virtually no effect on the scores of American students. If
differences in their initial responses were largely a function of different meanings attached to the questions and different styles of expression in the two cultures, it is hard to understand why those differences would have disappeared.

Postsecondary Plans

Comparing figures on postsecondary plans from the two High
School & Beyond studies reveals that similar proportions of students in both countries planned to go directly into the labor market,
to enter a vocational, trade, or business school, to go to a two-year
college, or to finish college or go to graduate school (see Table 7.5).

It is noteworthy that although the combined total proportions of students planning higher education were similar, the U.S. proportion aiming for graduate school was twice as large as that of Japan. For example, 44 percent of American and 55 percent of Japanese seniors planned to go to college or graduate school. However, in the case of the Japanese sample it is more precise to indicate that 72 percent of the males and 36 percent of the females had that plan. In the United States virtually identical proportions of boys and girls (47 and 45 percent, respectively) had such plans. Apropos this aspect of the data, two-thirds of the Japanese boys and one-quarter of the girls stated that their mothers wanted them to finish four or more years of college. In the United States 62 percent of the boys' and 58 percent of the girls' mothers had such wishes.

Table 7.5   High school seniors reporting various future plans, Japan and the United States, 1980 (percent)

Plan	Japan	United States
Labor market	18	22
Vocational, trade, or business school	15	19
Junior college	12	15
Four-year college (in Japan, national and private)	45	24
Postgraduate study	10	20

Twice as many young women as young men in the Japanese sample planned to go to vocational, trade, or business school (21 percent as compared with 10 percent). In the United States, however, virtually identical proportions of boys and girls had that plan. Similarly, in Japan 25 percent of female high school students planned to go to junior college, whereas only 2 percent of the males had that plan. But in the United States only a slightly higher percentage of females (18 percent) than of males (12 percent) planned to attend a two-year college.

In the United States two-year colleges have assumed a major role in vocational education. As Tamotsu Sengoku (1984) has pointed out, junior colleges may be viewed in the Japanese context as schools for marriage, which represents permanent employment for women in the traditional Japanese context.

When data were collected in the HS&B first follow-up, about half of the Japanese respondents[1] and 42 percent of the U.S. sample were going to two- or four-year colleges. (In Japan 40 percent of the follow-up sample had gone to a four-year college; in the United States the proportion was about 35 percent.) It is widely known that very few of the young people who enter college in Japan fail to complete the four-year course. Thus entrance figures closely resemble graduation figures. Such is not the case in the United States. Kolstad (1981) estimates that in the United States only about half of those who enter college earn baccalaureate degrees within seven years. I may be comparing the wrong numbers. When making system comparisons, one should perhaps look at the percentages of males in the appropriate age cohort who both enter and complete college. I hope that these glimpses of data will stimulate researchers to compare the two systems in ways that may not have been done before or to look more carefully at the factual base of our preconceptions.

Minor Collisions Between Preconceptions and Data

Working closely with the U.S. HS&B project and consulting with Tamotsu Sengoku on the Japanese HS&B presented opportunities to observe the slow change in preconceptions about both the U.S. and Japanese educational systems and some as yet unresolved minor collisions between preconceptions and data in both countries. I will illustrate this in two quite disparate areas, using examples from anecdote and from the HS&B surveys.

Youth Employment. The first area is youth employment. When researchers studying the NCES on the high school class of 1972 (the first cohort in the NCES longitudinal data series) reported that 62 percent of all high school seniors in the United States worked six or more hours a week, many people dismissed the finding. The actual wording of the question, "On the average over the school year, how many hours per week do you work in a paid or unpaid job? (exclude vacation)," seemed to allow bits of work done around the house, such as washing dishes, to be included in the positive responses.

In 1978, when the HS&B instruments were being developed, special attention was given to the question about students who held jobs while still in high school. The question used was: "Did you do any work for pay last week, not counting work around the house?" This was followed by a detailed series of questions about number of hours worked, earnings, type of work, and so on. Responses to the question indicated that 63 percent of high school students worked while seniors in high school. Now that figure and similar figures in other data are widely accepted in the United States. I present this as an example of a changing preconception of students in the United States. We must now think of the average high school senior as holding a part-time job while attending school.

When I spoke with Japanese experts, I was told that virtually no Japanese students worked while attending upper secondary school and that Japanese high schools forbid students to hold part-time jobs. At most it was possible that a few students worked during school vacations. Because I was told this by Japanese scholars and U.S. experts on Japan, I assumed that it was accurate. Then I looked at the Japanese data.

They revealed that my advisers were correct in one respect. No school administrator reported allowing students to hold part-time jobs. But only three (of 46) reported that they prohibited all part-time jobs. Thirty reported prohibiting work but made exceptions, and 13 administrators reported that they allowed students to hold jobs but prohibited specific ones. I have no way of knowing whether language and cultural barriers hinder my understanding of these answers, but I do propose that Japanese secondary schools do not necessarily prohibit students from working.

My hypothesis is confirmed by the finding that 56 percent of Japanese students in the sample reported having had jobs during school term or vacations while they were in high school. Of these, 38 percent worked during term. Thus about 20 percent of all Japanese seniors reported working during the school term while they were in high school. The kinds of jobs students reported holding were about equally distributed among labor, delivery, sales, and service categories.

Before making hypotheses about the kinds of Japanese secondary schools that allow part-time jobs, let us again consult the data. I categorized schools by the proportion of graduates who went on to postsecondary education. I found that about half of the schools in the two higher categories allow part-time jobs. In the category of school where the smallest proportion of students attend postsecondary education, only one school in seven allows part-time jobs (see Table 7.6).

The difference in percentages of students who had never worked for pay (44 percent in Japan, 5 percent in the United States) is very great, as is the contrast between the proportion of students who worked during the school term (21 and 63 percent, respectively). But these data reveal that Japanese high school students do hold jobs. It would seem that the situation in Japan has changed in recent years more quickly than has the Japanese perception.

Table 7.6   High school administrators' reports on rules about student jobs, Japan, 1980

School type	Allows any job	Allows most (but prohibits some)	Prohibits most (but allows some)	Prohibits all
1. ≥95% of graduates continue to postsecondary education (*N* = 11)	0	5	4	2
2. 75-94% of graduates continue to postsecondary education (*N* = 12)	0	5	7	0
3. ≤74% of graduates continue to postsecondary education (*N* = 7)	0	1	6	0
4. Vocational or technical schools (*N* = 16)	0	2	13	1

High School Counseling. The second area where I have observed preconceptions to collide with data is that of counseling in high schools. One often reads that U.S. high school students *choose* their program with the advice of a counselor. According to the U.S. data, however, 38 percent of seniors in 1982 reported that they had been simply assigned to a high school program and another 28 percent reported that they had chosen a program without any consultation at all. It is possible that counselors had some behind-the-scenes role, but the students' responses indicate the role was not the one depicted in the stereotype.

The U.S. stereotype has also surfaced in Japan. In speaking with colleagues there about the American and Japanese educational systems, I have found that Japanese scholars often admire the U.S. counseling system, which assists students in negotiating the transition from high school to the complex and differentiated postsecondary educational system. But the U.S. HS&B data show that only 10 percent of the students reported that counselors had influenced them a great deal. Half of the students (51 percent) reported that counselors had influenced their postsecondary plans "not at all." In response to another question, about one-fourth of the U.S. students reported that they did not know what counselors thought they should do after high school, and another 7 percent said that their counselors did not care what they did.

The role of counseling in U.S. high schools is being critically reviewed. For example, the U.S. College Board recently announced the appointment of a Commission on Precollege Guidance and Counseling to conduct a two-year study and then make recommendations about ways to improve the quality and availability of counseling in high schools.

What about counseling in Japanese high schools? Although the functions of counseling in Japan may be quite different from those in the United States, the amount of counseling in Japan may come as a surprise to American researchers. Japanese school administrators were asked to report the average number of counseling sessions arranged for each student per year. Table 7.7 shows that even first-year high school students had two individual sessions and that the average increased each year. The higher averages in the last year may partly reflect the role of the high school in job placement.

Table 7.7   Average numbers of individual guidance sessions about employment or college plans, Japan, 1980 (reported by school administrators)

School type	First-year students	Second-year students	Third-year students
1. ≥95% of graduates continue to postsecondary education	2.4	2.5	3.1
2. 75-94% of graduates continue to postsecondary education	2.3	2.7	4.0
3. ≤74% of graduates continue to postsecondary education	3.0	3.2	5.1
4. Vocational or technical schools	1.8	2.1	4.1

In the HS&B studies students in the two settings were asked their opinions about aspects of their schools and the things that their schools provided. Within each country male and female responses on many of the items were virtually the same. This was not the case in Japan when the topic was counseling. Ten percent more girls than boys reported being provided with counseling for both continuing their education and finding employment. About 80 percent of all Japanese seniors reported such counseling compared with only one-half to two-thirds of U.S. students (see Table 7.8).

Table 7.8 High school seniors agreeing with statements about high school counseling, Japan and the United States, 1980 (percent)

Statement	Japan			United States		
	All	Girls	Boys	All	Girls	Boys
School provided me with counseling for continuing education	82	88	77	66	65	67
School provided me with counseling for finding employment	81	86	76	49	48	50

It is not at all clear from the data that the counseling system in the United States is either more pervasive or more effective than that of Japan. What is clear is that we need to know more about its implementation and function in each context.

CONCLUSION

To seek models for improving our educational system is understandable and even desirable. But it is important that our understanding of the application of that model in its native setting be up to date and complete. Looking at aspects of systems as they are meant to work or as they may have worked in the past is only part of the task. We must seek to understand how they actually work now, with their particular strengths and weaknesses. It is hard to do this in our own culture. When studying educational systems in other cultures we are in danger of seeing only the general outlines and finding in them simplified solutions to our problems.

When social science data confirm our stereotypes or support our anecdotal knowledge, we readily accept the data but scorn them for being obvious or trivial. If such data are contrary to our notions, however, we often reject them. We scrutinize the data collection method, the sample, the presentation, and so on, seeking reasons to dismiss the surprising data. Such aspects of data collection and presentation should of course be reviewed. But data are sometimes dismissed even when no specific source of error can be found. There is a time lag between the publication of such data and their integration into our stereotypes.

It takes time for facts about one's own educational system to be assimilated by persons at one remove from it, even persons in the same culture. It takes even more time for information about one country to filter through to researchers and policymakers in another country. Meanwhile we often work with slightly outdated conceptions. Although both Mōmbushō and the U.S. Department of Education have detailed, accurate, timely information, our preconceptions are often not affected by its details. If we accept that this is true of our thinking about our own educational system, we can begin to see the problems in understanding the system of another country and the complexities involved in attempting to imitate or borrow aspects of that system for adaptation to our own.

NOTE

1. The Ministry of Education, Science, and Culture estimates that 36 percent of graduates attend postsecondary schools, including universities, junior colleges, and senior-level technical colleges (Japan, Mōmbushō 1983). The difference between this and the HS&B estimate of 51.5 percent may be the result of bias introduced by the response rate on the HS&B follow-up.

REFERENCES

Fetters, William B., Jeffrey A. Owings, Larry E. Suter, and Ricky T. Takai. 1983. "Schooling Experiences in Japan and the U.S.: A Cross-National Comparison of High School Students." Paper presented at the American Education Research Association meeting, Montreal, April.

Japan. Ministry of Education, Science, and Culture (Mōmbushō). 1983. *Statistical Abstract of Education, Science and Culture.* Tokyo: Ashai Shimbun.

Japan Youth Research Institute. 1981. *High School and Beyond Survey: Japan and USA Comparisons Using the Base Year Data about High School Life and Future Occupational Life* (in Japanese). Tokyo.

_____. 1984. *High School and Beyond Study: Comparisons Including Follow-up Data* (in Japanese). Tokyo.

Jones, Calvin, Miriam Clark, Geraldine Mooney, Harold McWilliams, Ioanna Crawford, Bruce Stephenson, and Roger Tourangeau. 1983. *Data File User's Manual, High School and*

Beyond, 1980 Senior Cohort, First Follow-Up (1982). Washington, D.C.: National Center for Education Statistics.

Kolstad, Andrew J. 1981. "What College Dropout and Dropin Rates Tell Us." *American Education* 17 (August-September): 31-33.

Sengoku, Tamotsu. 1984. "Japanese Education and Permanent Employment Structure." Paper presented at the Thirteenth International Conference on the Unity of the Sciences, Washington, D.C., September.

PART III
DECLINE

8
THE DECLINE AND REFORM OF EDUCATION IN JAPAN: A COMPARATIVE PERSPECTIVE
Kazuyuki Kitamura

In both Japan and the United States, the two most highly schooled societies in the world, a "crisis in education" has attracted national attention and "educational reform" has become a major policy issue for their respective governments. Various commissions and study groups have been established in the two countries to examine the problem, and many recommendations have been made for dealing with it.

JAPAN'S REFORM MOVEMENT

In the Japanese case, "educational reform" was raised as a national policy issue by Prime Minister Yasuhiro Nakasone. During the 1983 general election campaign for the House of Representatives, he found that educational problems were of major concern to voters. In spite of the apparent superiority of Japanese primary and secondary school education—as evidenced by the superior achievement of Japanese students in international mathematics and science tests—he was surprised to hear many voters expressing dissatisfaction with the current situation of schools and colleges. Their complaints led Nakasone to conclude that educational reform should be an important policy issue, along with the reform of governmental administration and public finance, which he had initially featured in his campaign.

Prime Minister Nakasone also realized that the fundamental structure of the Japanese educational system had not changed since it

153

was reformed under strong U.S. influence in the years following World War II. It seems ironic that, 35 years later, when proponents of U.S. educational reform are looking to the Japanese system as a model to be studied and learned from, Japanese reformers are critical of their own educational system because, among other reasons, it was established in accordance with American models during the Occupation. It is also ironic that Japanese reformers wish to make the Japanese school curriculum less demanding, while American reformers seek to make theirs more so, by strengthening the high school and college requirements for graduation.

And so, in 1983, there was widespread concern among the leaders of the reform movement and the general public that the Japanese educational system as a whole was not effective in developing its students to compete in the complex world of the twenty-first century. "Creative talent, diversity, and international awareness" are what Japanese industry will need most from its work force (Ranbom 1985, p. 32), and this need is of deepest concern to Japanese political and economic leaders. The internationalization of Japanese education and society was another theme of concern.

In August 1984 the Japanese Diet enacted a bill to establish an Ad Hoc Council on Educational Reform (Rinji Kyoiku Shingikai), responsible to the prime minister. Nakasone immediately appointed 25 representatives from various fields to the council, which began its deliberations. Because it reports directly to the prime minister, the council is the most powerful advisory body on educational affairs to have been established since 1951. Formerly, national educational policy was the purview of the Central Council for Education (Chuo Kyoiku Shingikai), which advised the minister of education. The prime minister required that this new council report directly to him so that he could become intimately involved in reform. The Education Council consists of four committees, which address the issues out-lined in Exhibit 8.1.

Although Japan's current educational reform movement was born in the political arena, it reflects legitimate concern about the recent decline of the Japanese educational system. In this chapter I attempt first to describe the decline and explain why it is occurring and then to outline my own view of the direction that reform efforts should take.

SIGNS OF EDUCATIONAL DECLINE

The Japanese educational system enjoyed a rapid, unprecedented, and continuous expansion of both enrollment and financial resources during the 1960s, which reached a plateau by the early 1970s. But in the mid-1970s it entered a period of no expansion and even of decline. The population of the kindergarten-age cohort has recently reached its lowest level since the World War II "baby boom." As a result, most kindergartens have canceled nearly half of their classes. This decrease will soon hit the primary schools, and later it will affect secondary and higher education.

Exhibit 8.1   Issues addressed by the four committees of the Ad Hoc Council on Educational Reform

First Committee	*Education for the twenty-first century*, in particular education for high technology and for an information-oriented, internationalized, liberalized, aging, and highly schooled society
Second Committee	*Revitalization of educational functions in society*, including the improvement of "degreeocracy," current education, the provision for lifelong learning, and the promotion of international cultural exchange
Third Committee	*Reform in primary and secondary education*, including the curriculum and school system
Fourth Committee	*Reform in higher education*, including the academic calendar, general education, college entrance examinations, and the relationship between public and private sectors
Third and Fourth Joint Committee	*Educational systems*, including 6-3-3-4[a] school system, admissions, international educational exchange, teacher education, and the education of the handicapped.

[a]6-3-3-4 relates to the number of years for primary, middle, secondary, and university education, respectively.

While enrollments are decreasing, the schools' financial problems are increasing because Japanese economic growth has declined in the wake of the 1973 oil crisis. Before the mid-1970s, budget officials regarded education and social welfare, along with the military, as "sanctuaries," off limits to budget cuts. Since the mid-1970s, however, the increasing deficit in government revenue has made these sanctuaries no longer exempt from cuts. Because the government's policy has been to restrain budget growth, the total budget for education has not increased in constant yen since then.

Other signs of educational decline include the increasing numbers of low achievers in primary and secondary schools; increased school violence, especially at junior high schools; and the emerging phenomenon of voluntary dropouts from senior high schools. The dropouts are adolescents who want to study at home or at cram schools in order to obtain the certificate for application to the college entrance examination without attending high school. Their action is a clear expression of declining trust of the effectiveness of formal education for realizing the educational needs of the public.

The declining faith in Japanese formal education can be seen from other evidence as well. According to a public opinion poll conducted in May 1984 by the newspaper *Asahi Shimbun*, more than half (55 percent) of the adult respondents felt "unsatisfied" with the primary and junior high schools, whereas only 24 percent were "satisfied." (In a similar survey conducted in 1977, 49 percent of respondents had been "satisfied" with the educational system and only 22 percent "unsatisfied.") Responding to the question, "Do you think school education has become better or worse when you compare it with your school days?" 32 percent of adults surveyed in 1984 answered "better," while 47 percent considered it "worse." (In 1977, 44 percent had said "better" and 32 percent had said "worse.") The more recent poll indicates that the Japanese public has come not only to feel increasing dissatisfaction with the schools but also to rely less on formal education since 1977 (*Asahi Shimbun* 1984).

In the field of higher education a trend toward diversification in the types of institutions selected by applicants began to occur in the mid-1970s. The assumption of the 1960s that there would be an almost endless increase in university applications suddenly became doubtful. More students have begun to choose noncollegiate institutions for postsecondary education, such as vocational and technical schools (*senshugakko*). Moreover, the past five years have seen a slight decline in the proportion of college-age students attending colleges and universities.

One important problem that disturbs university administrators is the demographic future. The population of 18-year-olds, who are the clients of higher education, will grow from 1.7 million to 2 million between 1984 and 1993. However, the size of this age group will shrink dramatically—from 2 million to 1.5 million—between 1993 and 2000. How to survive in an age of declining enrollments is a question that already deeply concerns university administrators (see Figure 8.1). Perhaps during the next decade Japan will enter the age of "student consumerism," in which colleges make desperate efforts to recruit student clients, as is currently happening in the United States.

Figure 8.1 Trends in Japanese higher education, 1960-83, and projected 18-year-old population, 1984-2000

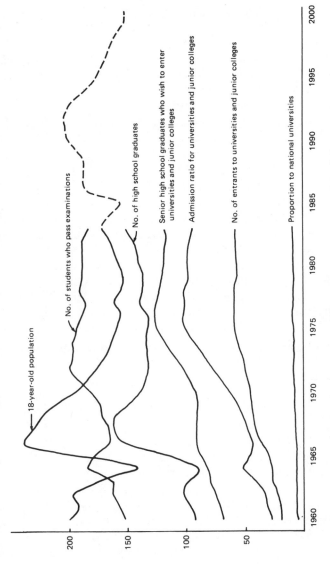

Source: Adapted from Mombushō (1977); Ministry of Education, Science, and Culture (1984, p. 11).

Note: Success rate = no. of entrants to universities and junior colleges/no. of high school students (including *rōnin*) wishing to enter universities and junior colleges.

157

Another sign of declining respect for Japanese higher education is the increasing criticism of it from abroad. Evaluations of Japanese education by Americans, especially the U.S. Japanologists, contain a common theme. In sharp contrast to the high marks they and others give to primary and secondary education in Japan—it is generally recognized that Japanese primary and secondary schools are "among the most effective in the world" (OECD 1971, p. 57) —higher education has come in for heavy criticism. Fiske (1983, p. 1), for example, considers the quality of Japanese universities to be "far below" that of U.S. colleges and universities.

A national opinion survey of foreign teachers at Japanese universities and colleges that was conducted by the Research Institute for Higher Education at Hiroshima University in 1979 (RIHE 1981; Kitamura 1983-84, 1984) found that many foreign teachers were extremely critical of Japanese professors' attitudes. Their criticism can be summarized as follows: (1) In general, Japanese professors seem to have more respect for research than for teaching, and thus their interest in teaching appears to be negligible. (2) The Japanese curriculum is unorganized and unstructured; most courses and programs seem to suit the convenience of the professors and do not necessarily meet students' needs. (3) Teaching methods and patterns are uniform and inflexible, and they are particularly unsuitable for teaching foreign languages. (4) In comparison with U.S. and European universities, little institutional consideration has been given to the teaching function of Japanese universities. For example, there are no staff development centers, and no evaluation of teaching and curriculum has been undertaken. Indeed, little research on teaching and learning in higher education has been conducted in Japan.

A recent *New York Times* article severely criticized university education in Japan. Written by an American professor who had spent four years at Japanese universities (Zeugner 1983), the article carried the shocking title "Japan's Noneducation." Its author wrote: "Although Japanese students demonstrate superiority in certain elementary and secondary school tests, their advantage slips drastically at the university level." He pointed out several weaknesses of Japanese universities, including the low rate of student class attendance, the high incidence of class cancellations by professors, and grade inflation. He concluded that "the combination of Japanese elementary and secondary education and corporate training seems to compensate for the emptiness of the Japanese university" (Zeugner 1983; see also Zeugner 1984).

These examples are typical of the criticism of Japan's higher education by American observers. It is noteworthy, however, that the same criticism has been directed against U.S. schools by American reformers. According to the several reports on higher education published recently by the National Institute of Education, the National Endowment for the Humanities, and the American Association of Colleges, U.S. higher education is also severely criticized because of the low quality of undergraduate education, the lack of a structured and coherent curriculum in general education, the overemphasis on research and insufficient emphasis on teaching among faculty members, and grade inflation of students' academic performance, among other faults (NIE 1984; Bennett 1984; AAC 1985). If these criticisms are fair, it may be that the American and Japanese systems of higher education face common problems.

DILEMMAS OF THE DUAL STRUCTURE

I would argue that the weaknesses and strengths of Japanese formal education stem from its dual structure. On the one hand, there is the contrast between the limited public sector and the market-driven private sector. On the other hand, there is the perverse complementarity of the formal and the nonformal systems. These structures were fairly well balanced until the mid-1970s but since then have been gradually disrupted by both social changes and the advent of student consumerism.

The Private and Public Sectors

The private sector, particularly in higher education, has been dominant, comprising nearly three-quarters of students and institutions (74.8 percent of students and 73.9 percent of institutions in 1983). Public higher education charges lower tuition and fees than private universities (on average less than 30 percent of private universities' fees in 1983) and generally has better conditions as measured by teacher-student ratios, floor space per student, and books per student (Ichikawa 1984). As public higher education is open to only 25 percent of the student population, the majority of young people are forced to attend the more costly but generally educationally disadvantaged and crowded private universities.

The traditional policy of the Japanese central government was to concentrate educational resources in the public sector in order to preserve academic quality, while leaving quantitative expansion to private institutions, which are more responsive to changing social demands. The rapid expansion of Japanese higher education without substantial investment in higher education from public funds has been due to this two-sector policy, which the central government maintained throughout Japan's 100-year bid for modernization until the end of the 1960s. Faced with the increasing imbalance of manpower needs in various fields, financial crises at private universities, and increased dissatisfaction of parents and students with the unequal academic conditions that existed between the private and public sectors, the government finally changed its policy of withholding support to the private sector. In 1970 it approved a new policy to provide direct financial assistance to private institutions, covering up to half of each institutions's current expenses. This was perhaps the greatest reversal of educational policy in Japan's history.

Since then the traditional hierarchy of universities and colleges in Japan has been gradually changing. The monopoly of prestige that top national and local public universities long enjoyed no longer exists. For instance, as a result of the introduction in 1979 of a new examination system for admission to universities, college-bound students applying to public universities are now required to take a nationally uniform achievement test consisting of seven subjects as a primary screening and then another test for the university of their choice. It is a one-time opportunity, and students may apply to only one public university. These rigid requirements have precipitated a dramatic change in college choice among students. Most of the major private universities, which require tests in only a few subjects, have attracted increasing numbers of able applicants, whereas many of the major public universities (except for top institutions like the University of Tokyo) have suffered from a decrease in both number and quality of applicants. Because almost none of the private universities (composing more than 70 percent of all universities) participates in the nationally uniform test, the reform has not succeeded in improving the university entrance examination system as a whole.

Thus the reform of the entrance examination system in the public sector has resulted only in pushing talented students away from the public system, just as the high school examination reform of the late 1960s, which was "a major drive to end the stratification of public high schools, only led to a strengthening of . . . private schools" (Rohlen 1983, p. 312). These two examples illustrate the close interaction between the public and private educational sectors and how the traditional hierarchy has been changing. The traditional balance between public and private institutions seems to have been lost with the advent of student consumerism. College choice is extremely responsive to changes in the educational world and the society at large. Such changes include not only the introduction of entrance examination systems but also shifts in employment market trends.

The Formal and Nonformal Educational Systems

A second dimension of the dual structure of Japanese education is the increasing interdependence of formal and nonformal education. If we look at the educational system from the broadest perspective, the formal schools (those that form the backbone of the system) and the nonformal institutions (those catering to special educational needs) are so mutually dependent and supportive that without the links that connect them the educational objectives of Japanese society could not be realized.

Japan's primary and secondary educational system often has been described as the most effective in the world (OECD 1971). But its supremacy could not be maintained without the huge nonformal supporting system, which compensates for the inflexibility of the formal system.

As shown in Exhibit 8.2, the relation between the formal and nonformal educational systems is like that between figure and ground in a painting. Each stage of formal schooling is closely connected with a supporting system that is continuously changing according to social demand. This supporting system is composed of private college preparatory and cram schools (*yobiko* and *juku*), proprietary technical and vocational schools, and various learning and training programs usually provided by corporations as part of on-the-job training.

The dominant values of the Japanese public primary school are egalitarianism and uniformity: Pupils are not classified according to their academic ability because all pupils are supposed to keep up with the progress of the class. There they are taught by means of a nationally controlled, uniform curriculum. Despite its principles of egalitarianism and uniformity, however, the school inevitably must produce high achievers and low achievers. The school and its teachers are unable to counter these disparities because they are bound by the two mandatory principles. So troubled teachers assume the role of traffic police, directing high achievers who are dissatisfied with the progress of the school class to attend a preparatory school for elite students, where they can take more advanced classes, while sending prospective dropouts to another type of cram school offering remedial classes. Then, thanks to the existence of these two kinds of supporting institutions, the formal school itself can continue to function according to the principles of egalitarianism and uniformity.

Exhibit 8.2   Dual structure of Japanese education as of May 1983

Formal education	Nonformal education
	Postgraduate education
Graduate schools	Government research institutes
268 schools	On-the-job training
62,000 students	Adult education
	Long-cycle higher education
Universities	Government's "grand schools" (*daigakko*)
457 universities	15,000 students
1.8 million students	University of the Air
	10,000 students expected
	Correspondence education at the
	university level
	13 universities
	100,000 students
	Short-cycle higher education
Junior colleges	Technical and vocational schools
532 colleges	(*senshûgakko*), postsecondary level
379,000 students	
Technical colleges	2,328 schools
(*kôtô semmon gakko*)	386,000 students
62 colleges	Correspondence education at the
	junior college level
47,000 students	10 colleges
	78,000 students
	Upper secondary education
Senior high schools	Technical and vocational schools
5,369 schools	(*senshûgakko*), high school level
4.7 million students	816 schools
	57,000 students
	Miscellaneous schools (*kakushu-gakko*)
	4,674 schools
	606,000 students
	Compulsory education
Junior high schools	Cram schools for able pupils
	(*gakushû-juku*)
10,950 schools	50,000 schools
5.7 million students	3.1 million students (estimated)
Primary schools	Remedial *juku* (*hoshû-juku*)
25,000 schools	Vocational and technical *"juku"*
11.7 million students	(*naraigoto-juku*)
	Infant education
Kindergartens	Nursery schools
15,000 schools	22,800 schools
2 million students	2.1 million students

Available data are somewhat outdated, but according to a national survey conducted by Japan's Ministry of Education, Science, and Culture (1977), the number of primary school and junior high school pupils attending *juku* was approximately 1.3 million (12 percent) and 1.8 million (38 percent), respectively. The number of such schools was estimated to be more than 50,000 (Japan, Ministry of Education 1977, p. 329). According to a survey of Tokyo children conducted by the Tokyo Metropolitan Agency in 1977, 24.4 percent of primary school children and 55.9 percent of junior high school pupils went to *juku* two or three time a week for one to three hours per day (Tokyo-to-Kyoiku-cho 1977, pp. 11-12).

One important reason why the new uniform entrance examination system has not been successful is that students' and parents' rely extensively on the major university preparatory schools (the so-called *juken sangyo*, or "examination industry") in developing their strategy for applying to and selecting universities. These schools have amassed huge data banks on the admission requirements and standards of all universities and colleges. Upon receiving their test results, students look to the preparatory schools for identifying colleges appropriate to their academic abilities, and these suggestions almost ensure their admission. Because admission requirements of private colleges vary greatly, unlike the rigid requirements of public universities, virtually any high school graduate can find a private school that will accept him. Even highly qualified students who aspire to Japan's most prestigious universities tend to prepare for entry to at least one other college where they have a high probability of being accepted, and that is almost invariably a private one. The choice of a public or private university is generally made in the last two years of high school, when academic preparation differs according to the type of institution an individual seeks to enter. With their ability to assess quite accurately students' chances for admission to certain universities, the nonformal institutions have in many cases a stronger influence over students' choices than do high school teachers, and even the teachers have found the information provided by this industry useful for advising students.

This nonformal educational system is no longer simply a subordinate system supporting the formal school system but an increasingly important means for high school students to make their college choice and to prepare for the entrance examinations. The nonformal sector plays such an important role in secondary education that the traditional balance between the formal and nonformal systems is teetering.

The Balance of Educational Levels

Higher education is seen by Americans as the worst and weakest part of the Japanese formal educational system. As an American observer put it, does "the combination of Japanese elementary and secondary education and corporative training compensate for the emptiness of the Japanese university?" (Zeugner 1983). In comparing Japanese and U.S. education, it is necessary to consider each nation's system of higher education in the context of the total educational enterprise.

As is well known, Japan's high school students have to work much harder than their U.S. counterparts in preparing for admission to universities and colleges. Thus, during high school, college-bound Japanese students have little opportunity to develop their non-cognitive qualities. Gaining admission to the group of one's choice is of such crucial importance in Japanese society that aspirants are prepared to devote extraordinary efforts (Nakane 1970, pp. 104-26). In the case of university admissions, youth study assiduously, and only afterward do they as students have enough free time to enjoy their youth and develop interests denied during 12 long years of schooling. The university thus provides a valuable opportunity for the young to enjoy their youth and to further their personal development.

In contrast, the U.S. high school provides much free time and a flexible curriculum. High school is "a fine time for the flourishing of friendships, romance, creativity, and independent choice" (Rohlen 1983, p. 135). Most American high school students are not required to undergo as strenuous a competition for admission to universities and colleges as their Japanese counterparts. Their academic education begins in earnest only after they are enrolled in college.

In Japan, after the all-out effort to prepare for the college entrance examination, competition abates until, after four years of college life, the young people graduate and once again vie with each other in the job market. In contrast, in the United States, the competition to survive in college life is maintained throughout the four-year period. Thus one of the major functions of Japanese higher education, especially for students in the humanities and social sciences, is to give the students greater freedom for independent study and personal development, both of which are lacking during their high school days.

School versus University

Since the days of Arinori Mori, Japan's first education minister (1885-89) in the Meiji Government, the school has been considered an institution in which the pupils' learning is heavily dependent on the aid of others, whereas the university is an institution in which students are supposed to have the capacity to learn independently.

Because the university is considered an institution of *higher* education that accepts only qualified students who need the least instruction and guidance from teachers, those students admitted by a university are considered to be members of an elite group who are presumed to have both definite goals for study and the capacity to learn independently; therefore, they have the least need for special teacher assistance.

In addition, another traditional concept of the university reinforces the downplaying of the teaching function. This is the idea that the functions of both research and teaching are in harmony, cannot be separated, and are not in a conflicting relationship with each other. Thus it is assumed that the professors' research activities automatically contribute to their students' educational progress. According to this theory, what professors should do is to deepen their research and scholarly activities and "to profess" what they have investigated without special regard to "how to teach" students. This is because it is considered the students' responsibility to learn something from what the professors "profess" and then to integrate what they obtain from various academic offerings into the total educational experience of their college life.

Although these traditional concepts of university education were maintained at the small number of elitist universities (fewer then ten institutions) before World War II, this consciousness continued without modification among a great number of younger professors at universities and colleges that were created just after the war. It is still prevalent today among most professors (120,000 full-time faculty members) at the almost 1,000 universities and junior colleges in Japan.

Another major reason why Japanese students are generally not forced to work as hard as American students (except for students in highly professional fields such as medicine and engineering) is the relatively weak relevance of the university curriculum to the needs of the business world and the employment practices of Japanese society. What Japanese businesses are interested in is not what students have learned in the university but the rank of the university from which they graduate—on the presumption that graduates from prestigious universities have greater abilities and therefore higher potential. In addition, employers in Japan usually prefer to recruit "generalists" rather than narrowly focused "specialists," as they themselves provide intensive courses to train employees for their particular needs (Ushiogi 1984).

Although seemingly "empty" to American observers, the relatively free and loose Japanese college or university functions as a place for the personal and social development of these young people, a "buffer zone" between the stringent demands of secondary education and the intensive vocational or professional on-the-job training in store for them in the business world.

If we examine Japanese higher education in the perspective of its vertical balance in the total educational ladder, it was able, until at least the end of the 1970s, to accommodate the high growth rate needs of the Japanese economy. However, this vertical balance of the different functions of Japanese secondary and higher education has increasingly been challenged by student consumerism and changing social demands.

Student Consumerism

In the book *Academic Revolution* (1968), Christopher Jencks and David Riesman describe the rise to power of the academic profession in the United States. In Riesman's recent book, *On Higher Education* (1980, p. xiv), he predicts the imminent rise of student consumerism. According to Clark Kerr, who wrote the preface to the book, this shift from academic merit to student consumerism is one of the greatest reversals in the history of American higher education. Because of the coming demographic decline, decreased financial support, and rising educational costs, Riesman asserts, students are ceasing to be "supplicants for admission" and becoming "courted customers"; they are gaining increased market power while faculty influence is declining. In an era of student hegemony, more and more students are "passive consumers" who want to buy only easily obtained educational services sold at "academic supermarkets," without setting their own curricula or integrating their own education as "active producers." Riesman believes that it is necessary to resist the prevailing mood of faculty demoralization and the desires of students to be entertained and awarded degrees after little effort. He concludes that students must be at once the producers and the consumers of their own educational development.

Riesman's view of historical developments in U.S. education has implications for Japanese higher education. I believe that in Japan also there are signs of a historical transition from the "university of teachers" to the "university of students." The university of teachers is a traditional university in which academics have supreme power over students, power that is legally defined and protected by the concepts of academic freedom and faculty autonomy. Today's Japanese university professors have substantial power not only in the academic affairs of teaching and research but also in governance and administration. Their recruitment and promotion are based on their academic productivity and research achievements rather than on their teaching ability. The curriculum, requirements, and admission standards are determined by faculty members' needs and convenience rather than by students' needs or demands. The university of teachers treats students as young adults who have already set their academic goals and can design their own curricula. It expects them to integrate what they have learned from fragmented academic offerings by individual professors without consultation among colleagues. Faculty members find no need to master any special teaching methods that would help students to learn.

If the university of teachers is the traditional model of Japanese universities, there are also many examples of the university of students. The major function of the university of students is to serve the needs and interests of students as clients. Teaching is more important than research, and students evaluate faculty members according to their teaching ability. To prevent declining enrollments, students are courted as customers who are interested only in buying the tasteful offerings of academic supermarkets. Curriculum, academic requirements, standards, and grading are all determined by students' needs and tastes. It is the students and not professional colleagues who evaluate the teachers' ability.

The following quotation from a campus guide for students issued by a Japanese private college offers a model of the university of students:

> It doesn't matter if you haven't yet decided
> "What should I become?"
> It also really doesn't matter if you don't know
> "Why I came to the College."
> Because here you have so much time, four years of
> campus life, to think about such problems.
>
> Here it is acceptable if you are still wondering
> "What should I do at college?"
> You shouldn't be self-conscious because you think
> "I am already a college student."
> For here is a campus that is always ready to accept you.
> —*Private College 1984 Campus Guide*

The characterization of the two types of universities may seem simplistic. Actual universities are probably somewhere between the two extremes. But it seems to me that a historical movement from traditional, faculty-centered higher education to higher education increasingly influenced by students' needs and tastes has indeed been occurring in Japan as well as in the United States. If I am correct in my assumption that this movement is not temporary but an inevitable and historical trend, then the most important challenge for universities is deciding how to adapt to the changes the trend is causing while maintaining their identity as traditional centers of learning.

I do not believe that all universities should attempt to become more like educational-service supermarkets for student consumers. However, if many universities and colleges cannot attract enough students, especially during the period of declining enrollments and resources that both countries face, it may become difficult for them to survive by adhering rigidly to their traditional functions. Students are the one indispensable resource of the university. They are its major source of funds and social prestige, and above all they are its *raison d'être*. Therefore it is important to consider which aspects of the university should be changed and which should be protected and maintained.

Eric Ashby (1958, p. 97) has stated that the university could be "destroyed either by resisting pressures to change and so losing its viability, or by yielding too rapidly to change and so losing its integrity." In an era of increasing social interdependence and rising student consumerism, the survival and development of the modern university is highly dependent on our finding a good balance between these extremes—in short, to provide the possibility for change without sacrificing the integrity of the university. This must be considered one of the most pressing problems of higher education in both Japan and the United States in the near future.

REFERENCES

American Association of Colleges (AAC). 1985. *Integrity in the College Curriculum: A Report on the Project in Redefining the Meaning and Purposes of Baccalaureate Degrees.* Washington, D.C.

Asahi Shimbun. 1984. "National Poll on Educational Problems" (in Japanese). June 6, pp. 10-11. Tokyo.

Ashby, Eric. 1958. *Technology and the Academics—An Essay on Universities and the Scientific Revolution.* London: Macmillan.

Bennett, William J. 1984. *To Reclaim a Legacy—A Report on the Humanities in Higher Education.* Washington, D.C.: National Endowment for the Humanities.

Fiske, Edward B. 1983. "Education in Japan: Lessons for America." *New York Times*, July 10, 1986, pp. 1, 28.

Ichikawa, Shogo. 1984. "Financing Higher Education in Japan." *Daigaku Ronshu—Research in Higher Education* 13: 19-38. Research Institute for Higher Education, Hiroshima University.

Japan. Ministry of Education, Science, and Culture (Mōmbushō). 1977. *Zenkoku no Gakushu-juku Gayoi no Jittai* (A Survey of Cram School-Going Among Primary School and Junior High School Pupils). MEJ 6903. Tokyo: Gyosei.

Jencks, Christopher, and David Riesman. 1968. *The Academic Revolution.* New York: Doubleday.

Kitamura, Kazuyuki. 1983-84. "The Internationalization of Higher Education in Japan." *Japan Foundation Newsletter*, May 1983, pp. 1-9; September 1983, pp. 6-7; August 1984, pp. 9-11.

____. 1984. *Daigaku Kyoiku no Kokusaika—Sotokaramita Nippon no Daigaku* (The Internationalization of University Education in Japan—Japanese Higher Education Observed from the Outside). Tokyo: Tamagawa University Press.

Nakane, Chie. 1970. *Japanese Society.* Berkeley: University of California Press.

National Institute of Education (NIE). 1984. *Involvement in Learning: Realizing the Potential of American Higher Education.* Final Report of the Study Group on the Condition of Excellence in American Higher Education. Washington, D.C.

Organization of Economic Cooperation and Development (OECD). 1971. *Reviews of National Policies for Education—Japan.* Paris.

Ranbom, Sheppard. 1985. "Schooling in Japan—The Paradox in the Pattern." *Education Week*, February 20 and 27, March 6.

Research Institute for Higher Education (RIHE), Hiroshima University. 1981. *The Internationalization of Higher Education—A Final Summary Report.* Hiroshima.

Riesman, David. 1980. *On Higher Education: The Academic Enterprise in an Era of Rising Student Consumerism.* San Francisco: Jossey-Bass.

Rohlen, Thomas P. 1983. *Japan's High Schools.* Berkeley: University of California Press.

Tokyo-to Kyoika-cho. 1977. Gakkogai Gakushu Katsudō Zitta Chōsa (Fact-Finding Survey on Pupils' Study Activities Outside Schools in Tokyo). March 15.

Ushiogi, Morikazu. 1984. *Transition from School to Work: Japanese Case.* Paper submitted to the Conference "Learning from Each Other." East-West Center, Honolulu.

Zeugner, John. 1983. "Japan's Noneducation." *New York Times,* June 24.

____. 1984. "The Puzzle of Higher Education in Japan." *Change Magazine,* January-February, pp. 24-31.

9
THE STATE OF HIGHER EDUCATION IN THE UNITED STATES
Martin Trow

In recent years much of the writing about American higher education has assumed that after its great period of expansion and innovation (variously identified as "the postwar years," "1955 to 1975," "the sixties") the system entered a period first of stagnation and then of decline. Some of the literature analyzes the causes of this decline; more of it addresses the problem of how to cope with it.

The theme of this chapter is that American higher education is not at all in decline but, on the contrary, is thriving and is perhaps stronger and more effective than ever before in its history. The latter is an arguable proposition and difficult, perhaps impossible, to demonstrate. But I hope in exploring that idea, and without minimizing the many difficulties that our colleges and universities face, to establish at least that American higher education is not, in any sense of the word, in "decline."

First, what do we mean by "decline"? In an age that worships bigness, and too often confuses quantity with quality, "decline" in higher education may mean a decrease in the numbers of students, or of institutions, or in the levels of financial support. Or it may refer to the alleged lowering of academic standards or of the quality of research done in universities. Or the word may point to changes for the worse in the quality or quantity of service that colleges and universities provide to the larger society. Or the concept may refer not so much to the recent past or present but to an anticipated future—

171

we are in decline, so to speak, when we stand at the top of a slip-
pery slope.

In this chapter I first consider whether American higher education is in decline in any of these meanings of the term and argue that
it is not. Then I want to try to explain why American higher education is not in decline, why, on the contrary, it is, I believe, singular-
ly well adapted to the demands and pressures of the late twentieth
century. Finally, lest I be thought a modern Pollyanna, I discuss the
substantial and continuing problems and difficulties faced by American colleges and universities, difficulties that are rooted in the fundamental structural characteristics of American higher education and
that are in a sense a product of its very virtues, strengths, and
successes.

RECENT AND PROJECTED ENROLLMENTS

Enrollments in American colleges and universities of all kinds
are currently (1984) running about 12.5 million and holding fairly
steady (Evangelauf 1984a, p. 1). And those enrollments are up over
6 percent since 1979, the peak year in the number of high school
graduates (Frances 1984, p. 3). Thus over the past five years the
overall level of enrollment in higher education has held up and indeed grown, despite predictions from so many sources about the
inevitable decline that was expected to accompany the decreased size
of college-age cohorts. Although the supply of high school graduates fell off from the peak of about 3 million in 1979 to a projected
2.6 million in 1984 (McConnell and Kaufman 1984, p. 29), enrollments of entering freshman classes in fall 1984 were off only slightly from record levels (Evangelauf 1984a, p. 14).

So it appears that between 1979 and 1984 American colleges and
universities weathered a decline of more than 13 percent in the number of high school graduates without an enrollment decline but rather
with an increase of more than 6 percent. As Frances (1984, p. 3)
has observed: "Colleges and universities have close to 1.5 million
more students and $6 billion more revenues than predicted by the
gloom and doomers."

But what of the future—what of the continued demographic decline in the size of the traditional college-age cohorts in the United
States? As one college president put it rather pessimistically, "The
future has been postponed, not cancelled." The demographic projections point to a further decline in the anticipated number of high
school graduates, down to a four-year trough in 1991-94 of about
2.3 million annually, or about 10 percent fewer than our current 2.6
million. By 1998, these projections suggest, the number of high

school graduates will have come back up to about their current levels (McConnell and Kaufman 1984, p. 29).

Although the system faces a further decline of 10 percent in the numbers of high school graduates by 1991, it is far from certain that college and university enrollments will in fact suffer an equivalent fall. Forecasts of enrollments in higher education are notoriously poor; hardly any have been accurate anywhere in the world. The only way a government can ensure the accuracy of its projections of college and university enrollments is to make them come true by fixing the number of places available, whatever the demand. But insofar as enrollments are permitted to respond to demand, they are highly unpredictable even a few years ahead. Clark Kerr has observed that "it takes a dash of bravado to make a projection; but it shows a touch of madness to believe too much in its invincibility" (Carnegie Council on Policy Studies in Higher Education 1975, p. 49). An interesting question is why such forecasts and projections are almost uniformly wrong, and usually by a good deal.

Among the reasons for not anticipating any large decline in American college and university enrollments over the next decade are these:

- There has been a steady growth over the past 15 years in enrollments of older students. During the decade 1972-82, the greatest percentage increase in enrollments was among people 25 years old and older; those 35 years and older increased by 77 percent, and the enrollments of 25- to 34-year-old students increased by 70 percent, as compared with a growth of 35 percent in total enrollments during that period (*Higher Education & National Affairs* 1984b, p. 3).
- Increasing numbers of students are enrolled part time. During the decade 1972-82, part-time enrollments increased by two-thirds, whereas full-time enrollments were growing by less than a fifth.
- The past decade has seen very large increases in the enrollments of women and minorities. The number of women in colleges and universities grew by 61 percent in that decade and minority enrollments by 85 percent, as compared with 15 percent for men and 30 percent for white students (*Higher Education & National Affairs* 1984b, p. 3).

The growing enrollments of older students, of working and part-time students, and of women and minorities are trends that are not dominated by the changing size of the college-age population. To take just one example: Relatively small proportions of Mexican

Americans (Chicanos) living in California currently go on to higher education. But the number of Chicanos in California's population, and especially among its youth, is very large. In 1981-82 about a quarter of all public school students were Hispanic, and by the year 2000 Hispanics will begin to outnumber whites in the under-20 age group (PACE Project 1984, p. 11 and exhibit 4). Even small changes in the propensity of Chicanos to graduate from high school and go to college would have a major impact on enrollment levels in California colleges and universities. One would predict a long-term growth in the numbers of Chicanos going on to college, simply on the basis of trends among other ethnic groups throughout American history. Add to this the widespread recognition that the United States is becoming an information society, one in which higher education is seen by growing numbers as an investment in the future of individuals as well as of the society at large. The growth of the knowledge and information industries increases the numbers of jobs that call for college-educated people. And many of our colleges and universities are more than eager to welcome back older people who want to upgrade their skills and equip themselves for jobs in the new industries as old ones are phased out.

Moreover, current efforts to strengthen secondary education, efforts that are almost wholly directed toward strengthening the courses that prepare students for college, may well lead both to increases in high school graduation rates and in the proportions of high school graduates who go on to college (National Commission on Excellence in Education 1983; Boyer 1983; Goodlad 1983; Trow 1985).

Enrollment levels may yet fall over the next few years. Moreover, population movements, changes in the economy, and change in the size of age cohorts will affect the various states and regions differently. In addition, these changes will affect different kinds of institutions even within the same region quite differently. There is not only the obvious contrast between, say, Ohio and Texas; equally great are differences in the effects of demographic and economic changes on public community colleges, minor private four-year colleges, and elite four-year colleges and research universities within the same region. There almost certainly will be closures of some private colleges over the next decade and perhaps some consolidation among public institutions, though recent figures show an increase in the number of private four-year colleges over the past four years, an event that one would not have predicted (see Chapter 5, Figure 5.3). But the birth and death of colleges in large numbers throughout our history have been and continue to be a natural outcome of giving the market a great influence over our diverse decentralized system of higher education. And while there may be closures, they will be mostly of weaker institutions and may well leave the system as a whole even stronger (Glenny 1983).

FINANCIAL SUPPORT

If we think of decline in terms of funding and support, we have no better reason for believing that higher education in America is in decline. In 1984-85 expenditures on colleges and universities were estimated to be more than $95 billion as compared with about $70 billion in 1981-82, a 36 percent increase (*Higher Education & National Affairs* 1984c, p. 3). Student aid from all sources in 1982-83 was running at more than $16 billion a year (Association Council for Policy Analysis and Research 1984, p. 18). The federal government in fiscal 1984 provided directly and indirectly about $20 billion to higher education, nearly 40 percent of that in a complex combination of student grants and loans (derived from *Chronicle of Higher Education* 1985, p. 32). And while the Reagan administration has proposed cuts in that aid, most of its proposals have been defeated; student aid has widespread support in Congress as well as in society at large. Many states did cut their support for public colleges and universities during the severe recession of 1980-82, but the levels of state support have tended to rise about as fast as economic recovery and rising revenues have permitted. State tax funds for higher education are more than $28 billion for 1984-85, up 16 percent since 1982-83. In constant dollars, state support to higher education increased 8 percent between 1974-75 and 1984-85 (Evangelauf 1984c, p. 1).

One should not underestimate the size or gravity of recent cuts or of continuing deficiencies in the support of higher education in many states. But higher education remains a popular institution in the United States, one that can count on continued public support in the future. For example, a national survey done in 1984 found that two-thirds of Americans considered the overall quality of higher education in the United States to be good or excellent, and increasing federal aid to higher education was third on their list of priorities for U.S. government spending, behind only increased aid for medical research and medical care for the aged (*Higher Education & National Affairs* 1984a, p. 12; Evangelauf 1984b, p. 3).

Moreover, contributions to colleges and universities from individuals, alumni, and business and industry have been rising steadily in recent years. Total voluntary support to higher education in 1928-83 was estimated at $5.8 billion, a 15 percent increase over 1981-82 and up from $2.2 billion a decade earlier (*Higher Education*

& *National Affairs* 1984d, p. 3; 1984c, p. 3). These figures provide little evidence for the proposition that support for American higher education, either in sentiment or money, is declining.

HIGHER AND SECONDARY EDUCATION

It may be useful to compare higher and secondary education in the United States in a way that illuminates both. In no other country is the difference between secondary and higher education as great, or as visible, as it is in the United States. Put simply, public secondary education is among the least successful institutions in American life, whereas our system of higher education is among the most successful. Why should that be?

In a recent essay, Burton Clark (1985) asks why American secondary schools are, as he puts it, "biased against excellence" in preparing students for higher education (p. 391). Clark finds the sources of this inherent bias against academic excellence in certain structural characteristics of American secondary education. Looked at from a comparative perspective, the characteristics that he points to compose a unique cluster that distinguishes American secondary education from that of other countries.

One of those characteristics is the commitment of American secondary schools to universal participation and thus to a great diversity in the school population.

> In 1980, among 18-year-olds (the normal age for completing the last year of upper-secondary schooling in Europe), the 10 member nations of the European Economic Community averaged 36% of this age group still in school. . . . The U.S., by contrast, has pressed hard to keep all youths in secondary school until they graduate. . . .
>
> School persistence rates for the various age groups in the U.S. have been double those of European schoolchildren. Virtually all U.S. students enter the first year of high school . . . and, in 1980, about 75% of the age group graduated from high school. Thus, in our extremely heterogeneous society, the secondary school system has to cope with youngsters from a variety of social and cultural backgrounds. The system has been compelled to accommodate the deprived and the disaffected, as well as the advantaged and the highly motivated—to accommodate those for whom the school diploma is a terminal credential, as well as those bound for higher education (a roughly 50-50 split in recent years). (Clark 1985, p. 392)

Another structural source of bias toward mediocrity in American secondary education, in Clark's view, is the relative absence of differentiation between and within schools.

> The advantages of specialization—and especially of distinctiveness—are largely lost; instead, education purpose has been dulled, and communities that share common interests have been dispersed.
>
> As educational tasks multiply, a school that is asked to do them all finds it very difficult, if not impossible, to maintain a clear sense of mission . . . Doctrines of education that might serve as statements of purpose become stretched beyond repair. (Clark 1985, p. 393)

Without differentiation, no school can sustain a marked sense of its own character and distinctiveness, and without that sense there can be no strong commitment to excellence. Although lack of differentiation still characterizes much of American secondary education, the situation in this respect may now be changing in response to the growth in the number of "magnet schools," which differ in important respects from the standard American comprehensive high schools (Doyle and Levine 1984).

A third feature of the American secondary school is its closer ties with primary education than with higher education. In other countries elite secondary schools are closely linked to the universities for which they prepare. But mass secondary education in the United States developed about the turn of the century as a terminal system, one that in its comprehensiveness and emphasis on "education for life" simply carries further the education of the elementary school of which it was an outgrowth (Trow 1961). American secondary schools are linked both philosophically and organizationally with primary schools; their staff recruitment, training, and conditions of work are much more like those of primary schools than like those of colleges and universities. Similarly, their modes of governance and finance much more closely resemble those of primary schools than those of colleges and universities.

A fourth feature of American secondary schools is the element of local and political control; their part-time lay school boards, their big administrative staffs, and increasingly active parents groups have a large influence on the working lives of secondary school teachers, an influence tending to undermine the teachers' commitment to high academic purpose.

All of these factors adversely affect the professional autonomy of U.S. teachers, and a malaise born of powerlessness becomes widespread. To a degree not widely recognized by Americans, the pattern of local control over secondary education contributes to a "deprofessionalization" of teaching. (Clark 1985, p. 394)

Finally, public secondary schools have a near monopoly over the educational services available to students in a given geographic area. Private schools are few and expensive, and thus "we have diminished the amount of choice left to parents and students, virtually eliminated competition among schools for enrollment, and rendered scholastic comparisons among schools operationally harmless" (Clark 1985, p. 394).

These characteristics that give most American high schools their distinctive character--universal secondary education; comprehensive school organization; close links with primary schools; local control, lay boards, and big bureaucratic staffs; and the local monopoly—all tend to weaken the academic and intellectual role of those schools and thus their links with higher education.

By contrast, American colleges and universities have enormous structural advantages precisely to the extent that their characteristics differ from those of the high school. One crucial difference is that enrollment in higher education is voluntary. While it is a mass system, it is not a universal system; less capable and less highly motivated students do not make the transition to college or university. Moreover, colleges and universities are highly differentiated among themselves, and the larger ones are differentiated internally (Trow 1976). They can and do cultivate distinctive images, purposes, and missions, and they can recruit and motivate faculty and students around those distinctive images. Thus they have the enormous advantage for intellectual life that arises out of academic differentiation. In addition, higher education, even at the undergraduate level, is pulled toward new knowledge, toward graduate education and research, and toward professional practice, both by its faculty and by the job/career orientations of its students. Colleges and universities differ from secondary schools further in their higher degree of autonomy in relation to government and their own boards of trustees. This autonomy, especially marked in the leading research universities, is rooted in the monopoly of expertise that academics have in the subjects they teach and study. Even in more modest institutions, faculty members not at the frontiers of their fields, who do little or no research, borrow their claim to autonomy from academics in the more prestigious institutions, which provide the models for all of academic life.

Unlike secondary schools, American colleges and universities compete actively for students, for financial support, and for prestige. And these kinds of competition make them responsive to a wide range of trends and forces in American life, some of them economic and demographic, others intellectual. As a result, American higher education exhibits an enormously dynamic character, both as a system and in its component institutions. We see this in many ways, among them the ability of many private American colleges to survive in circumstances that many observers have predicted would lead to their closure (Cheit 1971, 1973).

The responsiveness and adaptiveness of American higher education is not only a strength but also a potential weakness—it can result in the loss of institutional integrity and the softening of distinctive character and purpose. Our colleges and universities are so enmeshed and entwined with other institutions of the society that they run the risk of becoming simply instruments in the service of those other institutions—of state and federal government, private business, special interest groups, and funding agencies. Nevertheless, it is also true that flexibility, adaptiveness, and responsiveness are institutional strengths in a world of rapid social, economic, and technological change.

AMERICAN AND EUROPEAN HIGHER EDUCATION

If American higher education is different from American secondary education, it is different also from its counterparts abroad. And it differs from them especially in the way that the American system deals with the issue of academic standards.

When one raises the issue of standards in higher education, as one ordinarily does in connection with the quality of teaching and research, there is almost always the assumption that the higher the standards, the better. By standards we mean norms regarding the level of intellectual work demanded in various subjects and institutions, what students are expected to know or be able to do after completing a course of study or on earning a degree. But when we raise the question of standards in relation to American higher education, we accept that the degree to which academic work is difficult, complex, and sophisticated varies enormously from one institution to another and even from one department to another within the same institution.

On the whole, this is very different in European nations, where efforts are made to achieve and sustain high and common standards of achievement throughout the university systems, and where even nonuniversity forms of higher education, such as the British polytechnics and the French university institutes of technology (IUTs), strive to achieve university standards. Sometimes such common levels are gained through enforcing a common standard for honors degrees, backed up, as in Great Britain, by external examiners for university degrees and the Council for National Academic Awards for the nonuniversity institutions, or in France by a national examination for the higher degree. Institutions that cannot teach to those standards simply are not considered part of higher education and are not permitted to award the degree. In Britain, for example, this exclusionary rule applies to the whole of what is called "further education," which enrolls by far the largest numbers of mature students, is never considered part of higher education, and is treated as a kind of delayed secondary or vocational education, not worthy of offering degrees.

The maintenance of high common standards for the degree is a mark of European systems, which are still governed by elite conceptions of higher education. These standards have great consequences for the development of those systems. They constrain growth; access to these systems is limited either by an entry examination or by graduation from sectors of secondary education specifically designed to prepare students for university entry. The common degree standards require a high degree of standardization of work among institutions and among departments and courses in the same subject, as all students in the same subjects in all universities are expected to achieve the same standards of performance. Such assumptions inhibit the creation of departments in new or emerging fields because any new field has to prove itself worthy of being included within the elite course of study, as having a proper knowledge base and modes of inquiry similar in complexity and difficulty to those associated with existing, established fields of knowledge. And that tends to require that new fields be created by the establishment of chairs rather than by the infiltration of new recruits to academic life who have begun to work in new ways in their graduate training and early research.

The number of students prepared and able to do the demanding work required for entry to a selective university system is relatively small; indeed, if the number were much larger, that alone would suggest that the standards were "not high enough." Such an education tends to be expensive, and in societies like England, in which the state is expected to bear all or nearly all costs of university attendance, the per capita costs of instruction alone keep unlimited expansion in check. These intellectual and financial constraints on the number of undergraduate and graduate students result in a limited number of scientists and scholars who have the training and research experience necessary to teach such highly selected students. Moreover, such systems are not only restrictive in size but also have a bias toward students from middle- and upper-middle-class origins, where the culture of the school is propagated and supported in the home. Everywhere in Europe efforts have been made, with relatively little success, to democratize recruitment to these elite systems and to increase the proportions of working- and lower-middle-class students in the selective secondary schools from which their students are recruited (see, for example, Halsey, Heath, and Ridge 1980, table 10.8, p. 188; Neave 1984). But even changing the nature of secondary schools by making them more comprehensive, and creating new channels of access by adults to the university, have not substantially changed the class composition of those systems of higher education. Rather, on the whole they have increased the advantage of the middle classes, who respond to new educational opportunities quickly.

Most of the familiar characteristics of American higher education, those that set it off so sharply from other national systems, are made possible by its diversity, the decentralization of control, and the consequent absence of a common standard of performance. (Of course, causality is in both directions: Decentralization and diversity together preclude the maintenance of high common standards for the degree throughout the system. But the absence of a common standard permits decentralized control and diversity.)

American colleges and universities have other distinguishing characteristics as well:

- Strong college and university presidents and large internal administrative staffs responsible to the president rather than located in a government agency or ministry.
- Lay boards with their large formal powers and close relations to the president. Powerful boards and presidents exercise large discretionary powers, which increase the diversity among institutions by preventing the standardization of requirements for the degree or the content of the curriculum by central authorities.
- The large role of nonspecialized, liberal, or general education in the curriculum.
- The elective course system.
- The unit credit as the form of academic currency, which permits students to transfer between major fields of study and in-

stitutions and to accumulate credits in different institutions over many years.

- The relatively easy creation of interdisciplinary courses, new departments and professional schools, and educational innovations of all kinds.
- The widespread incorporation of recurrent education, or lifelong learning, into American higher education.
- The rapid growth of previously underrepresented minorities, including women, in American colleges and universities.

Together these characteristics make up a kind of functional system or web, mutually related and reinforcing, that both requires and results from the absence of a strong central governing and standardizing authority (Trow 1981).

So long as the governing assumption of a system of higher education is that only a minority of students can work at the required standard and can demonstrate that capacity in secondary school, just so long is that system constrained both in its size and in the variety of functions it can perform for its students and for the larger society. Such a system may perform the functions of elite selection, preparation, and certification, as most European universities have done and still do. But it cannot penetrate as deeply or broadly into the life of society as American higher education has.

FUNCTIONS AND CONSEQUENCES OF THE AMERICAN SYSTEM

Some of the effects of mass higher education on American society are not, I believe, well recognized. In our concern for the effects of higher education in America, which must be central to any serious assessment of it, we are overly influenced by the economist's conceptions of the costs and benefits of institutions, conceptions dominated in higher education by their focus on rates of return to the individual graduate. Economists have had a near monopoly on the study of the effects of higher education, but on the whole I believe they have obscured more than illuminated those relationships. Along with their many positive contributions to social and economic theory, economists, and especially econometricians, have bequeathed us at least one large error: the belief that if you cannot measure a phenomenon or put a price on it, it does not exist or—what comes to the same thing—that it need not be taken into account in plans and assessments.

Economists, especially those directly involved in central state planning or advising international aid organizations, ordinarily attend to the direct, measurable, purposeful, short-term effects of educational decisions. But the long-term effects of institutions are hard to measure, and they are influenced by a variety of forces and conditions that are not directly the outcome of decisions and do not result from activities of the institution in question.

Economists recognize that there are large unplanned and unintended effects of higher education in society. They even refer to these as "externalities," that is, effects "external" to the particular causal relationships that they are concerned with or are able to develop quantitative measures for. Economists are sometimes wise as well as clever, and those who are wise recognize that the measured effects of higher education are always a fraction, an unknown but small fraction, of the total impact of higher education on society. But they often go on to say that it is better to measure and assess carefully what can be measured, and leave to others—historians, sociologists, educators, politicians—the discussion of those larger effects of higher education on society that we cannot measure very precisely, are long delayed in their appearance, are "outcomes" rather than intended effects, and whose sources are only partly within the system of higher education and partly within the society at large. (For an economist whose views are similar to those described here, see Bowen 1977, pp. 359-87.)

Among the important effects of higher education that ordinarily escape the economist's attention are the following:

1. Higher education has substantial effects on the attitudes of those exposed to it. A large amount of research supports this assertion—and also that changes in attitudes occurring during the college years persist throughout life (Hyman, Wright, and Reed 1975; Feldman and Newcomb 1969). For example, higher education achieves some of what it intends by broadening the perspectives of students, giving them an appreciation of other cultures and groups, making them more tolerant of cultural differences, and weakening the prejudices and hostile stereotypes that are so characteristic of uneducated people. And those changed attitudes in a population in turn make possible real changes in social structures, if and when they are accompanied by changes in law and institutional behavior.

In the United States the years after World War II saw a steady decline in hostility toward black people and a growing readiness on the part of whites to give them equal and fair access to education, housing, and jobs (Hyman and Wright 1979; Stember 1961; Stouffer 1955; Clark et al. 1972). These changes can be seen in studies made of attitudes both in the general population and among college students during the college years and after. I believe that the considerable progress the United States has made in race relations since World War II has been made possible by the growth of mass higher education and the marked decline in racial prejudice that accompanied it. If that is true, then it represents a very great contribution of higher education to the life of the society, one that is almost never acknowledged by economists as a "benefit" of American higher education.

2. Other positive attitudes, values, and perceptions are engendered by the experience of higher education, quite apart from the intentions of a college or its courses. For example, people who have been to college or university on the whole have a longer time perspective regarding public issues than do less well-educated people. Time perspectives are basic and important ways of looking at the world, yet we do not measure them or give them value, certainly not as outcomes of higher education. Nations and industries cannot plan or develop programs without the help of people who have gained that longer time perspective, who can imagine the outcome of projects that may lie years in the future. And that perspective is very much a "benefit" of mass higher education.

In an increasingly complex society it is not enough that small elites in the planning offices of central government ministries have these longer time horizons. The successful development and implementation of plans require that people with those perspectives exist throughout the society, and especially at the middle levels of the civil service in central, regional, and local governments, and in public and private enterprises. Increasingly we recognize that long-range plans require continual adjustments and modifications at the levels where they are implemented; people at those levels must be able to understand the purposes of long-term programs and be able to implement and modify them within planning guidelines. The more intelligence and initiative that exist among middle managers, the more likely are those plans to succeed. And, again, those qualities are very much an outcome of mass higher education.

3. Another skill that is gained or enhanced by exposure to higher education is the capacity of a nation's citizens to learn how to learn. In a world marked by rapid social and technological change, where so much of what we learn in college or university is obsolescent in ten years and obsolete in twenty-five, it is possible to exaggerate the importance of the ability to continue to learn after finishing formal schooling. Wherever facilities are provided for adult education, they are quickly filled by people who already have a first degree or higher credential, who already belong to the class of lifelong

learners (see Neave 1985). Modern societies need all of those people that they can get; and that quality of mind, that ability to learn how to learn, is also a product, if often a by-product, of higher education. I believe that mass higher education in the United States, and especially its generous provision of education for adults, engenders and distributes more widely the habit of "lifelong learning" than is true in most other countries.

These qualities of mind (they are more than attitudes) that I have mentioned—tolerance of cultural and class differences, a longer time perspective, greater initiative among middle- and lower-level administrators, the ability to learn how to learn—are all created or enhanced by exposure to postsecondary education. As I have suggested, they are usually by-products of that education, but immensely important by-products for the life and progress of any society.

4. In the political life of the nation higher education has two distinct roles. The more familiar one is the university as the radical critic of the established political order, the nursery of radical and even revolutionary student movements. But less dramatically and less visibly, the expansion and democratization of access to higher education may work in the other direction, to strengthen and legitimate the political and social order by giving concrete evidence that it rewards talent and effort rather than serving merely as the cultural apparatus of the "ruling classes" to ensure the passage of power and privilege across generations.

In a time of rising expectations through all social strata, nations must provide real opportunities for social mobility to able and talented people from poor and modest origins—and they must do so for social and political reasons as well as for economic growth. In many countries the armed forces have provided that avenue of mobility and have often gained the support of the poor even when other institutions in the society have lost it. But the army is not the most satisfactory solution to the great problems of political legitimacy and social order. Higher education may be a better instrument for social change and democracy. Again, where it performs that vital function, as it has in the United States, it goes unrecorded on the accounting sheets of the cost-benefits analyst.

5. Another large benefit of American higher education, still to be achieved, still tentative, is the effect of current efforts by American colleges and universities to come to the aid of secondary education in other ways than through teacher training and the production of educational research in schools and departments of education. The many reports and books on public secondary education that

have appeared since 1983 (for example, National Commission on Excellence in Education 1983; Boyer 1983; Goodlad 1983) have led to the creation of a large number of programs by colleges and universities that establish new links between higher and secondary education. Some of those programs are designed to strengthen the academic and college preparatory work of the high schools, not just provide remediation for ill-prepared students after they reach college. It may be that the task is too large even for American higher education and that the structural characteristics of American high schools will defeat all efforts to overcome their "bias against excellence" (Clark 1985, p. 391). But it will not be for want of trying: Already the staff of the National Commission on Excellence in Education has put together two volumes that catalog and describe hundreds of programs developed by colleges and universities that aim to correct or ameliorate deficiencies in the schools (Adelman 1984).

This heightened attention to secondary education need not be a repetition of the *Sputnik* era. Then the response was limited to small groups of scientists and scholars from elite universities who developed new curricula and teaching materials in their subjects—the new math, the new physics, biology, history, English, and so on—without any real regard for the training and abilities of teachers in the schools or the conditions of learning that prevailed. Current efforts are much more realistic and substantial and involve genuine and continuing connections between colleges and universities on one hand and neighboring secondary schools on the other (Trow 1985). Some results can already be seen in individual schools, but the larger effects will be long delayed and obscured by many other inputs and forces. Still, my point here is not so much to demonstrate an achieved effect as to illustrate the continuing propensity of American higher education to respond to national needs of almost every kind—to try to provide some service, some program, to meet those needs. Whatever else that may be—and it may be foolhardy or even a threat to the core functions of teaching and research—it is not the mark of a system in decline.

TEACHING AND RESEARCH

Criticisms of teaching in American colleges and universities have revolved around several themes:

- The impersonality and mass "people-processing" of undergraduate education in big state colleges and universities.

- The incoherence of the curriculum, the absence of any common conception of what knowledge is of most worth, which gives every subject, every discipline, a spurious and anarchic equality in the intellectual supermarkets that American colleges and universities have become.
- The increased preponderance of professional and vocational studies in the undergraduate curriculum, especially the growth of undergraduate majors in business administration, engineering, and pre- and paramedical studies.
- The alleged inattention to undergraduate teaching by college and university faculty, either out of laziness or incompetence or because the system of academic rewards requires faculty to "publish or perish" and rewards research achievement over effective teaching.

These are genuine issues, but I do not see them as elements of any general "decline" in American higher education. These problems are being broadly discussed, and many efforts are being made to meet and ameliorate them. (For example, three sharply critical reports on U.S. higher education appeared within a few months of one another in 1984 and 1985. See the Study Group on the Conditions of Excellence in American Higher Education 1984; Bennett 1984; and Association of American Colleges 1985.) Like other big research universities, my own university, Berkeley, is less cold and bureaucratic, less indifferent to student needs and concerns than it was 20 years ago at the time of the "free speech movement." Every kind of student interest, concern, and problem is reflected in its impressive structure of counseling and student services. As for the curriculum, American colleges and universities are currently undergoing a modest move away from voluntarism toward a reintroduction of academic requirements, both in the general education component and in many major fields of study—a new phase in our cyclical swing between the poles of curricular freedom and constraint.

If criticism is directed at American research, any analysis of the health or decline of higher education would have to acknowledge the enormous and rapid gains being made in many academic disciplines in American universities, from biology and bioengineering to mathematics, the informational sciences, cognitive studies, astrophysics, geology, and so on. Surely any discussion of a supposed decline in a university system should consider its research capabilities and achievements (Smith and Karlesky 1977). Of course, it can be argued that we are living on our intellectual capital, and that our achievements and Nobel Prize winners reflect past scientific strengths that are not being reproduced. I do not think that is the judgment of the academics closest to the frontiers of science and scholarship, and the burden of proof rests on those who would make the case that our capacity for pure science and scholarship is in decline.

CONTINUING PROBLEMS

In this chapter I have stressed the continuing strength of American higher education, especially when considered in comparative perspective. But I cannot close without reference to some serious and persistent problems of American higher education. Let me list just a few.

- Some public universities and state systems are and remain underfunded after the severe cuts of the late 1970s and early 1980s. In some cases these cuts have damaged the academic quality of the institutions and are not being restored quickly enough.
- Colleges and universities throughout the country report a serious backlog of capital improvements and maintenance, an area that took a disproportionate share of cuts during the lean years of 1976-83.
- Repeated cuts in some institutional budgets have led to declines in the adequacy of scientific instruments in university laboratories, with the result that the state-of-the-art instruments in some areas of research are too often overseas or in industry rather than in American universities.
- American higher education is marked by an aging and largely tenured faculty. Low retirement rates lead to poor job opportunities in some fields for even very able young scholars and scientists. Attention has been drawn to the danger of a "lost generation" of scholars and scientists; and while the problem is of varying severity in different fields, it is widespread enough to be a source of concern throughout the system.
- Colleges and universities face growing competition from industry for certain kinds of potential academics—for example, electrical engineers, accountants, economists, certain kinds of biologists. It is difficult and in some cases impossible for colleges and universities to compete successfully against industry for such people, and already the capacity of some colleges to teach in those subjects has been weakened.
- A variety of problems arises out of the emerging relationships between universities and industry, problems associated with potential conflicts of interest for involved faculty members

over secrecy and confidentiality and with biasing of problem
selection and research orientations in unversity-based research
that is supported by industry.

- In some states a problem for public higher education is posed
  by a rapidly changing ethnic mix in the general population.
  Such demographic changes are not yet reflected in the proportions of minority students who go on to higher education. The
  problems here are largely but not exclusively political. So far,
  in most places the discrepancy between the ethnic mix in the
  university and in the general population has been a source of
  concern, creating pressure for "affirmative discrimination" in
  favor of members of "underrepresented" groups. The pressure may grow as these ethnic groups begin to gain political
  power appropriate to their numbers.
- American colleges and universities are doing more and more
  remedial work, a tendency rising out of the growing recognition of the inadequate academic preparation available in many
  secondary schools. If current reform efforts improve the
  quality of academic preparation in secondary school, this problem may solve itself. But if those efforts are not successful,
  colleges and universities will be taking on more and more such
  remedial work, and this work will come to represent serious
  competition for resources with their core functions of teaching
  and research (Trow 1985).
- The growing popularity of specialized and vocational subjects
  among undergraduates has led to a concern in many colleges
  and universities for the survival of liberal or general education.
  Since the introduction of the elective principle, students have
  had a strong influence on the undergraduate curriculum
  through their freedom to choose their major fields and many
  elective courses. The balance of freedom and constraint in the
  curriculum will have a bearing on the future of liberal studies
  in this age of popular "relevant" vocational studies.
- A perennial problem for American higher education is the
  difficulty of developing a coherent core program of liberal
  studies. An incoherent curriculum is an inevitable outcome of
  the growing complexity and differentiation of studies in the
  absence of widespread consensus around intellectual values.
  The very hetereogeneity of the society and of the college-going
  population in a system of mass higher education makes the
  idea of "liberal education" in the older sense almost impossible
  to realize. Yet that idea survives and prevents a total surrender
  to student preferences (Rothblatt 1985). Again, this problem

takes quite different forms in different kinds of institutions, as do the responses to it.

But these problems, I believe, arise out of the vigor, not the decline, of American higher education and are consequences of trying to do too much rather than too little. All social institutions have their characteristic faults that arise out of their very nature, their very successes. When we look at American higher education, both comparatively and historically, we see how impressively our colleges and universities have continued to struggle against their own frailties. Academics, administrators, civil servants, and journalists have analyzed these problems interminably, worried about them continually, and tried to overcome or ameliorate them persistently. How much is written, for example, about the supposed death of liberal education, even as we educate half the college-age population, a large proportion of it in universities of 30- or 50- or 60,000. Americans still seek, and not always in vain, for a more humane education that broadens perspectives, refines sensibilities, strengthens critical and independent judgment, and provides a clearer understanding of the power and limits of reason. Those goals of higher education are still pursued in American colleges and universities, even under the least promising circumstances.

CONCLUSIONS

I do not believe it is fair to say that American higher education is complacent; if anything, we are overly critical of our own achievements and too little aware of how successful and effective our institutions are when compared with those of other countries. If we judge American higher education by the quality and integrity of its ongoing processes, or by its outcomes, or by its effects on the students who have gone through the system or on the society that supports those institutions, we must come to a generally favorable assessment. The critics of American higher education, and they are many, almost always compare it not with its own real past or the real institutions of other societies but with some utopian notion of how things "ought to be" (see, for example, Finn 1984). Often those critics have as their implicit reference a small elite university system of very high quality, approximated perhaps only by the British universities before World War II, by the best German universities before World War I, or by the French *grandes écoles*. But these critics rarely give credit to American higher education for the varied and wide-ranging functions it serves for the society as a whole. Against that criterion, the preeminent criterion, our system of higher education must be seen not only as not in decline but as healthy and strong —surely the most successful system of higher education in the world. What other American institution can make that claim?

NOTE

I am grateful to my colleague Janet Ruyle for her help with this chapter.

REFERENCES

Adelman, Clifford. 1984. *Starting with Students*, 2 vols. Washington, D.C.: National Institute of Education.

Association of American Colleges. 1985. *Integrity in the College Curriculum: A Report to the Academic Community*. Washington, D.C.

Association Council for Policy Analysis and Research. 1984. *American Has a New Urgency*. Washington, D.C.: American Council on Education.

Bennett, William J. 1984. *To Reclaim a Legacy—Report on the Humanities in Higher Education*. Washington, D.C.: National Endowment for the Humanities.

Bowen, Howard R. 1977. *Investment in Learning: The Individual and Social Value of American Higher Education*. San Francisco: Jossey-Bass.

Boyer, Ernest. 1983. *High School: A Report on Secondary Education in America*. New York: Harper & Row.

Carnegie Council on Policy Studies in Higher Education. 1975. *More Than Survival: Prospects for Higher Education in a Period of Uncertainty*. San Francisco: Jossey-Bass.

Cheit, Earl F. 1971. *The New Depression in Higher Education: A Study of Financial Conditions at 41 Colleges and Universities*. A report for the Carnegie Commission on Higher Education and the Ford Foundation. New York: McGraw-Hill.

_____. 1973. *The New Depression in Higher Education—Two Years Later*. Berkeley: Carnegie Commission on Higher Education.

Chronicle of Higher Education. 1985. "Fact File, Higher-Education Funds in President Reagan's 1986 Budget." February 13, p. 32.

Clark, Burton R. 1985. "The High School and the University: What Went Wrong in America, Part I." *Phi Delta Kappan* 66 (6): 391-97.

Clark, Burton R., Paul Heist, T. R. McConnel, Martin A. Trow, and George Yonge. 1972. *Students and Colleges: Interaction and Change*. Berkeley: Center for Research and Development in Higher Education, University of California.

Doyle, Denis P., and Marsh Levine. 1984. "Magnet Schools: Choice and Quality in Public Education." *Phi Delta Kappan* 66 (4): 265-69.

Evangelauf, Jean. 1984a. "Enrollments Stable This Fall; Faculty Salaries Up 7 Pct., Outpacing Inflation Rate." *Chronicle of Higher Education*, December 12, pp. 1 ff.

_____. 1984b. "Poll Finds 63 Pct. Want More Aid for Colleges." *Chronicle of Higher Education*. October 24, p. 3.

_____. 1984c. "States' Tax Funds for Colleges Top $28-Billion, Up 16 Pct. in 2 Years." *Chronicle of Higher Education*, October 31, pp. 1 ff.

Feldman, Kenneth A., and Theodore M. Newcomb. 1969. *The Impact of College on Students*, 2 vols. San Francisco: Jossey-Bass.

Finn, Chester E., Jr. 1984. "Trying Higher Education: An Eight Count Indictment." *Change* (May/June): 29-51.

Frances, Carol. 1984. "1985: The Economic Outlook for Higher Education." *American Association of Higher Education Bulletin* (December): 3-6.

Glenny, Lyman A. 1983. "Higher Education for Students: Forecast of a Golden Age." Paper delivered at a seminar sponsored by the Higher Education Steering Committee, University of California, Berkeley, July.

Goodlad, John I. 1983. *A Place Called School: Prospect for the Future*. New York: McGraw-Hill.

Halsey, A. H., A. F. Heath, and J. M. Ridge. 1980. *Origins and Destinations: Family, Class and Education in Modern Britain*. Oxford: Oxford University Press.

Higher Education & National Affairs. 1984a. "Americans Support More Federal Aid for Higher Education." November 5, p. 12.

____. 1984b. "Growth in Nontraditional Students, 1972 to 1982." June 18, p. 3.

____. 1984c. "Higher Education as an Industry." November 19, p. 3.

____. 1984d. "Voluntary Support to Higher Education." September 24, p. 3.

Hyman, Herbert H., and Charles R. Wright. 1979. *Education's Lasting Influence on Values*. Chicago: University of Chicago Press.

Hyman, Herbert H., Charles R. Wright, and John Shelton Reed. 1975. *The Enduring Effects of Education*. Chicago: University of Chicago Press.

McConnell, William R., and Norman Kaufman. 1984. *High School Graduates: Projections for the Fifty States (1982-2000)*. Boulder, Colo.: Western Interstate Commission for Higher Education, January.

National Commission on Excellence in Education. 1983. *A Nation at Risk: The Imperative for Educational Reform*. Washington, D.C.: U.S. Department of Education.

Neave, Guy. 1984. "External Reforms vs. Internal Continuity: Some Perspectives on the Links Between Secondary and Higher Education in Certain European Countries." Paper delivered at the first international meeting of the American National Academy of Education, Lidingo, Sweden, June 4-6.

____. 1985. "Elite and Mass Higher Education in Britain: A Regressive Mode?" *Comparative Education Review*, August (in press).

PACE Project. 1984. *Conditions of Education in California, 1984*, no. 84-1. Berkeley: School of Education, University of California.

Rothblatt, Sheldon. 1985. "Standing Antagonisms: The Relationship of Undergraduate to Graduate Education." In *Project 2000*, edited by David Wilson and Leslie Koepplin. New Brunswick, N.J.: Rutgers University Press.

Smith, Bruce L. R., and Joseph J. Karlesky, eds. 1977. *The State of Academic Science. Vol. 1. The Universities in the Nation's Research Effort*. Vol. 2. *Background Papers*. New York: Change Magazine Press.

Stember, Charles H. 1961. *Education and Attitude Change*. New York: Institute of Human Relations Press.

Stouffer, Samuel A. 1955. *Communism, Conformity and Civil Liberties*. Garden City, N.Y.: Doubleday.

Study Group on the Conditions of Excellence in American Higher Education. 1984. *Involvement in Learning: Realizing the Potential of American Higher Education*. Washington, D.C.: National Institute of Education.

Trow, Martin A. 1961. "The Second Transformation of American Secondary Education." *International Journal of Comparative Sociology* 11 (September): 144-66.

____. 1976. "Elite Higher Education: An Endangered Species?" *Minerva* 14 (3): 355-76.

____. 1981. "Comparative Perspectives on Access." In *Access to Higher Education*, edited by Oliver Fulton, pp. 89-121. Guildford, England: Society for Research into Higher Education.

____. 1985. "Underprepared Students and Public Research Universities." In *Challenge to American Schools*, edited by John H. Bunzel, pp. 191-215. New York: Oxford University Press.

PART IV
EDUCATION AND WORK

10
TRANSITION FROM SCHOOL TO WORK: THE JAPANESE CASE
Morikazu Ushiogi

THE IMPACT OF EDUCATIONAL EXPANSION ON THE JAPANESE LABOR MARKET

During the last 20 years or so the Japanese educational system has experienced an unprecedented expansion. The proportion of the high school-age population enrolled in high schools increased from 57.7 percent in 1960 to 94.3 percent in 1982. The proportion of college-age persons enrolled in institutions of higher education increased from 10.3 percent in 1960 to 36.3 percent in 1982. This rapid expansion of the educational system has had major effects on the Japanese labor market, the most significant being the decreasing supply of low-wage, middle school graduates and the increasing supply of higher education graduates who earn relatively high salaries. Japanese employers have had to adjust to the new situation by changing their recruitment policies, work organization, training systems, and wage systems.

Before the relationship between the labor market and the educational system can be understood, it is necessary to know a little about the educational system in Japan. The system consists of nine years of compulsory education (six in primary school and three in middle school); three years of high school; two years of junior college or four years of university education (for students pursuing medical degrees six years of undergraduate study are required); and, at the graduate level, two years for a master's degree and five years for a doctorate. Put another way, the educational system provides five kinds of school leavers to the labor force: middle school graduates, and postgraduates, high school graduates, junior college graduates, university graduates, and postgraduates (see Figure 10.1). Among these groups the smallest comprises graduates of graduate schools. In 1981 Japanese graduate schools produced only 16,201 masters and 6,599 doctors, who represented only 1.5 percent of their age group. The main market for this group is academic; except for graduates of professional schools such as engineering schools, it is still rare for persons with a doctorate or master's degree to be absorbed into the nonacademic sector.

Figure 10.1   New entrants into the labor force and their educational background, Japan, 1981

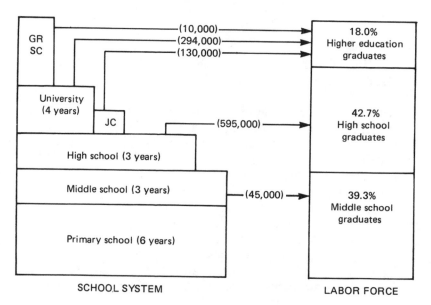

Source: Ministry of Labor.
Note: GR SC = graduate school; JC = junior college.

Therefore, most of Japan's labor force comes from the remaining four groups, who represent essentially four labor force strata. What has been most important for the labor market is the dramatic change in the educational background of new entrants from the educational system. In 1960, for example, more than 57 percent of Japan's middle school graduates enrolled in high school, and the rest (684,000 in number) entered the labor market as new job seekers (see Table 10.1). As for the high school graduates, 17 percent enrolled in institutions of higher education and the rest (573,000 in number) sought jobs. In comparison, the new job seekers who had graduated from junior colleges numbered only 18,000 and those from universities numbered 99,700. Thus 50 percent of new job seekers in 1960 were middle school graduates, 42 percent were high school graduates, and only 9 percent were junior college or university graduates. This means that the main suppliers of labor within the educational system were middle schools and high schools.

Table 10.1   New entrants to the labor force by educational level, Japan, selected years, 1960-83 (% distribution)

Year	Middle school graduates	High school graduates	Junior college graduates	University graduates	All levels[a]
1960	49.6	41.6	1.3	7.3	99.8
1965	41.8	46.8	2.4	9.1	100.1
1970	20.0	60.2	6.0	13.9	100.1
1975	9.2	57.9	10.1	22.8	100.0
1980	6.2	55.5	11.9	26.4	100.0
1983	6.5	56.6	11.6	25.3	100.0

[a]Percentages may not sum to 100.0 because of rounding.
Source: Japan, Ministry of Education (various years).

In 1960 the starting salary of male middle school graduates was less than half that of the university graduates (see Table 10.2). Middle school graduates, whom the educational system supplied in plenty, were therefore attractive to employers because the employers could hire them for low wages.

Sixty percent of those middle school graduates were absorbed into manufacturing, mostly as production process workers. Manufacturing in the 1960s was a leading industry for the Japanese economy. We can see from the recruitment policy of the industry how heavily Japanese manufacturers depended on middle school graduates (see Table 10.3). In 1960 the rapidly expanding manufacturing industry recruited 47 percent of new graduates from the educational system at all levels. Of those, 63 percent were middle school graduates and 32 percent were high school graduates, whereas only 6 percent had completed higher education. Thus middle school graduates were the key labor force for the Japanese manufacturing industry.

Table 10.2   Starting salaries of male school graduates, Japan, selected years, 1960-82 (index of university and high school graduates to middle school graduates)

Year	University graduates	High school graduates	Middle school graduates
1960	221	138	100
1965	174	125	100
1970	157	119	100
1975	144	121	100
1980	141	114	100
1982	140	114	100

Source: Japan, Ministry of Labor (various years).

Table 10.3   New entrants into manufacturing by educational level, Japan, selected years, 1960-82 (no. and % distribution)

Year	Middle school graduates No.	%	High school graduates No.	%	Junior college graduates No.	%	University graduates No.	%	All levels[a] No.	%
1960	407,494	62.7	204,732	31.5	4,523	0.7	32,727	5.0	649,476	99.9
1970	162,479	29.3	301,040	54.2	18,107	3.4	72,789	13.1	555,009	100.0
1980	41,393[b]	13.2	178,431	57.1	23,309	7.5	69,308	22.2	312,441	100.0
1982	36,701[b]	10.3	213,619	60.0	25,345	7.1	80,606	22.6	356,271	100.0

[a]Percentages may not sum to 100.0 because of rounding.
[b]Includes new entrants into the construction industry.
Source: Japan, Ministry of Education (various years).

During the last 20 years, however, the situation has changed dramatically. In 1982, 60 percent of new entrants from the educational system into the manufacturing industry were high school graduates and 30 percent were graduates of junior colleges and universities, whereas only 10 percent were middle school graduates. As a result of the educational system's expansion, employers are no longer able to employ low-wage middle school graduates as production process workers. Robots are now performing many of the tasks formerly done by those workers.

The expansion of high schools and colleges in the 1960s and 1970s can be explained by various factors. Among them, the rapid income increase was most significant. Gross national product (GNP) per capita in real terms increased six times from 1960 to 1980. Most parents preferred to send their children to high school rather than to low-wage jobs after the children completed middle school. Thus both the central and the local governments tried to meet the demand for more high schools. Although some employers' organizations criticized these expansion policies, they had no effect. Employers therefore changed their recruitment policies, shifting from dependence on low-wage middle school graduates for manual labor to automation. They began to hire more high school graduates as operators of automated production processes.

CAREER GOALS OF UNIVERSITY GRADUATES

Many Japanese young people try to find jobs in big companies. Generally speaking, big companies are those with more than 1,000 employees. The reason why young people are attracted to them is that they offer much greater salaries, fringe benefits, social prestige, and stability than do smaller firms. For example, a 45- to 49-year-old male university graduate who works in a company employing 1,000 or more employees is paid 1.5 times as much in salary and bonuses as a similar worker in a company employing only 10 to 99 employees (see Table 10.4). In the case of male high school graduates, the income difference is approximately 1.55. The difference is due mostly to the larger bonuses paid by the bigger firm. When we compare only the salaries of male university graduates working in big and small firms, for every 100 yen earned by the employee of the big firm, the employee in the small firm is paid 78 yen. When bonuses are compared, however, the difference is 100 to 45.

Not only are there income differences between large and small firms, there are also differences in employees' prospects for future development and in the stability of the firms. Many middle-sized and small companies go bankrupt, but few of the big companies have such a risk. Because a lifelong employment system prevails in Japan, and moving from one company to another is discouraged, new workers are attracted to firms likely to offer stability. According to a survey by the Nihon Rikurūto Senta (1984, p. 98), 45 percent of university graduates reported that job stability is a very important consideration when choosing an employer. That item was singled out more than any other.

Table 10.4 Annual income (in yen) of university and high school graduates, by size of company, Japan, 1982
(salary and bonus of male workers 45 to 49 years of age)

	No. of employees in company		
Educational level and income	1,000	100-999	10-99
University graduates			
Salary	5,580,000	4,723,200	4,334,400
Bonus	2,772,900	1,894,200	1,249,500
Total	8,352,900	6,617,400	5,583,900
High school graduates			
Salary	3,640,800	3,111,600	2,726,400
Bonus	1,116,600	789,700	488,400
Total	4,757,400	3,901,300	3,214,800

Source: Japan, Ministry of Labor (1982, p. 234).

Another difference between large companies and middle-sized and small ones is in the chances of promotion. Major companies are highly organized and usually have large numbers of supervisory and managerial positions. In most cases competition for such top positions is open to anyone within the company. In contrast, middle-sized and small companies are often privately owned, and family members hold the supervisory and managerial positions. Ambitious workers are therefore drawn to big companies.

Statistics are not available on the differences in fringe benefits between large and small companies. But housing conditions differ greatly, depending on whether one works in a major company or in a middle-sized or small firm. Major companies generally offer special housing arrangements for their employees. Big companies also have special housing arrangements for their employees. Big companies also have special loan arrangements, including interest-free loans, for employees wishing to purchase their own homes. Moreover, large firms are more likely than small ones to have recreation facilities for employees and to offer long vacations.

These differences in salaries, bonuses, chances of promotion, stability, and fringe benefits add up to differences in social prestige associated with working at large and small firms. Graduates attracted to prestige positions aim to work at major companies.

The chances of joining a major company improve with greater education. In 1982 only 18 percent of middle school graduates joined companies with more than 500 employees, compared with 43 percent of high school graduates and 68 percent of university graduates (see Table 10.5). Twenty-seven percent of university graduates were hired by top companies with more than 5,000 employees. In the nonagricultural sector, 36 percent of Japanese workers are employed in companies with more than 500 employees or in central or local government (Japan, Ministry of Labor 1983). Those who work in companies with fewer than 99 employees account for 49 percent of the labor force. From these statistics one may conclude that university graduates have a better chance of being hired by big companies than do high school or middle school graduates.

Table 10.5 Companies where new graduates found jobs, by company size and type of graduate, Japan, 1982 (% distribution)

Type of graduate	No. of employees in company				All sizes
	≤ 29	30-99	100-499	500+	
Middle school	34.2	22.6	25.3	17.9	100.0
High school	12.2	16.3	28.2	43.3	100.0
University		7.5[a]	20.4	67.6	100.0

[a]Percentage for firms employing 30-99 includes smaller firms.

Sources: Figures for middle and high school graduates from Japan, Ministry of Labor (1983, p. 32 of annex); those for university graduates from Nihon Rikurūto Senta (1984a, p. 27).

RECRUITMENT POLICIES OF JAPANESE ENTERPRISES

Japanese firms try to meet their needs for more employees by hiring new school graduates rather than by employing former employees of other companies. When companies need to retrench, they stop hiring new graduates. By not employing new graduates they can usually make necessary adjustments in the size of their work force, as older workers retire when they reach an upper age limit. When a hiring freeze fails to achieve a sufficient reduction of the work force, Japanese enterprises nevertheless try to avoid dismissing employees. The reason is that executives know how difficult it is, under the Japanese lifelong employment system, for dismissed workers to find jobs with other companies. Even if the laid-off workers find new jobs, they usually face disadvantages because of the prevailing lifelong employment system.

The policy of adjusting the size of a company's work force by controlling the number of new hires is particularly conspicuous among major companies. In 1981 big companies hired a total of 1.2 million workers (see Table 10.6). Thirty-nine percent of their new hires were recent school graduates, and 37 percent were workers who had changed jobs. (The rest, 24 percent, were entrants from the nonworking population.) In the case of companies employing fewer than 30 workers, 11 percent of new hires were recent school leavers and 61 percent were former employees of other companies. (The remaining 28 percent were entrants from the nonworking population.) These figures indicate that major enterprises rely much more than small firms on school leavers for new employees.

Table 10.6   New entrants into the labor force, by company size and entrants' origin, Japan, 1981 (% distribution)

No. of employees	Entrants' origin			
	School	Nonworking population	Another company	All origins
≥ 300 employees	39.2	23.5	37.3	100.0 (1,221,300)
30-299 employees	22.8	24.3	52.9	100.0 (1,305,100)
< 29 employees	10.5	29.0	60.5	100.0 (1,110,300)
All companies	24.8	25.4	49.8	100.0 (3,262,000)

Source: Japan, Ministry of Labor (1983, p. 80 of annex).

Most employees in the major companies secure their positions after graduating from school, and afterward they remain in those firms, spending most of their lives in the same company. The number of workers who change jobs is very small.

According to a 1973 survey (Shokugyo Kenkyūjyo 1974, p. 9), Japanese workers between ages 40 and 54 had changed jobs an average of only 1.4 times. The average age of that group of workers was 46.7, and they had, on average, 29.1 years of working experience. According to those statistics, the typical Japanese worker changes jobs only once in 20 years. Moreover, among the workers surveyed, the proportion of those who had ever changed jobs was 67.7 percent; nearly one-third (32.3 percent) had no experience of changing employers.

This survey revealed the following: Although the cohort that was between ages 40 and 54 in 1973 experienced World War II and therefore had more opportunities for changing jobs than younger age cohorts, the proportion of workers between ages 30 and 39 who had even changed jobs was 58.7 percent, compared with 41.3 percent who had not.

Companies hiring new graduates give them training tailored to the companies' needs and intended to maximize the employees' productivity. No accurate statistics exist on how much money Japanese companies invest in their employees' training, but it is commonly believed that the amounts invested are substantial. Because employees work for long periods in the same company, the investments are profitable.

Japanese firms also try to hire the most promising employees, inasmuch as the new hires may work for them a very long time. Therefore, many firms recruit graduates from the best high schools and universities. Hiring graduates of top universities heightens the firms' prestige. It is also believed to reduce the cost of on-the-job training.

Graduates from faculties of law, economics, business management, commerce, and engineering are preferred to those from faculties of literature and science. The reason does not seem that the former have more practical knowledge required by employers. On the contrary, Japanese businesses and even the society as a whole have a low regard for the practicality of a university education. Randall Collins (1971, p. 1008) suggests that the reason is that executives believe graduates from those faculties have a higher regard for the values of the business world.

The way Japanese enterprises hire university graduates varies according to the faculty from which the students are recruited. When companies hire graduates from a faculty of technology at a leading university, they rely heavily on the recommendation of a professor. Such professors usually have personal connections with major businesses, and their opinions are therefore trusted. Social science graduates, on the other hand, normally must pass a company-administered entrance examination before being hired. Graduates of only certain universities and faculties—faculties of law, economics, commerce, business, and management—are eligible to take the entrance examinations of major companies.

These recruitment policies have been criticized as being discriminatory, and recently a fair number of major companies have permitted graduates from other faculties and less prestigious universities to take the entrance exams. Graduates from top universities still enjoy an advantage in hiring decisions, however. According to the results of a 1979 survey (Nihon Rikurūto Senta 1984a, p. 13), 28 percent of Japanese business permitted graduates of only particular departments or faculties of particular universities to take their entrance examinations, 22 percent opened their examinations to graduates of all universities but not of all faculties and departments, 36 percent opened their entrance examinations to all faculties of all universities.

University graduation in Japan occurs in March, but recruitment by corporations begins in November of the previous year. Major companies administer their examinations early in November, usually on the same day, in order to recruit the best students as soon as possible. Consequently, within the first five days of November, 80 percent of university seniors decide where to work after they graduate (see Table 10.7). Those who are not offered jobs during this period must take the entrance examinations of the second-rank companies, mostly the middle-sized and small companies.

Table 10.7   Timing of university graduates' company choice, Japan, 1984
(% distribution)

Date of choice[a]	%
Before November 5	79.8
November 6-10	5.2
November 11-20	5.0
November 21-30	3.3
After December 1	5.6

[a]For April 1985 graduates.
Source: Nihon Rikurūto Senta (1984a, p. 35).

For their selection, Japanese enterprises use a written test, an interview, and sometimes an aptitude test as well. Almost all enterprises interview applicants, and 84 percent give a written test. The test is not designed to assess the examinees' professional knowledge but rather their knowledge of general and current topics and their motivation, personality, leadership, appearance, and loyalty to business in general and to the company. A common jest is that the applicant who is most sought after by Japanese companies is the leader of an athletic club at a major university.

Whereas companies are interested in hiring as many graduates from the best universities as they can, the universities are concerned about maximizing the number of their graduates who end up at the major firms in order to attract the best high school graduates. Many universities therefore have an independent job opportunity office that engages in active public relations with the business community. This practice is more conspicuous at private universities than at national ones. Some 46 percent of private universities offer their seniors mock examinations, and 34 percent conduct mock interviews to prepare the students for the companies' entrance examinations.

The university's job opportunity office also assists companies in selecting job applicants. The companies ask the major universities to recommend a certain number of students for employment. If the job opportunity office recommends undistinguished students to an employer, the university loses its good reputation and may not be asked for a recommendation the next year. The job opportunity office therefore tries to select the best students for referral. Thirty-eight percent of private universities recommend students with good academic records, and 69 percent recommend students on the basis of both academic achievement and other attributes determined by a special selection committee.

As the result of these recruitment procedures, most of the graduates of the best universities are recruited by the major companies, and those from less prestigious universities find jobs in smaller companies. In 1980, for example, 52 percent of graduates from former Imperial universities found jobs in businesses with more than 5,000 employees, but only 6 percent of graduates from private universities established after World War II were hired by such firms (see Table 10.8). Correspondingly, only 2 percent of graduates from former Imperial universities joined the staffs of companies with fewer than 499 employees, compared with 54 percent of graduates from private universities established after World War II.

Table 10.8   Companies absorbing university graduates, by company size and
type of university, Japan, 1980
(% distribution, male graduates)

Type of university	No. of employees					
	≤499	500-999	1,000-4,999	5,000+	Public sector	Total
Former Imperial university	2.2	2.8	25.3	52.2	17.6	100.0
First-rank national university	7.3	9.4	27.8	36.8	18.7	100.0
Second-rank national university	17.5	9.3	27.2	28.9	16.8	100.0
Private university established before World War II	21.1	9.7	28.5	30.6	9.9	100.0
Private university established after World War II	54.2	13.4	16.2	6.4	9.8	100.0
All universities	27.0	10.2	25.4	26.1	11.3	100.0

Source: Nihon Rikurūto Senta (1980, p. 20).

Opinions are currently divided about whether the hierarchical
structure of the university system and the unequal life chances it
produces create dissatisfaction or frustration among Japanese
youths. So far, at least, there has been no youth revolt against the
system, and the reason why is believed to be that economic conditions in Japan are reasonably good. If the present economic prosperity and social stability were to collapse, it is difficult to predict
what would happen to the system.

REFERENCES

Collins, Randall. 1971. "Functional and Conflict Theories of Edu-
    cational Stratification." *American Sociological Review* 36:
    1002-19.

Japan. Ministry of Education. Annual. *Gakkō Kihon Chōsa*
    (Basic Survey of Education). Tokyo.

___. Ministry of Labor. Annual. *Chingin Kōzo Kihon Chōsa* (Basic Survey of Wage Structure). Tokyo.

___. 1983. *Rōdō Hakusho* (White Paper on Labor). Tokyo.

Nihon Rikurūto Senta. 1980. *Rikurūto Chōsa Sōran, Shinki Gakusotsu Rodo Shijyo Henka* (Recruit Survey: The Changing Labor Market for University Graduates). Tokyo.

___. 1984a. *Gakureki ni Kansuru Kigyō no Iken Chōsa* (Opinions of Enterprises on Educational Credentials). Tokyo.

___. 1984b. *Rikurūto Chōsa Geppo* (Monthly Report on Recruitment Survey) 9 (1).

Shokugyo Kenkyūjyo. 1974. *Nihonjin no Shokugyō Keireki* (Occupational Careers of the Japanese). Tokyo.

11

THE TRANSITION FROM SCHOOL TO WORK IN THE UNITED STATES

Robert Evans, Jr.

Every year several million young men and women graduate from high school in the United States and begin their transition from full-time student to full-time member of the work force. (In 1981 the number of high school graduates was 3.04 million.) For some, years of additional education lie ahead, while for others (38.2 percent in 1982) entrance into the world of work begins immediately. Between these alternatives are myriad patterns that intermix work, unemployment, education, and time out of the labor force. These life-cycle stages in an individual's life have long fascinated scholars and poets. From Scripture comes the observation:

> To every thing there is a season, and a time to every purpose under Heaven: A time to be born, and a time to die; a time to plant, and a time to pluck up that which is planted. (Ecclesiastes 3:1-2)

Or we can turn to Shakespeare:

> All the world's a stage,
> And all the men and women merely players
> They have their exits and their entrances;
> And one man in his time plays many parts,
> His Acts being seven ages. (*As You Like It*, act 2, sc. 7)

In recent years we seem to have become even more interested in the transitions from one age or season to the next, for bookshelves abound with such titles as *Passages* (Sheehy 1976) and *Transformations* (Gould 1978).

This chapter is concerned with the process and patterns involved as young men and women move from the role of student to the season of being mature and full-time contributors to economic production and growth. The examination involves (1) review of the general patterns of labor force participation, employment and unemployment, and occupational mobility; (2) an analysis of the job-search process of young men and women as they move from school to work, especially the degree to which the process differs from that of older, more mature workers; (3) consideration of the special problems of youth unemployment; and (4) an evaluation of the degree to which particular states within the transition process—for example, military service and marriage—affect young people, especially over the long run.

Any transition involves a beginning, a process and time of change, and a conclusion. The transition from school to work begins when an individual receives his or her terminal degree. For the Ph.D. or professional-school graduate, the beginning of the transition is clear. Problems arise for those whose school and work patterns are less straightforward—for example, the individual who completes one level of schooling, works for a while, and then returns to school, or the person who accepts full-time work before completing a particular level of schooling. During the 11 years from 1968 to 1978 the proportion of part-time college students in the United States rose from 31 to 41 percent, and by 1979 one-third of all U.S. college students were 25 years of age or older (Corman 1983, p. 249). Earlier Beverly Duncan had estimated that one-tenth of all high school graduates who discontinued their schooling would subsequently seek more education (Sewell, Hauser, and Featherman 1976, p. 136).

Are these initial periods of work part of the transition years, or must one wait until the terminal degree is actually received to begin them? What about the individual who is employed full time while going to school? In Japan, at least for most males employed by major corporations, the completion of formal education outside the firm and acceptance into the firm for a long period of continuous employment are clearly identified events. In the United States, and increasingly in Japan, the identification of these events can be quite complex.

Similar questions may be asked about the conclusion of the transition process. Does it occur when the individual obtains his or her first full-time job? If so, then most transitions are very short. Or is it when the individual is well settled into a job in which he or she may achieve considerable tenure? The latter event is more realistic but may be difficult to measure since some individuals will remain with an initial employer for many years, whereas others will change jobs frequently. An alternative approach would be to say that the process has been completed when an individual has achieved a specific age, say, 25 years of age. The difficulty here is that at age 25 a lawyer is just starting to work and a would-be physician is still in medical school. At the same age a high school graduate who began working after graduation has been in the labor force for up to seven years, the median white woman has been a mother for one-third of a year, and the median black woman has a child almost ready for kindergarten (Mott 1982, p. 4).

According to Marcia Freeman (1976), transition assumptions for men and women in the early post-World War II years had little variation. A young man assumed that he would finish high school and go to work full time or join the military. In his twenties he would marry and settle down to raise a family. A young woman, too, was expected to complete high school and accept full-time employment, but only until the birth of her first child, when she would withdraw from the active labor force. She might return to a job after her children entered school or even later, but her income was not expected to provide the major financial support for her family (Freeman 1976, p. 21). For nonprofessionals the period between full-time participation in the labor market and settling down to raise a family was characterized by frequent job changes. Moving into jobs suitable for long-term employment and settling down tended to occur at the same time.

That these years should be ones of trial and error, of testing and learning, has seemed natural for at least half a century. Davidson and Anderson (1937, p. 39) characterized the period immediately following the completion of school as a "floundering period," whereas Hollingshead (1975, p. 277) wrote

> The typical worker passes through a two phase cycle in his adjustment to the work world. The first normally lasts from a year to a year and a half after he leaves school. The average boy holds five jobs in this phase. . . . Once experience and age requirements are met a youth enters the second phase of his work career. This phase is marked by better performance on the job, higher pay, and a steady job by local standards.

Despite many changes over the postwar years, a long transition period has characterized the idealized pattern for noncollege young men. For young women there have been major changes, largely placing more emphasis on their participation in the labor force and less on the role of nonworking mother. A similar but less protracted trend can be expected for college-educated men and women because today many graduate without completely defined interests or much knowledge concerning the world of work.

CONTEMPORARY PATTERNS

Contemporary patterns of participation in the labor force, employment, and unemployment are presented in Tables 11.1, 11.2, and 11.3, which show not only the powerful influences of age, education, and marriage upon these aspects of the world at work but also the differences between men and women and between whites and blacks.

Labor Force Participation

Typically during the transition period, labor force participation rates of out-of-school youth rise between the usual ages of high school graduation (18 to 19) and the mid-twenties, except for white women, whose lower rates reflect the impact of marriage and childbirth on those age groups (see Table 11.1). A similar pattern is observed in Japan, with participation rates rising for males 25 to 29 years of age but falling for women in that same age group (Japan, Ministry of Labor 1982, p. 21).

Unemployment

In the United States, unemployment has been in many ways a young person's monopoly. In 1982 the average unemployment level for U.S. men was 9.9 percent, but for 16- to 17-year-olds, the rate was 24.4 percent. Yet, by age 65 and older, the unemployment rate was down to 3.2 percent (U.S. Department of Labor 1983, p. 70). Similar patterns were recorded for women and for blacks and whites, though black unemployment levels tended to be twice as high as those of whites. In Japan, in contrast, older workers suffer the greatest level of unemployment. Although unemployment levels of persons 15 to 24 and over age 55 are similar, the ratio of job offers to job applicants at the Employment Service in 1981 was 2.4 jobs for each applicant 19 years old and younger and only one job for each ten applicants of age 55 and over (Japan, Ministry of Labor 1982, pp. 34, 41).

Table 11.1   Labor force participation of young whites and blacks, by sex and age, United States, 1982 (%)

Age group	Whites		Blacks	
	Males	Females	Males	Females
Not in school				
16-17	76.4	50.3	n.a.	n.a.
18-19	87.7	75.0	71.4	56.8
20-21	82.4	77.0	87.4	62.6
22-24	95.7	72.9	85.4	69.2
25-29	96.8	70.7	88.6	71.6
30-34	97.1	67.1	88.6	72.8
Single (in school and not in school)				
16-19	58.0	52.3	37.9	31.5
20-24	81.2	77.0	75.1	58.6
25-34	90.2	86.9	79.6	68.1
Married (in school and not in school)				
16-19	94.8	46.7	n.a.	n.a.
20-24	97.0	62.0	97.2	63.5
25-34	97.9	60.9	94.7	72.6

n.a. = data not available
Sources: Not in school: Young (1983, pp. 18-19); single and married: Hayghe (1983, p. 11).

In addition to age, educational levels pay an important role in determining levels of unemployment. In 1981, 27.1 percent of 20- to 24-year-old U.S. male high school dropouts were unemployed, but among 16- to 24-year-olds with four and more years of college only 8.4 percent were unemployed (see Table 11.2).

Occupational Mobility

Workers in transition revolve through a number of jobs and occupations. Among all U.S. men of ages 18 to 19 who were employed in January 1981, some six or seven out of ten (64.6 percent) had less than a year of job tenure, as did about half (48.2 percent) of men aged 20 to 24. Yet, by ages 25 to 34, mature job stability, by

U.S. standards, appears to have been achieved. Some 82.4 percent of men held the same occupation from one year to the next (Rytina 1983, pp. 5, 14) (see Table 11.3). Data from the University of Michigan's Panel Study of Income Dynamics suggest that for heads of household job mobility declines more as a function of work experience than of age at all educational levels, high school dropouts tending to have about twice as much job mobility as college graduates (Johnson 1978). An occupational shift of about 10 percent per year still occurs at older ages and levels of experience among men with stable ties to the labor force. This proportion of job changes among the stably employed in the United States is approximately the same as the proportion recorded for all Japanese men in 1982. Even among younger men in Japan the proportion who change jobs within a year has been quite small. In 1979 the figure was only 7.6 percent for men 20 to 24 years of age (Umetani and Reubens 1983, p. 214). Thus the higher occupational mobility patterns in the United States reported before (Evans 1971, pp. 84-87; Cole 1979, p. 67) appear still to be valid.

Table 11.2   Labor force participation and unemployment of out-of-school individuals, United States, October 1982 (%)

Sex, age group, and educational level	In labor force	Unemployed
Males		
16-19, no high school	78.0	38.8
20-24, no high school	88.1	27.1
16-24, high school	92.5	17.3
16-24, 1-3 years of college	94.7	11.7
16-24, 4+ years of college	98.0	8.4
Females		
16-19, no high school	48.6	38.9
20-24, no high school	46.5	29.5
16-24, high school	75.6	17.2
16-24, 1-3 years of college	84.4	11.2
16-24, 4+ years of college	93.0	9.8

Source: Young (1983, p. 1)

Table 11.3 Occupational mobility of out-of-school males and females, United
States, 1980-81 (%)

Age group	In same occupation		In different occupation		Unemployed		Not in labor force	
	Males	Females	Males	Females	Males	Females	Males	Females
18-19	43.3	37.8	21.4	21.8	8.5	8.9	26.8	31.4
20-24	63.5	61.9	19.3	18.0	7.1	6.0	10.1	14.2
25-34	82.4	73.8	11.6	11.9	3.2	3.9	2.7	10.4

Source: Rytina (1983, p. 5).

In addition to holding various jobs, men and women improve their occupational positions during the transition years. An analysis of U.S. occupational distribution indicates that high school graduates who entered the work force in 1981-82 upgraded their positions after several years in the labor force (Young 1983, pp. 24-25).

The pattern of improved occupational rank with additional labor force experience, at least for white males, emerged from an analysis of the experience of 1,600 men 30 to 39 years of age who were interviewed in the spring of 1968 (Ornstein 1976). Over an eight-year period following their labor force entry, the prestige scores of their occupations increased from an average of 29.3 points at entry to an average 37.1. For black males the entry position was lower, 24.8, and the extent of increase was smaller, for the average score after eight years being only 28.5. According to one analysis, about one-third of the black-white differences can be explained by differences in family background and another third by a combination of other known factors; the rest is unexplained (Ornstein 1976, pp. 8, 138, 168). A similar survey of 4,600 Japanese males, aged 20 to 70, who were interviewed in 1973 by the National Institute of Vocational Research reported restricted occupational mobility between the first job and the one held in 1973. The major change was in the composition of total employment; for example, over the period examined, agriculture lost workers and transportation and communication gained them (Umetani and Reubens 1983, p. 227).

THE PROCESS OF FINDING A JOB

Viewed broadly, graduating students' search for employment really begins in school when they make decisions about the high

school program—academic, vocational, commercial, or general—
and whether their occupational interests require schooling beyond
the secondary level. These decisions are influenced by the individuals' inherent abilities and preferences, on one hand, and by wage
and job-market characteristics on the other (Freeman 1971, p. 3).
Expectations, risk, and family influence also play a role. The family
influences the future labor-market activities of a child largely
through its influence on the kind of education received and the degree pursued rather than directly on labor-market events.

According to Young (1983, p. 13), slightly more than half of
U.S. high school seniors in May 1981 were enrolled in college in
October 1981 (54.7 percent of the men and 53.1 percent of the
women). A great majority of those in college were initially there on
a full-time basis (92.3 percent). But the proportion of blacks in
college (43 percent) was considerably below that of Hispanics (52
percent) and whites (54.6 percent). This pattern has been typical in
recent years. Another source (U.S. Department of Commerce 1984,
p. 158) suggests higher rates of college attendance in 1981 (63 percent for all groups combined), which is typical of U.S. rates since
1970 but considerably above the 41 percent rate in 1950. National
longitudinal data, however, suggest that only 43 percent of all high
school seniors in 1979 were enrolled in postsecondary education a
year later (Hahn and Lerman 1983, p. 22). These different estimates of continuation rates complicate efforts to understand the transition from high school to college, for they suggest serious data or
definitional problems.

Japan, too, has seen an increasing proportion of students obtaining education beyond the secondary level. In 1955, 42 percent of
junior high school graduates left school for employment, while 55
percent of high school graduates took jobs. In 1981, only 0.4 percent of junior high school graduates took jobs and 41.1 percent of
high school graduates went into employment. Between 1955 and
1981 the number of college graduates (including junior college
graduates) increased by 5.2 times (Japan, Ministry of Labor 1982,
p. 37). This phenomenon is discussed in more detail in Chapter
10.

The transition years include movements back and forth between
school and work. In the United States about one in every six teenaged males who have left school return. Individuals who have had
"some college" particularly seem to engage in a back-and-forth pattern; about one in three are involved in it. One reason may be that
additional years at college offer more levels of certification and enable participants to begin their full-time labor force activity in jobs of

higher social standing (Featherman and Canter 1976, pp. 136, 160).

Education beyond high school is more apt to occur for men than for women. Among children from the same family, almost 75 percent of the men who completed high school also completed some college, compared with only 57 percent of the women. Yet, once in college, women have had the greater staying power. The probability of completing college for those who completed high school was 33 percent for women and 37 percent for men (Mott and Haurin 1982, p. 25).

For both black and white women the probability of actually entering college was higher with higher intelligence (IQ). The probability nearly doubled for white women as IQ rose from 90 to 130, and for black women the pattern was about the same. The decision to enter college was a positive function of parents' education, educational attainment, family income, and mental ability. For whites, the number of siblings produced a negative effect, but not so for black women (U.S. Department of Labor 1978, p. 39).

In Japan the differences between the educational experiences of men and women are more marked. In 1980, 25.2 percent of men in the 25 to 34 age group were college graduates; the corresponding proportion among women was 6.9 percent. Inclusion of junior college graduates in these statistics would have increased significantly the female percentage. In the United States the equivalent percentages for college graduates in 1978 were 27.7 percent for men and 20.0 percent for women (Evans 1984, p. 35).

Information in the Labor Market

The process of seeking and finding a job is largely an exercise in the exchange of information and therefore needs to be viewed from the perspective of the employee and prospective employers. The desired information consists of the existence of a job and an applicant and related data that are useful in deciding whether to apply for a given job, offer a job to an applicant, and accept a particular job offer. Decision-making information can be divided into two types, factual and subjective. Factual data include wages, occupations, age, and formal certification. Subjective information includes such matters as whether the firm is a good place to work and whether an individual would be a good employee. The usefulness of subjective data depends largely on the confidence placed in the reliability of the sources.

The process just described suggests that the extent to which any source of labor-market information is used depends on the relative importance of factual or subjective knowledge about existing jobs. Such information is obtained from a variety of sources—friends, relatives, current employees, newspapers, posters, school officials, public and private employment agencies, and so on.

A relative or friend will have personal knowledge of the subjective job factors, whereas an employment office, whose source of data is the employer, is ill-prepared to assess such factors. An experienced job counselor at an employment office may have his or her own ideas about the relative merits of different employers, but various pressures restrict the degree to which such information can be conveyed to the applicant. A similar situation affects the employer. A recommendation by a current employee or a trusted third party implies a favorable assessment of subjective factors. Even more important than the informal source's more complete knowledge of subjective factors is the receiver's ability to assess the reliability of the information (Evans 1976, p. 165). That employers in some countries want applicants to call at the gate indicates the importance they attach to such subjective factors as personal observation and having a "feel" for the state of the market.

A large theoretical literature has grown up to analyze the process of job search, but it does not yet correspond closely to the real world, especially to jobs not filled by sought-after college graduates. As Dunlop (1977, p. 279) has noted

> While all kinds of ingenious models of job search, labor market signaling and training costs and benefits have emerged, I am not aware that any useful system of organizing new or available data or any viable programs have been developed from this source to deal with the pressing issues of youth unemployment, minority hiring, and upgrading the low productivity groups.

Tables 11.4 and 11.5 present data on job-seeking methods and their effectiveness for individuals in the transition years. Among individuals who sought new jobs in 1976 while employed, younger workers seem to have used the various sources of job information in roughly the same proportions as did older workers (see Table 11.4). Similarly, among young people who found jobs in 1972 differences were not marked, except that women 20 to 24 years of age made greater use of school, private employment agencies, and want ads than did other groups. Their use of want ads and private employment agencies is consistent with the clerical nature of so much of women's employment and mirrors findings of earlier studies (see, for example, Lurie and Rayack 1966, p. 94).

Table 11.4   Job-seeking methods used by U.S. workers, 1972 and 1976 (%)

Characteristic	Employer directly	Friends, relatives	School	Public employ-ment agency	Private employ-ment agency	Want ads	Other
Found job in 1972							
All persons	66.0	50.8	12.5	33.5	21.0	45.9	11.8
Men, 16-19	64.4	65.8	12.1	27.3	9.7	37.1	12.5
Men, 20-24	69.1	59.2	17.1	41.9	18.1	46.7	10.4
Women, 16-19	62.8	59.7	12.5	24.3	18.1	40.8	10.4
Women, 20-24	64.8	56.1	21.2	31.2	30.2	51.0	13.1
Employed May 1976							
16-19	74.3	20.4	N/C	9.9	2.4	20.1	7.5
20-24	72.1	20.0	N/C	11.2	4.5	25.0	7.1
25-44	69.1	15.9	N/C	8.7	7.8	26.9	8.1
Looking for work because left school							
All persons	66.2	58.5	38.2	29.3	23.8	40.9	11.4
≤ 8 years of education	68.9	47.1	2.0	33.6	8.5	29.4	10.8
1-3 years of high school	67.1	53.1	6.7	31.9	10.6	40.7	10.7
High school only	63.9	51.5	7.3	35.9	19.1	48.9	11.7
1-3 years college	65.3	51.2	12.0	35.0	29.6	53.4	10.7
College+	69.4	48.0	38.4	29.1	24.1	43.3	14.6

Sources: Rosenfeld (1977, p. 61); U.S. Department of Labor (1975, pp. 20-21, 27-28).

Table 11.5 shows that in the United States, in 1972, by far the most effective way for persons with eight years of education or less to find work was through friends and relatives, whereas for those with more education direct employer contact and "other" methods (such as, professional meetings) were more successful. The precise process by which people actually found their jobs is not clear. If a relative saw an advertisement (want ad) for a job vacancy and told an individual about it, and the individual then contacted the employer, the job seeker could have reported any one of the three sources as the method used to find the job, though perhaps the most likely one would be the employer. The actual survey question was "Which one method in this list was most useful in getting your present job?" (U.S. Department of Labor 1975, p. 54). The effectiveness results were fairly consistent among age groups. Direct employer contact appears to have been the most effective approach, about half of those who used it finding it successful. The rest of the methods were about half as effective as direct employer contact, except for the public employment services, which were the least useful, and "other" methods, which were second most useful. Public employment services provided jobs for only about 15 of every 100 who used the service. School sources proved more effective than employment services, for those who used them, but not outstandingly so.

Table 11.5   Effectiveness of job-seeking methods, United States, 1972 (%, derived from number of persons obtaining job by educational level and method)

Educational level and age group	Employer directly	Friends, relatives	School	Public employment	Private employment	Want ads	Other
≤ 8 years of education	57.2	79.2	0.0	18.9	5.3	23.1	36.8
1-3 years of high school	49.3	26.1	20.0	15.0	14.4	27.9	31.1
High school	47.3	21.9	17.2	15.4	29.2	25.4	36.9
1-3 years of college	45.3	21.7	31.2	11.2	27.8	24.5	41.4
4+ years of college	44.3	20.0	21.0	6.5	18.5	15.6	52.5
All ages[a]	52.8	24.4	24.0	15.2	26.6	26.6	44.0
Ages 16-19[b]	50.9	29.1	28.4	15.5	22.9	20.8	33.9
Ages 20-24	51.5	19.2	26.8	15.2	26.9	20.9	45.3
Looked for work because left school	47.7	21.1	27.3	15.0	21.8	14.7	48.2

[a]Taken directly from source.
[b]Calculated from tables in source. For unknown reasons the calculations are not equivalent to those obtained for categories for which effectiveness tables were presented.
Source: U.S. Department of Labor (1975, pp. 20, 29, 36, 42).

The Special Role of Schools

Schools play a modest role in the direct preparation of students for the world of work. About 11 percent of all U.S. graduates are identified as having had vocational preparation, defined as six or more courses in direct occupational skills or in the exploration of work through experience. Students took most of those courses (90 percent) in comprehensive high schools, where the level of sophistication and variety of the courses were more limited than in vocational high schools (Hills and Reubens 1983, p. 278). According to reports by students themselves, the average high school graduate on the academic track in 1982 had taken two occupationally related courses (Boyer 1983, p. 12). In addition to occupational and vocational courses, most high schools provide some counseling and career guidance, though a guidance department tends to emphasize issues directly related to the high school and the needs of the college-bound student. Thus, in contrast to Japanese schools, where administrators and teachers play an important role in job search and placement for those graduating from school, U.S. schools play a minor role.

Perhaps the most important preparation for work during the high school years is employment itself. The labor force survey of October 1980 conducted by the Bureau of the Census for the Department of Labor reported that 39 percent of 18- to 19-year-old youths in school were also employed, but a special panel survey of high school seniors reported a much higher rate, 63 percent (National Center for Educational Statistics 1984, p. 114).

It is sometimes argued that the principal contribution of schools to employment is the socialization to work standards, teaching respect for authority, and similar value shaping. Certainly punctuality, neatness, and effort, which help an individual to do well in school, are also attributes desired by employers. Possession of these attributes may explain in large part why high school graduates have higher levels of employment than students who did not complete high school. Yet it is also true that individuals with ability and these attributes are most likely to graduate. Which is more important, the individual or the school? Do the graduates of the best schools, for example, Harvard or Tokyo University, achieve success because of the education they received or because of their innate abilities, abilities that would have led to success even if their education had not been so good? The question is impossible to answer, though a recent article on Catholic and public education intelligently discussed ways to evaluate some of the issues concerning the individual versus the institution (Murnane 1984).

A 1965 survey in Japan identified the school as the source of information that led to jobs for 38.5 percent of those surveyed, though for job searches after the graduation period schools played a much smaller role (Evans 1973, p. 161). Under the Japanese Employment Security Law, school principals may share part of the duties of the Public Employment Service. More than three-fifths of the high schools conduct free placement services for their graduates, in cooperation with the Ministry of Labor. Career guidance within the high school, however, is less developed than in the United States and is a responsibility of the classroom teacher (Umetani and Reubens 1983, p. 192). Although Japanese schools are more involved than U.S. schools in direct job placement, the high school years in Japan provide much less work experience than those in the United States. Few Japanese teenagers hold jobs during the academic term except in family enterprises, where workers in school uniforms are often seen. Even university students are seldom employed except during vacation periods (Umetani and Reubens 1983, p. 187).

Although direct employer contact was for nearly all the groups the most effective, as well as the most widely used source of information, schools were generally as effective as friends and relatives and more effective than the public employment services (Table 11.5). Among U.S. residents who looked for and found work in 1972, 12.5 percent used their school was one source of information about jobs. If one considers only those who indicated that their reason for seeking a job was that they had left school, the proportion was 38.2 percent. A substantial portion of those using their school will have been college graduates, for five times as many persons with at least a college education used that source than did high school students (Table 11.4).

Schools were used to the same degree and were as effective as private employment agencies. The similarity in usage levels between schools and private employment agencies is hardly surprising, for the placement role of most school employment activities is similar to that of private agencies. One difference, of course, is that school placement activities are free to both employers and students or graduates. A more important difference is that colleges typically see career planning, including efforts to help students think through their goals and learn how to search for employment, rather than job placement as a principal task. Various factors convinced many individuals, especially in government, that special programs to develop job-seeking skills would alleviate what were perceived as the special problems of the unemployed. These special programs included the widespread existence of career planning and placement offices in colleges, extensive commercial literature on seeking and finding employment, the apparent success of job-finding clubs, and a study that found that white youths spent more time searching for jobs than black youths and contacted more employers per day of searching than did black youths (Stephenson 1976, p. 110).

A special course or program in job search may benefit youths in various ways. Increased knowledge of the job market and search techniques may lead individuals to obtain more appropriate jobs and higher wages or to experience less job turnover. Alternatively, the program may lead to more intensive job seeking. Almost two-thirds of all persons finding employment in the United States in 1972 spent five or fewer hours per week looking for work and used four different sources of information. Those who entered the labor force from a school in that year looked a little harder (but not much), averaging 4.8 sources of information (U.S. Department of Labor 1975, pp. 50-51).

Evidence exists that increased knowledge and effort in job search have produced success (Burgess and Kingston 1974). One study of unemployment claimants in Tucson and San Francisco found that an individual's knowledge about work search was statistically significant in a regression explaining earnings. At its most favorable result, it added $1,119 to the individual's annual income (Burgess and Kingston 1974, p. 309).

The belief that individuals could be taught search skills led, in the 1970s to the organization of so-called job factories, which were a combination of school, psychological group, and work group whose goal was to teach individuals how to search for jobs and encourage them to search by paying them to search. Results were modest. High school graduates and dropouts who satisfied the Comprehensive Employment Training Act (CETA) family-income requirement initially found jobs quicker than did youths in a control group, and the jobs were slightly better. As time went on the advantages for the job factory youths disappeared. It seems that all youth eventually find jobs; the factory only accelerated that process by encouraging a more intense search (Hahn et al. 1981, pp. x, xii).

YOUTH UNEMPLOYMENT: HAS IT CHANGED?

Countless words have been devoted to the idea that special problems are associated with youth unemployment rates. As Trow (1979, p. 130) has noted, the attention paid to the problem reflects a concern that the high unemployment rates may be more or less permanent. It also reflects an anxiety about the special problems of inner-city minority youth and a more general concern about the ineffective role being played by such institutions as the family, church, and school, which traditionally have fostered the transition between youth and adulthood. The Carnegie Council on Policy Studies in Higher Education (1979) saw deeper problems for youth, problems that had been partially obscured by the attention given to the issue of their unemployment. These problems were talents lost because some individuals completed too few years of education, too many were caught up in delinquency and criminal activity, and not enough attention was being given to the qualifications and motivations of those who were entering crafts and other occupations that did not require a college education.

A variety of responses has occurred. In 1977 Congress passed the Youth Employment and Demonstration Project Act, an amendment of the Comprehensive Employment and Training Act. In 1982 it was replaced by the Job Training Partnership Act. Under the youth legislation, the Labor Department was charged with finding out what works best for unemployed youths. The department mounted several large- and many small-scale demonstration projects and commissioned research studies designed to provide a better understanding of youth unemployment (Hahn and Lerman 1983, p. 1). Although the Youth Act as separate legislation is gone, proposals for special attention to youth still exist. For example, President Ronald Reagan has advocated a subminimum wage as a solution to one aspect of youth unemployment.

In contrast with those who believe that high unemployment among youths may be permanent, some writers have suggested that no functional changes in youths' attitudes toward work or in the structure of youth employment have occurred, except for the significant decline in the number of black youths working in southern agriculture. According to these authors, the problem of youth unemployment has resulted from a combination of factors: the impact of the "baby-boom" generation reaching the teen years, rapid increases in the labor force participation of women, slower economic growth, and cyclical economic factors. One can hardly settle such an extensive debate in a few pages, but a clear delineation of the issues may be possible.

Concentration of Unemployment

Despite the high levels of youth unemployment, such unemployment tends to be concentrated among particular subgroups. Using national longitudinal survey data, Osterman (1980, p. 7) estimated that between 1966 and 1971 white male out-of-school youths averaged 2.66 weeks of unemployment at age 18 and less than half that amount at age 24. For blacks, the averages were about twice those for whites. A study by Ellwood based on the same surveys showed that out-of-school youths had an average unemployment rate of 5.4 percent during the first four years after they left school (Ellwood 1982, pp. 353-54). Yet an average youth's probability of being unemployed in any given year was about .25. Thus low average rates of unemployment mask the bi-modal nature of the unemployment, for some youths are unemployed for long periods while others experience little or no unemployment. In 1972-73 about half of all school leavers experienced between zero and five weeks of unemployment, a substantial proportion having found jobs prior to graduation. In the spring of 1980, 53.5 percent of seniors who expected to be employed immediately after graduation already had jobs (Coleman 1982, p. 135). Among persons aged 18 to 34 with a college education in 1971, 77.8 percent had experienced no unemployment. Among college students only 2.8 percent experienced 26 or more weeks of unemployment in 1971, compared with 7.1 percent for all educational levels (Reubens 1979, p. 85). Among all out-of-school youths, 63.7 percent reported no unemployment in 1975, whereas 8.3 percent reported being unemployed for more than 26 weeks. The latter group's unemployment constituted 50.7 percent of the unemployment experienced by out-of-school youth in 1975 (Feldstein and Ellwood 1982, p. 23).

Part of the observed high unemployment rates for youth reflects higher levels of job turnover, which causes greater proportions of these young job changers to move into the ranks of the unemployed. Overall, 3.4 percent of workers who were occupationally mobile in 1980-81 moved into the ranks of the unemployed. An additional 6.1 percent of males and 9.3 percent of females moved out of the labor force. Yet among out-of-school 18- to 19-year-old men, 8.5 percent were unemployed and 26.8 percent were out of the labor force. For women the percentages were similar, 8.9 and 31.4 percent, respectively (Rytina 1983, p. 5). These findings tend to confirm the view that major parts of the transition process consist of learning about jobs by trying them and becoming more committed to labor force participation (Eck 1984, p. 5). They also suggest that moving in and out of the labor force raises the unemployment rate because people seemingly have more difficulty finding a job when entering the labor force than when they are already in the labor force.

Why this should be so is not clear. It may only reflect the importance of searching for a new job while holding an existing job in order to minimize time spent unemployed. It also is consistent with Granovetter's conclusion that, other things being equal, for professionals long periods of employment with a single employer reduce mobility because such tenure diminishes contacts with others who know about openings (Granovetter 1974, p. 89).

The Long-Term Implications of Teenage Unemployment

Does unemployment during the transition years adversely affect the future careers of individuals who experience it? A study of males during the 1966-71 period found, as expected, that young white men's pay, occupational status, and skill level advanced as they gained experience and especially as they gained tenure with an employer (U.S. Department of Labor, 1977, p. 84). Among young women, those who remained with their employers over the years 1968-71 had higher wages in 1971 than did those who were mobile; the wages were 14 percent higher for whites and 18 percent higher for blacks (Parnes and Kohen 1976, pp. 67, 69, 75). These data suggest a lasting impact of unemployment, but other studies have not been able to isolate that impact. Ellwood (1982) looked at what happened to 750 young men who left school during 1965-67 with less than 14 years of education. During 1967-71 their overall unemployment rate varied little from year to year, though the probability of their being unemployed during a given year did decline. Time out of the labor force declined significantly over the period from a probability of .40 during the first year out of school to .24 during the fourth year. Controlling for various individual characteristics of the young men sampled eliminated any influence of labor force states from the unemployment equation (Ellwood 1982, pp. 353-73). This finding suggests that even extensive periods of unemployment did not have a persistent impact.

On the less positive side, however, the data suggested that early experience in the labor force meant 10 to 20 percent more wages in the latter years (Ellwood 1982, pp. 353-54, 373, 382). Thus lost employment opportunities in the early transition years may be seen as a forerunner of future wage loss for the individual, but not of greater levels of unemployment. The wage loss could reflect lesser amounts of experience or a continuation of learning about jobs by trying them; this possibility is consistent with a human-capital view of how the labor market operates. Alternatively, those with high unemployment levels during their early transition years may have subsequently been shunted into less desirable jobs because of a balkanized labor market or discrimination.

A more pessimistic picture emerges if one considers men who suffered chronic unemployment over the years 1968-76. Those men, 4 percent of a national sample, had, on average, at least 1.25 years of unemployment during the eight-year period. They earned

$1.43 per hour less in 1976 than did similarly situated young men who experienced no unemployment. This wage loss was proportionately much greater than that experienced by chronically unemployed men 55 to 69 years of age, who earned $0.73 less. Comparable losses were observed for women; young (26 to 34 in 1976), chronically unemployed women earned $1.86 less than similar women who had experienced no unemployment, and older women (46 to 54) showed a much smaller shortfall (Parnes 1982, pp. 36-77).

Another study looked at young men who were 16 to 19 years old and out of school in 1967 and 24 to 29 years of age and employed in 1975. Using a standard human-capital approach, including various control variables, Becker and Hills (1980) tried to explain hourly earnings in 1975. They concluded that the hourly wage rate for those men was significantly related to the degree of extra training they had received, their region of the country, the unemployment rate in the area of the country in which they worked, and an index of personal initiative (pp. 360, 363, 366). An individual's earlier unemployment affected the results in two ways. Overall, the length of time an individual had been unemployed in 1967 was negatively related to 1975 wages, suggesting that an individual did not catch up. The number of weeks unemployed had less effect on white youths than on black. Limited unemployment was not harmful, for white youths who had experienced as many as 15 weeks of unemployment still earned 6.1 percent more than the average white individual, whereas after only six weeks of unemployment a black male fell below the average wage for black youths. Yet a positive relationship emerged between current wages and the number of times an individual had been unemployed. The latter finding is consistent with the view that mobility and job turnover among young people have positive effects. Individuals learn about the labor market and themselves as employees by such changes, thus improving their position (Becker and Hills 1980, pp. 360, 363, 366).

These same authors made a similar study (1983) of wages in 1976 for males who had been in school during 1966-67, 1967-68, and 1968-69. Among white males those who had experienced no unemployment and had had frequent job changes earned the highest wages in 1976. This finding was again consistent with the labor-market-learning hypothesis. Some unemployment (one to five weeks) was associated with higher wages than those received by individuals who had neither been unemployed nor had had frequent job changes. For blacks the highest wages in 1976 were earned by those who had had short periods of unemployment or, alternatively, a large number of job changes and no unemployment. For blacks, having a high school degree bore an important and significant relationship to wages, but not so for whites. Veteran status was associated with lower wages for blacks, but again not for whites. Married youths had higher wages if they were white, but not if they were black. Job tenure was important for both, but more so for blacks than for whites (Becker and Hills 1983, pp. 204-6).

For women the situation has been little different. Ten years after completing school, a woman who spent two years out of the labor force earned 3 to 5 percent less than a woman who had been continuously employed (Corcoran 1982, p. 392). Such a result hardly supports the argument that male-female wage differentials are due to women's time out of the labor force. It may be, however, that women choose jobs where absence is not important, for six of seven women in the Corcoran study spent time both in and out of the labor force after completing school.

Overall, while not definitive, available evidence suggests that unemployment associated with the transition years does not play an important and significant independent role in future labor-market success. That those who are chronically unemployed during transition may need assistance is a different issue. Assistance for the chronically unemployed should be directed to those individuals' underlying problems and not to one of the outcomes, excessive unemployment.

Special Youth Programs

A key objective of the 1977 Youth Employment and Demonstration Project Act was to experiment with new approaches to the problems of youth unemployment. More than 80 demonstration projects were mounted, involving in 1978-79 alone over half a billion dollars. The results of the demonstrations and experiments fill many volumes. Among the conclusions drawn by Hahn and Lerman (1983) in their review of the studies are the following:

Training. As earlier studies had found, training was an effective strategy for improving labor-market outcomes for poorly prepared individuals when direct links existed between the training and the needs of employers, when employers had some confidence in the value of the training, and when trainees had reached a point in their personal transition where they were committed to the training and to subsequent employment in work areas consistent with the education and training they had received (Hahn and Lerman 1983, pp. 139-40).

Work Experience. Work experience programs by themselves did not seem to be very successful. The largest and most elaborate, the Supported Work Demonstration, did not produce positive results for young people, men released from prison, or drug addicts. Only women on welfare obtained strongly positive results from the supported work program (Board of Directors 1980, p. 107). Evidently, elaborate work experience was no more successful than earlier attempts, for the results were similar to those of the early CETA no-frills work experience programs (Hahn and Lerman 1983, p. 220).

Job Placement. In addition to the job factories' job-placement approach already discussed, placement activities included Jobs for Delaware Graduates, which assisted students who were neither college-bound nor clearly trade-oriented; Jobs for Youth; and a program called 70001. Young people who participated in these programs did find jobs faster than nonparticipants, but any gains were short-lived and probably reflected the job-outreach activities of the programs as much as anything else (Hahn and Lerman 1983, pp. 348-49, 355-56). Again, these results are consistent with those of the job factories reported earlier.

Youth Entitlement. One of the largest programs under the Youth Act involved an experimental program in 17 local labor markets in which low-income youth were guaranteed jobs after school hours and during the summer, provided they remained in school or, if they were dropouts, returned to school. Early returns indicated that it was necessary to offer nine jobs in order to keep one additional youth from dropping out of school, the other eight being held by individuals who would have been in school anyway. The ratio of jobs to students was lower for dropouts, 2.5 jobs per dropout who returned, but only one in ten eligible dropouts was attracted back to school through this program. Put another way, out of 100 eligible low-income youths, an additional 5.5 returned to school at the cost of offering about 30 jobs. If each of the jobs had to be created, and allowing for substitution of program youths for other youths, some 60 jobs would have to have been funded in order to ensure that five to six students obtained an additional year of high school education (Hahn and Lerman 1983, pp. 355-56). Results of a longer range study of the program's impact are still to come.

The Job Corps: A Success. Since its inception under the Economic Opportunity Act of 1964, the Job Corps has provided an intensive program of basic education, vocational skills training, and health assistance in a residential setting to low-income out-of-school youths. In 1980, 77 percent of the participants were dropouts. Four aspects of the program have been unusual: (1) its service mix, combining education, work, and training; (2) the provision of support services; (3) its balance between a regular curriculum and the opportunity for a person to make individual progress; and (4) the intensity of the programming. It is also possible that the program's centralized administration has given it advantages over the more decentralized approaches characterizing other youth programs. Careful evaluations of the outcomes have shown that participants who in fiscal 1978 had spent more than a year in the Corps (the average was 5.7 months) had postprogram employment rates of 79 percent compared with 65 percent rates for those who had been in the Corps for less than three months. In addition, their average hourly earnings were $3.47 per hour compared with $2.85 per hour for those in the program for one to three months (Hahn and Lerman n.d., p. 21). Overall there were positive social benefit-cost ratios for the Job Corps, though it was only the existence of nonmonetary values such as reduced criminal involvement that caused the ratios to be positive (Mallar and Thornton 1980, pp. 10-11).

It seems clear that combination programs that sought to provide education, training, and placement assistance did achieve some gains in dealing with the problems of youth. For the more motivated youth the programs offered a second chance. Yet, overall, their success was not very great.

SPECIAL CIRCUMSTANCES

In addition to such standard variables of age and education, which affect the labor-supply responses of all individuals, there are special features that affect a portion of the labor force. It is not possible in the space allowed to discuss all of them, but two important ones are marriage and military service.

Marriage

Marriage has long been seen as an important part of the transition process. For men, it marks acceptance of new levels of responsibility; for women, childbirth and lower levels of labor force participation have usually followed marriage. A clue to the impact of marriage on labor force participation can be found in the lower portion of Table 11.1. For both black and white men, marriage is associated with high levels of labor force participation even at young ages. This suggests that substantial portions of the differences between black and white males in the overall participation shown in the upper portion of Table 11.1 reflect different marriage patterns. At ages 24 to 25, when almost all men had completed their schooling, there was a difference of only 3 percentage points between the participation rates of black and white married men in 1982. For single men of the same ages the difference between black and white participation rates was 11 percentage points.

For white women, being married has a distinct effect on their participation in the labor force. Married white women 25 to 34 years of age had a participation rate 26 percentage points lower than that of their single counterparts in 1982. For black women the difference runs in the opposite direction; in 1982, nearly 5 percent more married women than single women in the 25 to 34 age group participated in the labor force (Table 11.1). For women more than for men substantial changes have occurred in the nature of employment since World War II. The median age of school leaving for women rose by about two years between 1948 and 1973, but for white women the age at first marriage changed hardly at all. This means that, whereas once white women had about three years of labor force activity between schooling and marriage, by 1973 that work period was down to just over one year. The length of time between their median age at school leaving and when they first gave birth stayed approximately constant at five years. But part of the time once spent in the labor force was now spent in school, and more of that time was spent in marriage. For blacks over the same period the median age at first marriage rose but that at first childbirth declined, so that typically the first birth occurred less than a year after women left school (Mott 1982, p. 4).

Other differences can be found in the marriage patterns between black and white women. A sample of women who were 14 to 24 years of age in 1965 and 22 to 32 years of age in 1973 showed that the proportion who were married and living with their husbands doubled over the years for both black and white women but that the proportion was much higher for white women, 64.2 percent compared with 39.1 percent for black women (U.S. Department of Labor 1978, pp. 3-8). Part of this difference reflected a higher level of divorce among blacks. For whites 90.3 percent of the women who had been living with their husbands in 1968 were still living with them in 1973, but for blacks the figure was only 67.1 percent, implying a divorce rate of one-third.

Military Service

Depending on the year of high school graduation, military service has been a part of the transition process from student to mature adult for some males. In some periods it has been nearly universal; in others it has affected only some males. Studies of military service in World War II and the Korean conflict have concluded that military service was associated with such advantages as postmilitary employment results and higher wages (Berger and Hirsch 1983, p. 457). Whether those favorable results reflect skills and knowledge gained while in the military, opportunities such as the G.I. Bill that were available to veterans after the completion of military service, or the initial higher human-capital attributes of those who became veterans has never been quite clear. For the Vietnam veteran the results have not appeared to be so positive. Over the years 1968-77, among some 73,000 Vietnam veterans, those who had high school diplomas and one to three years of college earned 1.9 and 1.8 percent less, respectively, than nonveterans with comparable education. Only veterans with less than a high school education received a wage advantage. This finding suggests that veteran status was a substitute for a high school education in the eyes of employers (Berger and Hirsch 1983, p. 467).

CONCLUSION

The basic patterns in the transition from school to work seem not to have changed in the United States since World War II. During the transition, which generally occurs between the ages of 18 and 25, individuals typically complete their education, hold several jobs, move out of the parental home, and marry. Most women give birth to their first child during the transitional period.

At ages 16 to 17 about 90 percent of Americans are enrolled in school. This proportion has increased over the years as the proportion of Americans over age 25 who were high school graduates has risen from 24.5 percent in 1940 to 71.0 percent in 1982.

Concurrently but probably independently, age at first marriage has shifted upward. As recently as 1970 one-half of men and two-thirds of women in the 20 to 24 age group were married. A decade later only about one-quarter of the men and 43 percent of the women in that age group were married (U.S. Department of Commerce 1984, p. 46).

Military service has often been a part of the transition years for men, but enlistment, too, has declined. In the 1950s about one-half of black men and 60 percent of white men served in the military (Ornstein 1976, p. 169), but in 1979 only about 7 percent of men in the 18 to 21 age group were in the military.

Compared with post-transitional years, the transitional period is characterized by higher overall unemployment and higher probability of being unemployed during a given year. The relatively high levels of unemployment at younger ages have declined markedly at older ages during the postwar years. Apart from concern over the existence of generally high levels of unemployment among young people, there has been fear that young people who experienced extensive unemployment in their teens and early twenties would continue that pattern at older ages. Research does not support this concern for most individuals. Average amounts of unemployment during the teen years do not seem to cause unemployment in their older years, except among a handful of people who were chronically unemployed as youth.

Transition results vary according to the extent of an individual's additional education. The best results seem to be experienced by individuals with the most education, especially those who have earned college degrees. The temptation is to suggest a policy of encouraging additional years of education. Yet many measures show the differences between the high school dropout and the high school graduate to be rather small, whereas the cost of increased grade-level retention is high. Moreover, there is still doubt as to whether the differences are due to the additional value of a year of education or other, unknown factors associated with individuals who have chosen to continue their education. Where transition problems exist, they mostly affect minorities. For them the situation is not easy to improve, nor do the problems appear to be directly tied to the labor market, schools, or the normal transition process. Rather they seem tied to social values, family structure, and events in individuals' lives at earlier ages. It is there that solutions must be sought. On balance, the transition process from school to work in the United States seems to work well, though the active involvement of educational institutions in the process appears quite small.

REFERENCES

Becker, Brian E., and Stephen M. Hills. 1980. "Teenage Unemployment: Some Evidence of the Long Run Effect on Wages." *Journal of Human Resources* 15 (Summer): 354-72.

____. 1983. "The Long Run Effects of Job Changes and Unemployment Among Male Teenagers." *Journal of Human Resources* 18 (Spring): 197-212.

Berger, Mark C., and Barry T. Hirsch. 1983. "The Civilian Earnings Experience of Vietnam-Era Veterans." *Journal of Human Resources* 18 (Fall): 455-79.

Board of Directors. 1980. *Summary and Findings of the National Supported Work Demonstration.* Cambridge, Mass.: Ballinger.

Boyer, Ernest L. 1983. *High School.* New York: Harper & Row.

Burgess, Paul L., and Jerry L. Kingston. 1974. "Work Search Knowledge, Schooling and Earnings." *Industrial Relations* 13 (October): 308-12.

Carnegie Council on Policy Studies in High Education. 1979. *Giving Youth a Better Chance.* San Francisco: Jossey-Bass.

Cole, Robert E., ed. 1979. *Work Mobility and Participation.* Berkeley: University of California Press.

Coleman, James D., Thomas Hoffer, and Sally Kilgore. 1982. *High School Achievement.* New York: Basic Books.

Corcoran, Mary. 1982. "The Employment and Wage Consequences of Teenage Women's Non-Employment." In *The Youth Labor Market Problem: Its Nature, Causes, and Consequences*, edited by Richard B. Freeman and David A. Wise, pp. 391-425. Chicago: University of Chicago Press.

Corman, Hope. 1983. "Post Secondary Education Enrollment Responses by Recent High School Graduates and Older Adults." *Journal of Human Resources* 17 (Spring):245-67.

Davidson, Percy, and Dewey H. Anderson. 1937. *Occupational Mobility in an American Community.* Palo Alto, Calif.: Stanford University Press.

Dunlop, John T. 1977. "Policy Decision and Research in Economics and Industrial Relations." *Industrial and Labor Relations* 30 (April): 275-82.

Eck, Alan. 1984. "New Occupational Separation Data Improve Estimates of Job Replacement Needs." *Monthly Labor Review* 107 (March): 3-10.

Ellwood, David T. 1982. "Teenage Unemployment: Permanent Scars or Temporary Blemishes?" In *The Youth Labor Market Problem: Its Nature, Causes, and Consequences,* edited by Richard B. Freeman and David A. Wise, pp. 349-84. Chicago: University of Chicago Press.

Evans, Robert, Jr. 1971. *The Labor Economics of Japan and the United States.* New York: Praeger.

____. 1973. "Labor Market Information in Japanese Labor Markets." In *Industrialization and Manpower Policy in Asian Countries,* pp. 157-72. Tokyo: Japan Institute of Labor.

____. 1976. "The Great Computer Bubble: Has It Burst?" *Industrial Relations* 15 (May): 158-67.

____. 1984. "'Lifetime Earnings' in Japan for the Class of 1985." *Monthly Labor Review* 107 (April): 32-36.

Featherman, David L., and T. Michael Canter. 1976. "Discontinuities in Schooling and Socio-Economic Life Cycle." In *Schooling and Achievement in American Society,* edited by William H. Sewell, Robert M. Hauser, and David L. Featherman, pp. 133-60. New York: Academic Press.

Feldstein, Martin, and David T. Ellwood. 1982. "Teenage Unemployment: What Is the Problem?" In *The Youth Labor Market Problem: Its Nature, Causes, and Consequences,* edited by Richard B. Freeman and David A. Wise, pp. 17-34. Chicago: University of Chicago Press.

Freeman, Marcia. 1976. "The Youth Labor Market." In National Commission for Manpower Policy, *From School to Work,* pp. 21-37. Washington, D.C.: U.S. Government Printing Office.

Freeman, Richard B. 1971. *The Market for College Trained Manpower.* Cambridge, Mass.: Harvard University Press.

Gould, Roger. 1978. *Transformations.* New York: Simon and Schuster.

Granovetter, Mark S. 1974. *Getting a Job*. Cambridge, Mass.: Harvard University Press.

Hahn, Andrew, Barry Friedman, Cecilia Rivera, and Robert Evans, Jr. 1981. "The Effectiveness of Two Job Search Assistance Programs for Disadvantaged Youth." Unpublished. Brandeis University (multilith).

Hahn, Andrew, and Robert Lerman. 1983. *The CETA Youth Employment Record*. Waltham, Mass.: Florence Heller Graduate School.

_____. n.d. *Representative Findings from YEDPA Discretionary Projects*. Waltham, Mass.: Florence Heller Graduate School.

Hayghe, Howard. 1983. "Marital and Family Patterns of Workers: An Update." *Special Labor Force Report 2163*. U.S. Department of Labor. Washington, D.C.: U.S. Government Printing Office.

Hills, Steven M., and Beatrice G. Reubens. 1983. "Youth Employment in the United States." In *Youth at Work*, edited by Beatrice G. Reubens, pp. 269-318. Totowa, N.J.: Rowman and Allenheld.

Hollingshead, August B. 1975. *Elmtown's Youth and Elmtown Revisited*. New York: Wiley.

Japan. Ministry of Labor. 1982. *Summary of Labor Statistics 1982* (in Japanese). Tokyo.

Johnson, William R. 1978. "A Theory of Job Shopping." *Quarterly Journal of Economics* 92 (May): 261-77.

Lurie, Melvin, and Elton Rayack. 1966. "Racial Differences in Migration and Job Search: A Case Study." *Southern Economic Journal* 33 (July): 81-95.

Mallar, Charles D., and Craig, V. D. Thornton. 1980. "Evaluations of the Economic Impact of the Job Corps with Other Youth Programs." Unpublished. Mathematica, Princeton, N.J. (ditto).

Mott, Frank L. 1982. "Women: The Employment Revolution." In *The Employment Revolution*, edited by Frank L. Mott, pp. 1-18. Cambridge, Mass.: MIT Press.

Mott, Frank L., and R. Jean Haurin. 1982. "Variations in the Educational Progress and Career Orientations of Brothers and Sisters." In *The Employment Revolution*, edited by Frank L. Mott, pp. 19-44. Cambridge, Mass.: MIT Press.

Murnane, Richard J. 1984. "A Review Essay—Comparisons of Public and Private Schools: Lessons from the Uproar." *Journal of Human Resources* 19 (Spring): 265-69.

National Center for Educational Statistics. 1984. *The Condition of Education*. Washington, D.C.

Ornstein, Michael D. 1976. *Entry into the American Labor Force*. New York: Academic Press.

Osterman, Paul. 1980. *Getting Started*. Cambridge, Mass.: MIT Press.

Parnes, Herbert S. 1982. *Unemployment Experience of Individuals Over a Decade*. Kalamazoo, Mich.: W. E. Upjohn Institute for Employment Research.

Parnes, Herbert S., and Andrew I. Kohen. 1976. "Labor Market Experience of Non-College Youth." In National Commission for Manpower Policy, *From School to Work*, pp. 57-88. Washington, D.C.: U.S. Government Printing Office.

Reubens, Beatrice G. 1979. *Bridge to Work*. Abridged in U.S. Department of Labor, *From Learning to Earning*, R & D Monograph 63. Washington, D.C.

Rosenfeld, Carl. 1977. "The Extent of Job Search by Employed Workers." Special Labor Force Report 202. Washington, D.C.: U.S. Department of Labor.

Rytina, Nancy F. 1983. "Occupational Changes and Tenure, 1981." In U.S. Department of Labor, *Job Tenure and Occupational Change, 1981: Special Labor Force Report*, pp. 4-34. Bulletin 2161. Washington, D.C.

Sewell, William H., Robert M. Hauser, and David L. Featherman. 1976. *Schooling and Achievement in American Society.* New York: Academic Press.

Sheehy, Gail. 1976. *Passages.* New York: Dutton.

Stephenson, Stanley P., Jr. 1976. "The Economics of Youth Job Search Behavior." *Review of Economics and Statistics* 58 (February): 104-:11.

Trow, Martin. 1979. "Reflections on Youth Problems and Policies in the United States." In *Youth Education and Unemployment Problems,* edited by Margaret Gordon and Martin Trow, pp. 127-64. San Francisco: Carnegie Council on Policy Studies in Higher Education.

Umetani, Shun'ichro, and Beatrice G. Reubens. 1983. "Youth Employment in Japan." In *Youth at Work,* edited by Beatrice G. Reubens, pp. 185-231. Totowa, N.J.: Rowman and Allenheld.

United States. Department of Commerce. 1984. *Statistical Abstract of the United States, 1984.* Washington, D.C.

United States. Department of Labor. 1978. *Years of Decision,* vol. 4. Research and Development Monograph 24. Washington, D.C.

_____. 1983. *Handbook of Labor Statistics.* Washington, D.C.

_____. Bureau of Labor Statistics. 1975. *Job Seeking Methods Used by American Workers.* Bulletin 1866. Washington, D.C.

_____. Employment and Training Administration. 1977. *Career Thresholds,* vol. 6. Research and Development Monograph. Washington, D.C.

Young, Anne M. 1983. "Students, Graduates and Dropouts, October 1980-82." In U.S. Department of Labor, *Special Labor Force Report,* Bulletin 2192, pp. 1-37. Washington, D.C.

PART V
IMAGES

12
AMERICAN PERCEPTIONS OF JAPANESE EDUCATION
Shogo Ichikawa

In this chapter I am concerned mainly with how Japanese education is perceived by American experts in the field of education. I have no data on the views of the general population other than reports in newspapers and popular magazines. American experts do not always see eye to eye with each other. Nor do they necessarily concur with reports in the mass media or with lay opinions, but experts cannot avoid being influenced to some extent by popular views (Tobin 1983). Correspondingly, the public is aware of the views of experts as conveyed through the mass media.

VARIATIONS IN U.S. PERCEPTIONS OF JAPANESE EDUCATION

American experts' perceptions of Japanese education that I have had occasion to study reveal wide variations, as expected. Some of the variations are due to the differences in the periods researched and others to differences in research focus. Obviously there are also disagreements about values.

Changes in Western Views of Japan

Japanese studies by Americans since the end of World War II can be classified into three periods. During the first period, from the Occupation to the renewal of the United States-Japan Security Treaty in 1960, the prevailing belief was that Japan was urgently in need of radical educational reform in conjunction with the process of democratization. Accordingly, American specialists criticized prewar Japanese education (Hall 1949; CIE 1946), reexamined the results of Occupation policy (Trainor 1983; Orr 1954), and showed great concern about the "reverse course" that followed the restoration of Japan's sovereignty (Brinkman 1955; Adams 1960). In all cases it was self-evident for them that Japan should accomplish educational reform upon the "perfect" model of U.S. education.

The next stage extended from the early 1960s to the early 1970s, when Japan enjoyed high economic growth. By that time, despite a scarcity of natural resources, it had miraculously overcome the postwar destitution and showed a steady economic development. As a result, the idea occurred to American specialists that Japan might serve as an example of nonsocialist modernization to developing countries (Jansen et al. 1965-71; Nagai 1984). Thus they saw Japan, which had been a naughty boy to be disciplined, turn out to be an exemplary pupil. In addition, they realized that Japan's huge investment in manpower planning accounted for its rapid modernization and economic development. Consequently, the role played by education attracted their attention, and they discovered some merit in Japanese prewar education (Passin 1965; Kinmonth 1981; Roden 1980; Rubinger 1982).

The third stage began in the mid-1970s, when Japan succeeded in catching up with the advanced countries. In the areas of national economy and technology it overtook the European powers, and currently it is competing closely with the United States. Foreign experts have come to recognize Japan as one of their rivals and consequently have turned their attention to the role played by the educational system in Japan's economic and technological success.

Even before the most recent developments, foreign experts began, in the 1960s, to be interested in the Japanese approach to company management, particularly in-service training, as this was considered to be an important factor in Japan's accelerated prosperity (Cole 1971; Abegglen 1958; Patrick and Rosovsky 1976; Levine and Kawada 1980). Since witnessing Japan ride out the oil crisis of 1973, the United States and Europe have paid special attention to Japanese training within firms. Two International Surveys on Educational Achievement conducted by the International Association for the Evaluation of Educational Achievement showed high mean scores for Japanese students in mathematics and science. Japan's low rates of juvenile delinquency and unemployment also drew attention in the West.

For all these reasons U.S. and European experts have turned their attention toward the Japanese school system (Rohlen 1983), joining the developing societies in examining both its strengths and its weaknesses (Cummings 1980; Cogan 1984). In contrast to the preceding period, when they concentrated on pointing out its flaws and remedies for them, nowadays Western experts are trying to learn lessons from Japan's mistakes. Thus the United States and Japan, who have acted respectively as teacher and learner, are preparing to shift their roles to those of classmates learning from each other.

Characteristics of Recent U.S. Studies

Recent U.S. studies of Japanese education have been highly specialized and analytical, in contrast to the past, when essays based on superficial observations were common. Focusing their efforts on narrow topics, however, specialists tend not to see Japanese education as a whole. This approach seems to have led to disagreements among the experts.

The fact is that even in Japan, a small country whose educational system is said to preserve uniformity, considerable differences exist at each level of education and also among school districts and individual schools. These variations are reflected in the researchers' reports. The researchers may correctly describe the situations they study, but they are liable to draw sweeping generalizations from insufficient data.

For example, some researchers place importance on the considerable efforts of high school students and teachers to prepare for the entrance examination (Rohlen 1983; Singleton 1967). Others see significance in the way in which Japanese children in kindergartens or primary schools are treated equally and encouraged to develop cooperative attitudes toward each other (Cummings 1980; Lewis 1984). Both observations are correct, but if one draws from them the conclusion that Japanese schools at all levels encourage competition or, conversely, that Japanese schools foster egalitarianism and cooperation, one can hardly escape criticism for having gone to extremes. The Japanese school system inculcates both values, as they are essential to political and cultural integration as well as the economic and social efficiency of a healthy society.

Japanese universities invite the criticism of visiting U.S. professors that students are neglected by the teaching staff (Zeugner 1984); but that is due partly to the fact that most of the foreign appointees are in faculties of humanities, social studies, and liberal arts, where the pressures on students are not very great. American appointees in faculties of science, technology, or medicine are likely to hold other opinions, however (Shimahara 1984). In a similar vein, the popular

U.S. view that a Japanese college graduate's success in landing a job in a top business firm is determined not by what the student has learned but by whether he has graduated from a reputable university also proves to be inaccurate. An international survey conducted in 1977 by the Youth Development Headquarters found that in response to the question "What do you think people generally value in college graduates?" 33 percent of Japanese youths (ages 18 to 24) stated "major field of study," compared with 26 percent who answered "having attended a top-rated college" and 11 percent who answered "school performance and school record" (YDH 1981b).

Distinctive Features of U.S. Views

Despite the disagreements about Japanese education among U.S. scholars, there do seem to be more commonalities. First, U.S. scholars have examined issues that the Japanese would hesitate to handle. Examples are Nikkyōso, the Japan Teachers' Union (Duke 1973; Thurston 1973); *zengakuren* or student radicals (Altbach 1963; Dowsey 1970; Krauss 1974; Wheeler 1979); *juku*, or cram courses (Rohlen 1980); and university reform (Cummings 1971; Pempel 1978)—all of which have generated doctoral dissertations. Japanese television and journalists have tended to treat these matters sensationally, and only rarely have scholarly works based on sufficient research appeared in Japan.

One reason for the reluctance of Japanese scholars to explore those issues is that research on controversial topics tends not to be regarded seriously by Japanese pedagogists. In addition, taking sides on delicate questions can place Japanese scholars in an awkward position and may even have negative repercussions on their careers. Non-Japanese are free from such concerns, and such studies by them may be regarded as accomplishments because of the value placed on research in a foreign country.

A second common element in U.S. research on Japanese education is that, in their research methods, U.S. scholars take full advantage of being outsiders. Americans have conducted such survey activities as interviews (Duke 1973; Krauss 1974; James and Benjamin 1984), school observations (Singleton 1967; Bettelheim and Takanishi 1976; Cummings 1980; Rohlen 1983; Lewis 1984), and questionnaires (Cummings 1971; Thurston 1973; Bowman 1981). These research methods may originate from their disciplines, for most of the scholars are in the fields of sociology, cultural anthropology, or psychology. Occasionally, however, their survey results do not compensate for their inability to read the Japanese literature. All the same, experts from abroad are privileged to be treated favorably by Japanese respondents, whereas the same respondents might reject a request by Japanese researchers to act as a sample. Non-Japanese scholars also have easier access to people in various positions and of different social levels than do Japanese scholars (Duke 1973).

Lastly, although some differences exist among foreign authors, most of them evaluate Japanese education objectively and impartially from an international perspective. Japanese scholars are well informed about domestic education, but, sticking to minor points, often fail to take a broad view. Their involvement in domestic education sometimes warps their judgment. People are apt to take familiar phenomena for granted, overlooking the distinctive characteristics of those phenomena. They also may regard trifling differences between their own and foreign situations, of which they are rather ignorant, as significant. Visiting specialists from other countries have the advantage of being less liable to fall into such a trap. In particular, Americans, whose cultural environment is extremely different from Japan's, enjoy great advantages in studying Japanese education.

ACCURACY OF U.S. PERCEPTIONS

It is very difficult to evaluate the objectivity of U.S. scholars' perceptions of Japanese education. One reason is that their perceptions are sometimes contradictory. Moreover, because of space limitations, this chapter cannot take into account all of the perceptions, which cover many areas of education. Hence, I concentrate here on examining two perceptions that appear to be nearly unanimous. One is a positive view of Japanese schooling, and the other is a negative view of the examination system.

Studies of the School System

Most U.S. scholars agree that the Japanese school system maintains high intellectual standards for all children and socializes children to be hardworking and disciplined. For evidence they cite the high enrollment rates in pre- and postcompulsory education, as well as in compulsory education, and the low ratio of dropouts; the high scholastic average and small variance measured by the International Survey on Educational Achievement; and Japan's high economic productivity and low crime rate.

No one in Japan would disagree with the view that the school system has expanded to reach the general population, but there are doubts about whether it has achieved remarkable qualitative improvement as well. Whether or not the results of the IEA survey are reliable for international comparisons, Japanese children possibly may have accomplished their admirable achievements by studying outside school in cram courses or with the assistance of tutors. Moreover, the industrious and cooperative character of the Japanese may originate in their national culture and racial homogeneity, or in discipline at home or training at office and factory, rather than in their experience at school.

A satisfactory case for dismissing these doubts should include an examination of why the Japanese school system is so fruitful. The following views prevail among American researchers:

- Schools offer demanding and balanced curricula, and students follow them during a longer school year. Besides basic subjects, the curricula include arts, physical education, and moral education, with the purpose of developing a positive balance of intelligence, emotional stability, and physical health in children. Japanese children also spend more hours at school then their American counterparts because of tight scheduling.
- Teachers dedicate themselves to their work and undertake interminable tasks, including extracurricular guidance activities. They also try to treat all pupils impartially. They have won the respect of the public and enjoy high social status, secure positions, and good salaries. Their professional independence and strong voice in the running of schools have contributed to their pride in their work.
- Most Japanese pupils are cooperative and well disciplined, and studious. Therefore, teachers need not spend much energy on maintaining order and instead can concentrate on giving well-prepared lessons. Assistance from elected class officers and daily rotating monitors promotes efficiency in running the classrooms.
- Differences in learning conditions are minor from one geographic area to another. School curricula, educational facilities, textbooks, and qualifications and salaries of teachers are almost the same throughout Japan. Standards are determined by the central government, budgeting is equalized among local governments, and primary and secondary education is administered by the prefectures. These factors help account for the level of educational uniformity.
- Thanks to their social homogeneity, the Japanese are comparatively free from such misfortunes as extreme poverty, unemployment, divorce, and ethnic tensions. Since premodern times they have valued education and shown respect for teach-

ers. They are eager to give their children better schooling and willing to invest heavily in education. Parents expect schools to contribute to their children's moral education and discipline, and therefore they lend their support to the schools, for example, by taking part in parent-teacher activities.

These are the general U.S. views of the Japanese school system, but the system has come in for some criticisms too. One of them is that, although all Japanese teachers are said to be engaged seriously in their jobs, some of them are interested in escaping their duties or are busy moonlighting. Critics also contend that teachers' lack of commitment has been encouraged by their being in secure positions under relaxed supervision and having too much autonomy in the running of schools (Rohlen 1983).

According to a survey conducted by NHK, the Japan Broadcast Corporation, in November 1983, 54 percent of adults believed that only a few schoolteachers are reliable at the compulsory education level, and the proportion of respondents who agreed that "many teachers are reliable" was only 14 percent (NHK 1984, p. 10). In another survey, in 1979, the Japan Youth Development Headquarters, in the Prime Minister's Office, sent a questionnaire to children 10 to 15 years old and found that 74 percent of those in the fourth grade of primary school and 42 percent of those in the third grade of junior high school respected their homeroom teachers. Both of those percentages proved to be very low in comparison with proportions of similar responses in Thailand, the United States, Great Britain, and South Korea (YDH 1981a, p. 109).

Furthermore, statistics disclosed by the National Police Agency for 1983 indicate that 929 cases of violence against schoolteachers had been reported, 128 teachers had been injured, and 1,989 pupils had been arrested; but they estimated the actual number of cases to have been five to ten times greater.

These findings do not seem to support the view that there are no problems in Japanese primary and secondary schools, despite the favorable conditions and excellent exam results.

Criticism of the Examination System

Prevailing among U.S. scholars is the view that in Japan one's occupation is usually determined by educational background and that this in turn causes keen competition for admission into institutions of higher education, impairment of students' physical and mental development, and warping of the school system itself. As evidence, those sharing this view make the following points:

- Most of the executives in government offices and large companies represent the cream of the graduates from the University of Tokyo and other reputable universities.
- Many unsuccessful candidates are produced every year because of the limited places in institutions of higher education.
- In addition to a high suicide frequency and increased juvenile delinquency, young people nowadays show selfish, mercenary, and cynical tendencies.
- School education makes children concentrate on rote learning for high examination scores and neglects the cultivation of their individuality and creativity.

Some of these arguments are valid, but others are not supported by the facts. Although Japan is rumored to suffer a "diploma disease," the difference in lifetime earnings between university graduates and persons without degrees is much smaller than that in the United States (Psacharopoulos 1973, p. 62), and initial salaries are not based on the educational institution an employee has attended, as in France.

The evidence contradicting some of the criticism of Japanese education is corroborated by the subjective opinions held by Japanese youths. In the 1977 international survey conducted by the Youth Development Headquarters, "a good education" was identified as being important for success by approximately 40 percent of respondents in India, Sweden, the Philippines, the United States, Australia, Great Britain, and Switzerland, whereas the proportion of Japanese youths choosing that answer was only 14 percent (YDH 1981b, p. 12). Only West Germany had a smaller percentage of respondents choosing that answer.

The entrance examinations for higher levels of education are not so severe as the term *examination hell* implies. Japanese high schools have places for all applicants, and institutions of higher education can accommodate 90 percent of new applicants from high schools. Approximately 70 percent of the candidates, including *rōnin*, succeed in gaining admission to universities. Only a small proportion of young people compete for admission to the prestigious universities. The proportion of high school leavers opting for a four-year university education is only about 30 percent, and half of them compete for places in public institutions. In other words, most teenagers do not face heavy examination pressure.

As for suicide, few people in the 15 to 24 age group take their lives in Japan. Japan recorded the fifth highest ratio of juvenile suicide among 48 countries in 1976; but when the figure is adjusted by frequency for all ages (frequency for youths divided by that for the whole population, multiplied by 100), Japan ranks twenty-fifth, below the United States. As regards suicide by children under age 15, Japan ranks in the middle of the 48 countries. The perception that Japan has a high ratio of juvenile suicide is based on data from the 1950s, and then the competition over entrance examinations was less than it is today (Watanabe 1979, pp. 127-29).

To attribute every difficulty of Japanese youths to examination pressure is simplistic. The incidence of reported juvenile delinquency is higher in the United States than in Japan. It is possible that increased educational opportunities and easier access to higher education have produced the increase in juvenile delinquency and the number of university students without academic bent. The tendency to act out of selfish motives, which Japanese adults share with young people, should not be blamed on competition for higher education but regarded as a general tendency in an advanced society. Egalitarianism in the classroom can lead to uniformity of school performance.

There can be no doubt that competition drives Japanese students to much rote learning, but it does not follow that the Japanese are imitators lacking creativity. Nor is the development of creativity or individuality necessarily impeded by rote learning. Foreign experts often assert, as evidence of a lack of creativity, that Japan has an enormous technological trade deficit. But all latecomers in the modernization process suffer from that phenomenon, and Japan is quickly moving toward a more favorable technological balance. Although Japan has not produced many world-renowned scientists, school education does not necessarily play a critical role in developing genius (Prause 1974). The Japanese have achieved academic distinction, as the activities of the quality-control circles demonstrate.[1]

LESSONS FROM JAPANESE EDUCATION

Although a few of the U.S. perceptions of Japanese education prove to be unsound, most of them are accurate. The following observations suggest, however, that the United States would have difficulty adopting the virtues of the Japanese education system just as Japan could not be expected to correct the defects of its system solely upon the U.S. experts' advice.

For one thing, the advantages and disadvantages of Japanese education cited by Americans are sometimes two sides of the same coin. As an example, parents' eagerness to give their children a good education at any expense deserves praise, but it also has intensified competition among students and led to the much-criticized "examination industry." Moreover, although it is generally conceded that intensive preparation for examinations is stressful to students, it also develops such positive habits as careful work, self-control, diligence, and endurance. It is claimed that egalitarianism and emphasis on group consciousness in education, on one hand, contribute to uniformly high student achievement but, on the other, hamper the development of individuality and creativity. Centralized administration and budgeting of the school system are considered helpful in maintaining a high national standard of education with few differences in conditions among districts, but is also considered a main cause of monotony in Japanese education. Therefore, it would be difficult for the United States to adopt the advantages of Japanese education without sharing its disadvantages.

For another thing, Japanese schools share some characteristics with other Japanese institutions. A Japanese pupil is promoted each year to the next grade regardless of achievement, just as a company or government employee is promoted mainly through seniority. Although students must exert themselves to gain admission to reputable universities, once admitted they are almost certain to graduate. This situation is similar to lifelong employment, which is guaranteed to successful applicants to large companies.

The procedure for decision making is another example. In Japanese companies and government offices, a decision or action seldom takes place without *ringi*, the system of circulating an intra-office memorandum to obtain the approval of all employees concerned. In Japanese schools any important decision takes place at a faculty meeting in which all staff members usually participate. Thus decision making is done through a bottom-up process instead of the top-down process characteristic of the United States.

These similarities between schools and other organizations in Japan imply that the ideology of egalitarianism or group consciousness, which supports *ringi*, is predominant in Japanese society. Little possibility exists that U.S. schools could adopt the Japanese systems, which are deeply rooted in a totally different social and cultural environment, without there being some carryover into other U.S. institutions.

Some of the characteristics of Japanese education noted by U.S. experts were imported originally from their own country. For example, at the beginning of the Meiji era, Japan adopted from America the instrumental view in education and class instruction, a view that many Americans now disapprove. Until then, personalism, emphasizing character development and the tutorial system, had been preferred. Moreover, after World War II the United States encouraged Japan to adopt a democratic method of administering schools, equality-oriented education, and independence within the

teaching profession. These things have been described as assets of
the Japanese educational system.

One of the reasons why those imports have come to be viewed
as features of Japanese education may be that they are in harmony
with Japanese culture. The main reason, however, is Japan's faith-
fulness in following the instructions of its teacher, the United States,
which was determined to impose its own ideals in Japan. Accordingly, before they attempt to learn from Japan, Americans ought to
consider why the ideals that their predecessors were not able to
realize at home have been fulfilled in a foreign country.

DIFFICULTIES IN MUTUAL UNDERSTANDING

With every passing year U.S. perceptions of Japanese education
have been growing more accurate, and U.S. studies have enlight-
ened and stimulated Japanese scholars. Nevertheless, some faulty
perceptions and biased opinions persist. Misconceptions seem to be
due to several factors.

Limited Sources of Information

One reason for the problem is limited sources of information.
Most of the visiting specialists depend for information mainly on
studies published in English or on Japanese people who can communicate in foreign languages. Because they have to squeeze information out of narrow sources, they can hardly avoid forming
biased views. Even foreigners with a good command of Japanese
do research under the instruction of or in collaboration with individual native scholars. The research focus and personal connections
of their Japanese contacts can have a major influence on the U.S.
research. Specialists from overseas must rely therefore on potentially inaccurate material outside their own fields. As a specialist in
educational governance and finance, I often find legal and administrative errors in their descriptions. Experts in other fields probably
notice mistakes made by foreign scholars in their disciplines too.

Visiting specialists tend to rely more heavily than native counterparts on secondhand information because they cannot afford to stay
in the country long enough for comprehensive surveys. Heresay information, which is often exaggerated or biased, can mislead foreign
specialists who have too little immediate information or experience
to recognize its unreliability.

Commercial journalism in Japan, as in other countries, tends to
report sensationally on such issues as juvenile delinquency and competition in entrance examinations. Such reports create the impres-

sion for naive readers and watchers that every Japanese pupil is under strong examination pressure or that Japanese schools have no useful function and are suffering from ever-increasing violence.

Professors, schoolteachers, journalists, and jurists assume an antigovernment attitude and pretend to be progressive intellectuals. Foreign researchers, having interviewed Japanese pedagogists and read newspaper articles and learned of decisions of the courts, understandably may form the opinion that a reactionary government is exercising strict control over the content of education in an attempt to foster ultranationalism or militarism (Livingston, Moore, and Oldfather 1973, p. 529). Those who have traced official courses of study or textbooks in social studies realize that educational materials are written from less biased points of view (Cummings 1980, p. 122; Rohlen 1983, p. 249).

Inadequate Interpretation

The difficulty of conducting research in a foreign country also results in misinterpretations of data. Most specialists from overseas try to develop overarching theories to make up for their poor opportunities for research. Consequently, their conclusions may sound logical but include some discrepancies from the real situation. They marshal facts according to their ideologies or disciplines. The idea of a single gigantic company, "Japan, Inc." controlled by the Ministry of International Trade and Industry, having a stranglehold on Japanese economic success typifies such rationalizations.

For example, Japanese experts agree that since World War II the Ministry of Education has had a laissez-faire policy toward higher education and the private sector, except for some temporary and futile expedients during emergencies. American experts, however, argue that the present situation vis-a-vis higher education and the private sector must have been created intentionally by the government because the consequences are beneficial to the dominant party and its supporters (Pempel 1977, p. 138; James and Benjamin 1984, pp. 10-12). Among Japanese pedagogists, some Marxists who have no direct contact with the policymaking mechanism are inclined to have similar views.

Misinterpretation is also caused by relying on out-of-date information and connecting it with contemporary situations. For instance, some foreigners, aware of statistics from the 1950s about high rates of juvenile suicide in Japan, have concluded that present-day competition in entrance examinations is responsible (Christopher 1983, p. 153; Vogel 1963, p. 44; Reischauer 1977, p. 153; Ranbom 1985, p. 16).

Similar flaws are found in the belief that Japan spends less on its schools than other industrial nations. Some Americans try to demonstrate this view by citing the percentage of gross national product (GNP) or of national income devoted to public education, educational expenditure per pupil, or teachers' salaries (Cummings 1980, p. 8; Christopher 1983, p. 71). But their calculations are based on data from the 1950s and 1960s, or they have made improper comparisons. Nowadays Japan spends almost the same proportion of its GNP or national income on public education as the United States, and statistics that include expenditures in the private sector demonstrate that Japan has been more lavish. Moreover, the share of government expenditure on education has been much greater in Japan than in the United States. Educational outlay per pupil and teachers' salaries now equal or even surpass those prevailing in most of Western Europe and the United States (Japan, Ministry of Education 1984).

Cultural Bonds and Historical Legacy

The cultural bonds and the historical relationship between Japan and a researcher's own country often affect the researcher's perceptions. Although foreign specialists can take a broad view of their subject, as mentioned before, they cannot sweep away preconceptions drawn from their own cultural or social contexts. American perceptions of Japanese education are no exception.

For example, numerous U.S. scholars have pointed out (1) that Japan's educational administration is extremely centralized; (2) that its prewar education, based on nationalism, was partly responsible for Japan's aggressive role in the war; (3) that the former dual school system, being behind the times, caused considerable inequality in educational opportunity; and (4) that Japanese parents spoil their children. All of these statements can be challenged by a more global perspective: France has a more centralized educational system than does Japan (Hough 1984, p. 71); a recent study from India has revealed that Japan's success in its modernization benefitted from nationalism nurtured through education (Murthy 1973, p. iii); in comparison with Great Britain's school system during the same period, Japanese education might be regarded as a single-track system and more accessible to ordinary people (Dore 1975, p. 36; and Korea (Lee 1982) shares with Japan such characteristics as a "vertical society" (Nakane 1970, p. 146), a "syndrome of dependency or indulgence" (Doi 1981, p. 28), and a "shame culture" (Benedict 1946, p. 224).

Japanese studies by Americans are bound up with the close relations between the two nations. As is well known, U.S. education has had a deep influence over Japan during the process of Japanese modernization. Were it not for this special relationship, the United States would not have produced so many experts in Japanese education. In tracing the history of Japanese education, some of them have asserted that Japan owes to the United States its success in establishing a modern educational system at the dawn of the Meiji era (during the 1870s), its popularization of new education after World War I, and the educational reform that followed World War II (Anderson 1959, 1975). Their publications relate U.S. involvement in Japanese educational policy under the U.S. Occupation Force (Hall 1949; Orr 1954; Trainor 1983).

It should be noted that the two nations have had a one-way relationship for more than a century: the United States a teacher and Japan a student. Although the Federal Republic of Germany shared with Japan defeat in war and a period of occupation, transatlantic communication has been very different from transpacific communication. Germany has had a close relationship with the United States since the last century, and the countries have influenced each other (Max Planck Institute 1983, pp. 1, 7).

Reports by U.S. missions on those two defeated countries clarify the distinctions. The report on Germany (U.S. Education Mission 1946a, p. 7) implies respect for German culture and education, but the report on Japan (U.S. Education Mission 1946b, p. 1) does not pay any attention to Japan's education and cultural tradition. The Occupation Force in Japan, in accordance with the report, carried out U.S. policy with the conviction that Japan should imitate the United States, which surpassed Japan in every aspect of education and culture (Gerhard 1956, p. 3).

Today no U.S. specialists show such a patronizing attitude toward Japan. However, the unequal relationship that the two countries have had for more than a hundred years remains unchanged. An unconscious superiority complex therefore may affect U.S. perceptions and evaluations of Japanese education (Tobin 1984, p. 19).

NOTE

1. Quality-control circles are groups of eight to twelve workers from the same division of a company who are encouraged to engage in regular brainstorming sessions in order to find ways of increasing their own productivity and the reliability of goods they produce. The idea of quality control originated in the United States but was imported by Japan and spread quickly.

REFERENCES

Abegglen, J. C. 1958. *The Japanese Factory: Aspects of Its Social Organization*. Glencoe, Ill.: Free Press.

Adams, Don. 1960. "Rebirth of Moral Education In Japan." *Comparative Education Review* 4 (June): 61-64.

Altbach, Philip. 1963. "Japanese Students and Japanese Politics." *Comparative Education Review* 7 (October): 181-88.

Anderson, R. S. 1959. *Japan: Three Epochs of Modern Education*. Washington, D.C.: U.S. Department of Health, Education, and Welfare.

____. 1975. *Education in Japan: A Century of Modern Development*. Washington, D.C.: U.S. Department of Health, Educa-tion, and Welfare.

Beauchamp, E. R. 1982. *Education in Contemporary Japan*. Bloomington, Ind.: Phi Delta Kappa Educational Foundation.

Benedict, Ruth. 1946. *The Chrysanthemum and the Sword: Patterns of Japanese Culture*. Reissued in 1954. Rutland, Vt.: Charles E. Tuttle.

Bettelheim, Ruth, and Ruby Takanishi. 1976. *Early Schooling in Asia*. New York: McGraw-Hill.

Bowman, M. J. 1981. *Educational Choice and Labor Markets in Japan*. Chicago: University of Chicago Press.

Brinkman, A. R. 1955. "Teachers, the Union, and Politics in Japan." *School and Society* 82 (August 6): 33-37.

Christopher, R. C. 1983. *The Japanese Mind*. London: Pan Books.

Civil Information and Education (CIE). 1946. *Education in Japan*. Tokyo: Supreme Commander Allied Powers, General Headquarters.

Cogan, J. J. 1984. "Should the U.S. Mimic Japanese Education? Let's Look Before We Leap." *Phi Delta Kappan* 65 (March): 464-68.

Cole, R. E. 1971. *Japanese Blue Collar*. Berkeley: University of California Press.

Cummings, W. K. 1971. "The Changing Academic Marketplace and University Reform in Japan." Ph.D. dissertation, Harvard University.

____. 1980. *Education and Equality in Japan*. Princeton, N.J.: Princeton University Press.

Doi, Takeo. 1981. *The Anatomy of Dependence*. New York: Kodansha International.

Dore, R. P. 1975. *The Diploma Disease*. Berkeley: University of California Press.

Dowsey, S. J. 1970. *Zengakuren: Japan's Revolutionary Students*. Berkeley: Ishi Press.

Duke, B. C. 1973. *Japan's Militant Teachers*. Honolulu: University Press of Hawaii.

Gerhard, R. H. 1956. "Some Observations on the Japanese Educational System." *North Japan College Review* (Sendai) 25 (December): 1-16.

Hall, R. K. 1949. *Education for a New Japan*. New Haven, Conn.: Yale University Press.

Hough, J. R. 1984. "France." In *Educational Policy: An International Survey*, edited by J. R. Hough, pp. 71-99. New York: St. Martin's Press.

James, Estelle, and Gail Benjamin. 1984. *Public Versus Private Education: The Japanese Experiment*. New Haven, Conn.: Institution for Social and Policy Studies, Yale University.

Jansen, M. B., et al. 1965-71. *Studies in the Modernization of Japan Series*. 6 vols. Princeton, N.J.: Princeton University Press.

Kinmonth, E. H. 1981. *The Self-Made Man in Meiji Japanese Thought: From Samurai to Salary Man.* Berkeley: University of California Press.

Krauss, E. S. 1974. *Japanese Radicals Revisited.* Berkeley: University of California Press.

Lee, O. Y. 1982. *"Chijimi" Shiko no Nihonjin.* Tokyo: Gakuseisha.

Levine, S. B., and H. Kawada. 1980. *Human Resources in Japanese Industrial Development.* Princeton, N.J.: Princeton University Press.

Lewis, C. C. 1984. "Cooperation and Control in Japanese Nursery Schools." *Comparative Education Review* 28 (February): 69-84.

Livingston, J., J. Moore, and F. Oldfather, eds. 1973. *Postwar Japan: 1945 to the Present.* New York: Pantheon.

Max Planck Institute for Human Development and Education. 1983. *Between Elite and Mass Education: Education in the Federal Republic of Germany.* Albany: State University of New York Press.

Murthy, P. A. N. 1973. *The Rise of Modern Nationalism in Japan.* New Delhi: Ashajanak Publications.

Nagai, Michio, ed. 1984. *Development in the Non-Western World.* Tokyo: University of Tokyo Press.

Nakane, Chie. 1970. *Japanese Society.* Berkeley: University of California.

Nihon Hōso Kyōkai (NHK). 1984. *Nihon no Joken.* Vol. 14, Kyoiku no. 3.

Orr, M. T. 1954. "Military Occupation in Japan (1945-52)." In *Year Book of Education: 1954*, pp. 413-24. London: Evans.

Passin, H. 1965. *Society and Education in Japan.* New York: Teachers College Press, Columbia University.

Patrick, H., and H. Rosovsky, eds. 1976. *Asia's New Giant.* Washington, D.C.: Brookings Institution.

Pempel, T. J. 1978. *Patterns of Japanese Policymaking: Experiences from Higher Education.* Boulder, Colo.: Westview Press.

_____, ed. 1977. *Policymaking in Contemporary Japan.* Ithaca, N.Y.: Cornell University Press.

Prause, Gerhard. 1974. *Genies in der Schule.* Dusseldorf: Econ Verlag Gmbff.

Psacharopoulos, George. 1973. *Returns to Education: An International Comparison.* New York: Elsevier.

Ranbom, S. 1985. "Schooling in Japan: The Paradox in the Patterns." Pt. 2. *Education Week,* February 27, 1985, pp. 11-26.

Reischauer, E. D. 1977. *The Japanese.* Cambridge, Mass.: Harvard University Press.

Roden, D. T. 1980. *Schooldays in Imperial Japan.* Berkeley: University of California Press.

Rohlen, T. P. 1980. "The *Juku* Phenomenon: An Exploratory Essay." *Journal of Japanese Studies* 6 (Summer): 207-40.

_____. 1983. *Japan's High Schools.* Berkeley: University of California Press.

Rubinger, R. 1982. *Private Academics of Tokugawa Japan.* Princeton, N.J.: Princeton University Press.

Shimahara, Nobuo. 1984. "The Puzzle of Higher Education in Japan: A Response." *IDE Journal* (September): 10-17.

Singleton, John. 1967. *Nichu: A Japanese School.* New York: Holt, Rinehart and Winston.

Thurston, D. R. 1973. *Teachers and Politics in Japan.* Princeton, N.J.: Princeton University Press

Tobin, J. J. 1983. *Strange Foreigners* (in Japanese). Tokyo: Kodansha.

_____. 1984. "American Images of Japanese Secondary and Higher Education." *IDE Journal* (September): 17-24.

Trainor, J. C. 1983. *Educational Reform in Occupied Japan: Trainors Memoir.* Tokyo: Meisei University Press.

U.S. Education Mission. 1946a. *Report of the United States Education Mission to Germany.* Washington, D.C.: U.S. Government Printing Office.

_____. 1946b. *Report of the United States Education Mission to Japan.* Washington, D.C.: U.S. Government Printing Office.

Vogel, E. F. 1963. *Japan's New Middle Class.* Berkeley: University of California Press.

Watanabe, Makoto. 1979. "An International Comparison of Suicide in Adolescence." *Journal of Educational Sociology* (Japan Society of Educational Sociology) 34: 126-37.

Wheeler, D. F. 1979. "Japan's Postmodern Student Movement." In *Changes in the Japanese University,* edited by W. K. Cummings, Ikuo Amano, and Kazuyuki Kitamura, pp. 202-16. New York: Praeger.

Youth Development Headquarters (YDH). Prime Minister's Office. 1981a. *Kokusai Hikaku--Nihon no Kodomo to Hahaoya.* Tokyo.

_____. 1981b. *Sekai Seinen Ishiki Chosa (dai ni kai) Saibunseki Hokokusho.* Tokyo.

Zeugner, J. F. 1984. "The Puzzle of Higher Education in Japan-- What Can We Learn from the Japanese?" *Change* 16 (January/ February): 24-31.

13
AMERICAN IMAGES OF JAPANESE SECONDARY AND HIGHER EDUCATION
Joseph J. Tobin

In cities big and small across the United States, upper-middle-class, education-minded Americans sit in their living rooms watching educational television programs and reading books and magazine articles with such titles as "The Human Face of Japan" and "Behind the Japanese Mask." Two or three years ago (during the *Japan as Number 1* days) the focus of most of these programs and articles was Japanese business: the Japanese economic miracle, Japanese quality-control circles, and Japanese management techniques. Currently the subject of these reports is more likely to be the Japanese educational system. What do Americans see on their television screens and read about in their newspapers and magazines about Japanese education? What images are Americans being offered of education in contemporary Japan?

At first glance, one gets the impression that Americans are impressed with Japanese education. But looking more closely, we discover that they actually have few kind things to say about Japanese educational methods. American accounts of the Japanese educational system describe its triumphs, in particular the diligence of Japanese students and their remarkable math and science achievements, and report that the Japanese school system is the primary force behind the Japanese economic miracle. But—and there is always a but—we are told, "this success comes at a great price. The Japanese are paying for this success with their children's happiness and even at times with their children's lives." The television documentaries, newspaper stories, magazine articles, and books Americans encounter about Japanese education usually begin with praise for Japan's success, then proceed to introduce an increasingly familiar set of villains and victims: the "education mama" and the fearsome *sensei* (teacher), on the one hand, and, on the other, the *rōnin* (high school graduates spending an extra year or more studying to gain admission to prestigious universities), the *bosozoku* (motorcycle-gang members), and the Harajuku rock 'n roller, who, we are told, are all victims of the school system, the defeated of the exam wars. We learn of cases of school-phobic patricide (and matricide), attacks on teachers with baseball bats, and "examination hell"-induced suicides.

Scholarly books on Japanese education generally offer a more somber and balanced view. Yet, though the rhetoric is usually more muted, even in U.S. academic writings on Japanese education all too often we encounter echoes of popular images: Japanese children being robbed of their childhoods, their imagination, their creativity —their very humanity being sacrificed on the altar of educational and economic success. Americans believe the Japanese have struck a Faustian pact, offering their children's lives in exchange for the prize of social and economic status. The American educator John Cogan (1984, p. 466) writes: ". . . the first weakness of Japanese education is its tendency to change students from happy, carefree children into serious, fatigued, and—too frequently—emotionally disturbed adolescents. The American scholar of comparative linguistics Roy Andrew Miller (1982, pp. 238-39) makes the same point in his hyperbolic style:

> [Japanese] society resolutely refuses to let fiscal considerations stand in its way when education is at issue, any more than it is willing to consider for a moment the appalling physical and mental costs that the whole system extracts from those tiny, sad-faced, listless boys and girls who may be observed every morning fighting for their own tiny places on overcrowded commuter trains and subways, their tiny backs weighted down with backpacks overflowing with dictionaries, pocket calculators, and notebooks. A society so willing to sacrifice its own children's health and happiness to "getting ahead" is quite obviously not going to quibble about anything so minor as money.

These American images of Japanese education are, to varying extents, shared by Japanese students, parents, teachers, scholars, and some politicians. Many of the images and protagonists (the *rōnin*, the education mama, the *bosozoku*) can be seen on Japanese television as well. And yet, although both Americans and Japanese are critical of Japanese education, the reasons for their criticisms are very different. The Japanese educational system and its problems have been around for a long time; it is only American interest in Japanese education that is new.

To understand American images of Japan and the sudden explosion of American interest in Japanese education we need to look not directly at Japan, but at America, for our images of Japanese education can teach us more about the United States than Japan, more of American anxieties, concerns, and thinking than about the Japanese. These images project the current issue of education onto long-standing American myths and stereotypes about Japan. The stereotypes, which were formerly used to criticize Japanese political and economic institutions, are now being applied to the educational system. As in the days of *The Chrysanthemum and the Sword*, Americans see the Japanese as drones, robots, selfless soldiers, a people without creativity or imagination, and Japan as a culture of sacrifice, a society antithetical to human feeling.

To Americans, the Japanese educational system has become a metaphor, an objective correlative, for the destructive power Americans see in Japanese society as a whole. Americans long have viewed Japanese young children as spoiled, overindulged, and undercontrolled and Japanese adults as repressed, self-denying, dull, and overcontrolled. We blame the Japanese school system for the transformation. We regard it as a monster that swallows up thousands of spoiled children each spring, chews them up for 12, 14, or 16 years, and then spits out an army of company men, bureaucrats, office ladies, and housewives.

Our images of foreigners serve complex social and psychological needs. Westerners have regarded Japan for centuries as the antipode, the "other," the nonself.[1] We cling to distorted images of Japan (and of its education) in order to save our image of ourselves. If we believe Japanese educational success comes at too great a price, then instead of envying the Japanese and seeing ourselves as lazy or failing, we can congratulate ourselves for having a more humane system. When we accuse the Japanese educational system of stamping out creativity, in a circuitous way we compliment ourselves, implying that we are a creative people and that our educational practices promote creativity. When we focus our attention on Japanese school violence and Japanese teenage suicide, we avoid thinking about our own pressing social problems or confronting the unhappiness and despair of many of our own young people.

In this chapter I consider some of the ways that American popular and scholarly writings on Japanese education, and specifically on Japanese high schools and universities, distort reality. I suggest that our errors in viewing Japanese education are not just the result of ignorance or random, idiosyncratic misunderstanding, but instead the result of culturally shared false assumptions and methodological mistakes. Because most Americans tend to see Japan through the same distorted lenses, we tend to corroborate one another's distortions.

CULTURE-BOUND ASSUMPTIONS

Distorted American views of Japanese education are rooted in the culture-bound assumptions we bring to our study of Japan in general. Most American writings on Japanese education begin with the assumption that there is something strange going on in Japan that needs explaining, something perhaps good, perhaps bad, but definitely strange. Japanese education is rarely simply described or analyzed in its own terms. Instead, it is either criticized or held up as an object of wonder, an oddity of the modern world.

Americans do not seem to realize that there is nothing inherently strange or wrong about starting the day by bowing to the teacher, or about wearing uniforms to school, or about families investing a great deal of time, money, and interest in their children's educational success, or about using examinations to determine admission to college. There is nothing inherently strange or wrong with examinations that test factual knowledge rather than the student's ability to write prose or interpret poetry. Nor is there anything inherently strange about a system in which many students spend an extra year studying to pass a university entrance exam or in which students study harder in high school than in college.

Most Americans writing about Japanese education begin with the conscious or unconscious assumptions that the primary business of schools is to promote students' individual creativity, that real learning has little to do with memorization, that standardized examinations, when used alone, are a bad way of determining college admissions, and that employment should not be determined too much by the university a student has attended. Miller (1982, p. 241) writes, "The Japanese university examinations are the ultimate, the most frightening rite of passage known to any modern society." Cogan (1984, p. 466) writes, "In many [Japanese] schools, instruction emphasizes only the rote memorization of factual material." Fiske (1983, July 10, p. 28) writes, ". . . the examinations, and thus the teaching within the schools, are oriented around factual knowledge such as the dates of battles in history and formulas in science, putting a premium on memorization rather than creativity and understanding."

Americans believe that Japanese children and parents have little choice in the children's education because the Japanese curriculum offers few electives and few routes for rising to the top. But does the fact that many American high school students may select one of several lunch periods, or choose between European history or introduction to philosophy as a senior elective really mean that they have more choice than Japanese students, who, though "stuck" with a standard curriculum, choose what kind of middle school, high school, *juku*,[2] and college to attend? We write that Japanese education (like Japanese society in general) stifles creativity, but this is based on our culture-bound assumption that creativity is incompatible with learning the value of discipline and perseverance, of learning to work harmoniously in a group, of learning to appreciate pattern and repetition, and of mastering basic skills.[3]

American beliefs about education are based on European notions of childhood, of learning, of society, of equality, and of individuality, notions we have no reason to assume to be universal. When we study Japanese education we explicitly or implicitly judge what we see according to both our culture-bound assumptions and our equally ethnocentric educational orientations, evidence in the writings of John Dewey, A. S. Neill, Mortimer Adler, Ivan Illich, and others. These assumptions determine the questions we ask, the topics we explore, the standards by which we measure, and the final judgments we reach about education in Japan.

IDEALIZATION AND REALITY

Another source of distorted American views of Japanese secondary and postsecondary education is the tendency of many Americans to compare an idealized image of education in America with an unvarnished view of education in Japan. For example, when Rohlen (1983) suggests that Japanese high school classes are excruciatingly boring, he is suggesting implicitly that U.S. high school classes are more interesting. (Cf. Beauchamp's [1984] and Cummings's [1985] reviews of Rohlen's book.) Rohlen's evaluation is based largely on his subjective experience of feeling bored as an adult American scholar sitting in a Japanese class. His perception tells us little about how a Japanese teenager might feel in the same situation.

The point is not that Rohlen is necessarily wrong in saying that Japanese high school classes are boring but rather that we lack adequate data to make such a judgment. To compare the interest or ennui produced by American and Japanese high school classes, an investigator would have to interview an adequate sample of high school students in both cultures about how they experience their education rather than to compare a firsthand view of Japanese education with one's memories of high school education in the United States.

A favorite target for American criticisms of Japanese secondary and postsecondary education is the Japanese teaching of English. Americans make fun of Japanese pronunciation of English; mixing up one's r's and l's at an American cocktail party in imitation of a Japanese speaking English seldom fails to get a laugh. American academicians who write about the study of English in Japan rarely have anything kind to say: The teachers have terrible accents, the English exams are ridiculous tests of memory that have nothing to do with learning English, the teaching methods are illogical, old-fashioned, and nonproductive. Miller (1982, p. 233) writes, for example,

> What are potentially the most valuable years for foreign-language learning are totally wasted in the course of hour after dreary hour in the English classroom with Japanese teachers, most of whom drone away in Japanese explaining the grammar and pronunciation of a language that they themselves have rarely even heard and certainly cannot speak.
>
> The spectacle of teachers busily engaged in attempting to teach youngsters what they themselves do not know—the charade of English education that goes on most of the day, six days a week, throughout all Japanese elementary and secondary foreign-language education—does not appear to strike either Japanese educators or even most Japanese parents as ludicrous or even illogical. The foreign visitor will find it extraordinary, but for most Japanese it is the only way that things have ever been and the only possible way they ought to be.

When we write that language teaching in Japan is uncreative at best and idiotic at worst, we imply that Americans are more creative and successful in our language teaching. But what really goes on in U.S. high school language classes? Creativity? Instead of comparing how well Japanese learn to speak English with how well we speak English, we should be comparing it with how well we learn to speak Japanese (or any other foreign language). American critics of Japanese education would respond that Japanese learn English *despite* their educational methods, through sheer force of will and perseverance. But is that an adequate explanation? Any meaningful comparison of Japanese and American language education must start with results, with a realistic assessment of the success each culture has in teaching its young people to use a foreign language. Boyer (1984, pp. 98-99) points out that only 15 percent of U.S. high school students are enrolled in any foreign-language class. Americans are full of excuses, of ways of putting down Japan's success in this area: "Yes, many Japanese can read English, but they can't speak it"—as if being able to read in a foreign language in itself is not an accomplishment. Or, "Yes, the Japanese can speak English, but their accents are terrible." Surely we must sound equally inept to native speakers when we speak Japanese.

A NARROWNESS OF FOCUS

American views of Japanese education are distorted also by a narrowness of focus. Too narrow a choice of topics is examined, too narrow a segment of society is emphasized, too narrow a portion of the life cycle is considered.

Sensational topics such as "exam hell," teenage suicide, and violence in the schools take up a disproportionate amount of space in American accounts of Japanese education. These topics are also widely covered by the Japanese popular media, which creates the illusion that these are the central issues in Japanese education. It is easier for publishers in both Japan and the United States to sell newspapers full of stories about suicide and school violence than ones containing stories about curricula and teaching methods. But scholars have the responsibility to avoid getting caught up in sensational and faddish topics and to focus instead on the most significant and enduring features of Japanese education.

In his appendix Rohlen (1983) makes an important contribution in this direction by carefully analyzing statistics on Japanese adolescent suicide. His analysis reveals that the Japanese adolescent suicide rate is not as high as the Western stereotype would have us believe, that it has fallen in the past 20 years even while exam pressures have grown, and that suicides do not tend to occur around exam time. One would hope that his discussion of this issue will prevent future references in scholarly writings to "the many Japanese children who kill themselves because they fail high school or college entrance examinations."

Another aspect of U.S. narrowness of focus in looking at Japanese education is the tendency of Americans to give disproportionate attention to the top quarter, or even the top 10 percent, of Japanese schools and students. American studies of Japanese education dwell too much on students' efforts to get into Todai (Tokyo University) and three or four other eminent schools. They create the impression that almost every Japanese high school student is aiming to enter one of those universities and that those who fail to do so are losers, victims of the Japanese educational system. But the number of applicants to Todai each year represents but a small fraction of Japanese students. It is true that entering Todai and eventually becoming employed by the government or by a leading Japanese firm is a widely shared Japanese dream. But, like American students' dream of becoming a movie star or a professional baseball player, attending Todai is not part of most Japanese young people's realistic life plans.

To understand the Japanese educational system well we need to hear less about the top 5 or 10 percent of Japanese students who aspire to attend the best universities and more about the rural students in Hokkaido, Shikoku, and Kyushu who plan to attend prefectural universities, more about blue-collar adolescents in Nagoya, Osaka, and Hiroshima who study in vocational programs, and more about the average students throughout Japan who study every day, but not so much as they should, who are ambitious, but not so ambitious as to hope to enter a prestigious national university, and who may have high hopes for the future, but who do not plan on realizing those hopes on the highest rungs of Japanese business. In short, we need to learn much more about the middle and bottom quartiles of Japanese high school classes.

Our tendency to focus on the top quartile of high school youths leads to distortions in U.S. studies that attempt to contrast the American and Japanese educational systems. When Americans (or Japanese) write that U.S. high school students enjoy more class discussions, compose more original essays, and experience a more creative overall education than Japanese students, who suffer under their exam-dominated system, they are considering only the top quarter or third of U.S. high schools and high school students. The more meaningful comparisons would be between a broader range of students in the two societies—for example, between the lower two quartiles of high schools and high school students in the United States and Japan, or between the educational experiences of students at the bottom of each society who are not concerned about entering a university, or writing original essays, or having a choice of foreign languages to study. We need more studies like that by Cummings (1980), which look at the educational experiences of a range of students and attempt to put contemporary features of Japanese education into a wider context of historical development and social change.

Related to this narrow focus on the strengths and weaknesses of the top students and institutions in the Japanese educational system is the tendency of Americans who study Japanese education to evaluate it from the limited perspective of current high school and college students rather than from a broader life-course perspective. We most need to know not how a Japanese student feels the day he learns that he has succeeded or failed to get into the university of his choice or to land a desired job but how he feels about his education five, ten, and twenty years later. Our image of Japanese youths who fail to enter the university of their choice is that they face a life of bitterness and frustration. Students who fail entrance exams no doubt feel crushed the day they hear their bad news, but certainly most of them recover from their disappointment. They share their bad news with their families, consider the possible explanations for and implications of their failure, and make plans for the future: to try again the next year as a *rōnin*, to attend a second- or third-choice college, or to use family ties to find a job.

We need to look at what happens ten years later to the student with low grades from a mediocre high school who becomes a delivery man or a blue-collar worker. If his educational system has given him at least minimal skills and a commitment to the work ethic, and if it has sorted him into a position in society, has it in fact failed him? Has it not served him as much as other graduates who have gone into more glamorous careers?

A wider, life-course perspective might help us to see that the Japanese educational system, including its entrance examinations, has an important function not only for those who succeed but for those who fail as well. The Japanese system, and indeed all educational systems, are more than a means of sorting out society's winners and losers. In addition to teaching academic subjects, high schools provide an organizing principle in young people's lives, a source of direction, of reality testing, of social skills, and of friendships that may last a lifetime. Plath (1980) brings such a life-course perspective to the study of contemporary Japanese culture. Like Plath, we need to focus not on the acute pain and disappointment of the youth who has just failed to get into Todai but on how Japanese people feel about their educations—and their lives—as adult members of their society (see Kato 1978).

In races on Japanese kindergarten field days (*yochien undo-kai*), the teachers and parents cheer hardest and pay most attention not to the children who win the races, but to those who bring up the rear. As the last children in a race near the finish line, people yell encouragement (*gambatte*). When the race is over, the winners are congratulated and the losers told, "*zannen, kedo yoku gambarimashita* (Tough luck, but it was a good try)." Those of us who wish to understand Japanese education would do well to learn to take our attention off the leaders and turn it on those in the back of the pack. Those who cross the finish line first may prove in the long run not to be the only winners of the race.

CONCLUSION

Recently there has been a surge of American interest in Japanese education. On the surface this interest seems to be a search for new ideas, for possible Japanese solutions to American educational problems. But, unfortunately, though we have a clearly expressed need to improve our educational system, we apparently feel an even more pressing need to defend and justify it. Many American writings that start out with the question, "What can we learn from Japanese education?" end up by congratulating ourselves on the individuality, creativity, and nonauthoritarian character of our schools and our society.

Thus U.S. popular and scholarly examinations of Japanese education end up revealing more about Americans and our concerns and values than about Japan. But this is not to suggest that it is impossible for Americans to come to know anything meaningful about Japan or to gain insight from looking at Japanese education. For us as outsiders to come to understand and learn from the Japanese educational system, we need to undertake studies that are truly comparative, studies that use the same methods to observe firsthand the educational systems in both cultures. And we must learn to ask research questions and to make judgments that are less culture-bound.

For starters, I suggest that we look critically at the limitations of the bicultural approach to comparative educational research. A bicultural study, as opposed to an ethnographic (emic) or a multinational study of Japanese education, tends to emphasize differences rather than similarities and to make Japan and the United States look more dissimilar than they really are. For example, when compared only with the U.S. adolescent suicide rates, Japanese rates have appeared at times to be disturbingly high, inviting invidious speculation by Americans and Japanese about the suicide-inducing character of Japanese education and society. But viewed from a multinational perspective, adolescent suicide rates in Japan and the United States look very similar. In both countries they are approximately 20 per 100,000 (Rohlen 1983, p. 329), much higher than in parts of Europe, Africa, and South America and much lower than, for example, in Micronesia, where the rates approach 200 per 100,000 (Rubinstein 1983, p. 658).

If we are to appreciate the special strengths and weaknesses of education in Japan and the United States, we also must overcome our overreliance on gross barometers of failure and success, such as suicide rates and Todai admissions, and develop more sensitive, salient measures of educational success and failure. If we are really interested in studying the human costs of Japanese or American educational pressures and in exploring the suffering that we hypothesize is caused by "examination hell," we should skip suicide statistics, which tell us something about only 16 out of 100,000 adolescents, and turn to more direct measures of the student experience, such as interviews with students in each country before and after they take their examinations and learn of their scores. We should give students in each country a chance to describe to us the pressures they feel not only from exams, but from other aspects of their educational and social lives as well.

Similarly, we need a much longer time frame. We need to ask people how they feel about their education years after they have completed them. What meanings have events such as examination success or failure and university admission or rejection taken on with the passing of months and years? How do individuals in each country move through high school and college and into the work force? The transitions between high school, college, and work are poorly understood in both the United States and Japan.

Today in both countries a majority of students continue their education beyond high school. It is thus somewhat artificial to compare Japanese and American high schools or Japanese and American universities as distinct entities. It would perhaps make more sense to think of high school and college as a seven- or eight-year educational system in each country and to evaluate the whole rather than the parts. In this light our educational systems begin to look more alike.

For example, some of the hypothesized weakness of the Japanese university begins to disappear when it is seen as part of an educational system that includes high school and company training, whereas some of the hypothesized laziness of U.S. high school students is compensated for by the relatively greater vigor of American postsecondary education and especially of American preprofessional training (preparation for admission to medical, law, and business schools). Many Japanese students study very hard and perhaps too narrowly in high school, and they attend *juku* to gain admission to prestigious universities and thereby guarantee a place for themselves in upper-middle-class Japanese society. American university graduates who fail to gain admission to medical school often spend a year or more as *rōnin*, taking additional premedical courses and attempting to improve their test scores, just as Japanese students often use this strategy to gain admission to the university of their choice.

When seen in this wider perspective, differences between the Japanese and U.S. educational systems begin to look more like differences in timing, in the scheduling of effort and selection, than like differences in Japanese and American students' willingness to work hard for the future. The exploration of issues of this sort calls for the rarest of comparative educational approaches: longitudinal studies, studies of students in each country moving through their school systems and on into the work force and their adult lives.

Finally, we need to look less at the top students and top schools in each society and more at the middle and bottom groups. We need fewer comparisons of Todai with Harvard and more of the University of Nebraska with Ehime University, or of urban institutions such as Malcolm X College in Chicago with Osaka Commercial University. We need to learn more of the experiences of average students in each country, of rural students, of minority students, of mediocre students, of students who do not make it, and of the recruitment of young people in each country into unskilled jobs and even into the worlds of unemployment and crime.

Studies of these types can help us to move beyond our image of Japanese education as consisting of education mamas forcing their pathetic, tired, unimaginative children to attend *juku* so that they can enter a good high school and thereby pass through the narrow gate to Todai, rather than failing and becoming a *rōnin*, a *bosozoku*, or, worse, an "exam hell"-induced suicide. Surely there are other, better stories to be told about education in Japan.

NOTES

1. Edward Fiske, for example, began his recent series of articles on Japanese education in the *New York Times* with the statement, "The education system in Japan, in its strengths and weaknesses, is virtually everything that its counterpart in the United States is not" (Fiske 1983, July 10, p. 1).

2. A *juku* is a "cram" school attended after the regular schoolday.

3. For an alternative to the usual American views on pedagogy, rote learning, and memorization, see Kobayashi (1984).

REFERENCES

Beauchamp, Edward R. 1984. "Review of *Japan's High Schools*, by Thomas Rohlen." *Comparative Education Review* 28 (2): 667-69.

Boyer, Ernest. 1984. *High School*. New York: Carnegie Commission.

Cogan, John J. 1984. "Should the U.S. Mimic Japanese Education? Let's Look Before We Leap." *Phi Delta Kappan* (March): 463-68.

Cummings, William K. 1980. *Education and Equality in Japan*. Princeton, N.J.: Princeton University Press.

_____. 1985. "Review of *Japan's High Schools*, by Thomas Rohlen." *Journal of Asian and African Studies* (in press).

Fiske, Edward B. 1983. "Education in Japan: Lessons for America. Japan's Schools: Intent About the Basics." *New York Times*, July 10, pp. 1, 28; "Japan's Schools: Stress Group and Discourage Individuality." *New York Times*, July 11, pp. 1, 6; "Japan's Schools: Exam Ordeal Rules Each Student's Destiny." *New York Times*, July 12, pp. 1, 8; "Japan's Schools: Not Very Much U.S. Can Borrow." *New York Times*, July 13, p. 10.

Kato, Hidetoshi. 1978. *Educational and Youth Employment in Japan*. New York: Carnegie Council on Policy Studies in Higher Education.

Kobayashi, Victor N. 1984. "The Secret of the Flower: Education in Traditional Aesthetic Forms in Contemporary Japan." Unpublished. College of Education, University of Hawaii.

Miller, Roy Andrew. 1982. *Japan's Modern Myth: The Language and Beyond*. New York: Weaherhill.

Plath, David. 1980. *Long Engagements: Maturity in Modern Japan*. Stanford, Calif.: Stanford University Press.

Rohlen, Thomas P. 1983. *Japan's High Schools*. Berkeley: University of California Press.

Rubinstein, Donald. 1983. "Epidemic Suicide Among Micronesian Adolescents." *Social Science and Medicine: An International Journal* 17 (10): 657-65.

14
JAPANESE IMAGES OF AMERICAN EDUCATION
William K. Cummings

Given the complexity of educational systems, descriptions of them inevitably simplify their characteristics and highlight certain features. Public opinion and professional knowledge within a country whose system is being described provide natural checks on excessive distortions. When the simplifications are made from another national context, however, the highlights and distortions become more interesting because there are fewer informed checks on the process of image creation. The simplifications can easily become uncontrolled projections of the personal and political values of the image makers. So, in an analysis of foreign, in this case Japanese, images of American education, it is important to search for the hidden agenda behind the imagery. What are the Japanese image makers trying to tell Japan through their caricatures of U.S. education? In an analysis of this kind it is just as important to keep in mind what is left out of the imagery as what is kept in.

Japan has been looking at American education much longer than America has been looking at Japanese education, and Japan therefore has far more information. But Japan's information surplus has not resulted in an accurate picture of U.S. education. Rather, the Japanese images of U.S. education have been shaped by internal political factors.

THE EARLY POSTWAR ERA

Japan has had a serious interest in U.S. education for more than 100 years, starting with the Japanese government's invitation to Murray and several other Americans to help structure the new Meiji educational system during the 1870s. Those early experiences taught the Japanese to be wary of American education. Unlike their U.S. counterparts, rural Japanese communities were not prepared to pay for or govern their schools in the manner of U.S. school boards. And Japanese teachers found German curricula and pedagogical approaches more to their liking. Possibly the only enduring outcome of that period was the Japanese fascination with the land-grant and liberal arts colleges of the U.S. system.

Throughout World War II Japan evidenced little interest in American education. Then, during the American Occupation, Japan once again had to come to terms with the U.S. educational system, for the Occupation government, in its wisdom, decided the best way to democratize and demilitarize Japan would be to dismantle whole-sale the "old system" and replace it with a new system based on "American" principles.

It is not necessary to go into the detail of these reforms. What we need to appreciate is that, from the very beginning, Japanese opinion was sharply divided on the wisdom of the reforms. To oversimplify, two polar viewpoints emerged. American education was seen, on the one hand, as expressive, individualistic, opulent, and creative and, on the other, as undisciplined, wasteful, and hedonistic. Those holding the former view welcomed the reforms as a liberating force that would enable individual Japanese to develop richer personalities and become more thoughtful and responsible citizens. Those holding the latter view feared the nation would be ruined by the reforms, or at least that the people would lose their admirable traits of hard work, loyalty, sense of duty, and willingness to sacrifice for the greater good.

The two viewpoints soon were crystallized in the extreme wings of what came to be the progressive and conservative political camps (see Nagai and Nishijima 1975). But of course within each camp there were more moderate voices. And so actual policy has tended to take something of a middle road, advancing some of the American reforms and closing out others. The Japanese imagery of U.S. education has been significantly shaped by the fact that elements of "American education" have become part of the Japanese system but are perceived differently by the respective political camps. Those camps have sought to distort the reality of U.S. education in order to advance their political programs.

Complicating the politics of image making was the recognized preeminence of the United States in the international system. From the day Japan chose to enter the modern era it has strived constantly to climb the international totem pole, relentlessly searching the globe for new institutional and technological models. During the immediate postwar period, the United States and American practices were a favorite referent; if America did something a particular way, so should Japan. Arguments of this kind were valid as long as the United States was number one. They become less salient as Japan becomes number one. Indeed, I believe that Japan's perception of its new ascendancy has significantly altered its images of American education.

Politics is not the only force behind image making. Commercial factors, such as the marketing of American higher education and personal dispositions for or against American ways of doing things, also enter into the process of image making. While recognizing the importance of these other factors, I do not devote equal attention to them in this account.

INSTITUTIONALIZATION OF IMAGE MAKING

Given Japan's long-standing familiarity with U.S. education and the political salience of U.S. educational images, American watching and image making have become institutionalized. Letters faculties of Japanese universities now have faculty positions in American studies, and faculties of education and philosophy teach Dewey philosophy. In the Ministry of Education, the National Institute of Education, the Prime Minister's Office, and the National Diet Library particular individuals have the responsibility of following developments in U.S. education. Similarly, NHK (the national broadcasting company) and several of the national newspapers have designated particular individuals to follow trends in American education.

Each of these America-watching centers has its constituencies. The universities, which are in many respects the weakest link in Japanese education, tend to envy conditions in American higher education. Moreover, many staff members of Japanese universities participate in the political activities of the progressive camp, which is favorably disposed to the "democratic" reforms of the U.S. Occupation. In contrast, the Prime Minister's Office is responsible to the prime minister, each of whom virtually throughout the postwar period has been from the conservative camp. The last several prime ministers have been beholden to the conservative wing of that camp, which favors the old elitist and manpower-oriented Japanese educational system. In between is the Ministry of Education, which must both please the prime minister and sustain a working relationship with the nation's teachers, three-fourths of whom belong to the progressive Japan Teachers' Union. Thus America watchers within the Ministry of Education have tended to take a somewhat moderate view in their America watching.

The institutionalization of America watching has resulted in a steady expansion of information about U.S. education. This does not mean, however, that there have been obvious improvements in the objectivity of the watching, for each of the institutionalized centers of America watching is at least as responsive to its indigenous constituency as it is to the reality of American education.

In addition to the institutionalized America watchers is the vast increase of private observers—scholars, teachers, students, tourists who visit the United States. This chapter provides some data on the volume of the visitor traffic and suggests that private observers approach America with definite images of what they expect to find. In most instances their American sojourn does little to alter their preconceptions. Thus I will be suggesting that the Japanese see U.S. education through their own highly developed filters, and it is my task here to describe those filters and their effects.

ACTUAL OBSERVATION OF AMERICAN EDUCATION

Established routes for the Japanese to learn about America include watching television, reading, reviewing official statistics, and traveling to the United States for study tours. The number of Japanese availing themselves of these opportunities has decreased substantially, especially during the past decade.

The Fulbright Program

Among scholarly exchanges, the oldest and possibly the most prestigious is the Fulbright program. Several of Japan's best-known America watchers have used this opportunity, including Michio Nagai, Hidetoshi Kato, Makoto Saito, and Makoto Oda. Nagai illustrates the immediate postwar generation. He selected Ohio State University over alternative choices so as to have a true middle America experience. His dissertation (Nagai 1976) examines the philosophical basis for the concept of educational neutrality, which the Occupation advanced as one of its reforms. Although he wrote it in the 1950s, at the peak of the McCarthy period, he did not use that development to focus on American education.

As soon as Nagai returned to Japan, however, he wrote extensively about American education. On the one hand, his writings expressed ambivalence about the managerial revolution in American education and the tendency toward specialization, noting both the positive aspects and the tendency to excess. On the other, he had much praise for America's liberal arts colleges because of their clear educational ideals and their concern for excellence. Nagai's initial writings about American education are reminiscent of the travelogue style used throughout Japan's modern history to report foreign practices: Peculiar foreign practices are identified, shown to be different from Japanese practice, and then proposed or rejected as practical alternatives to the Japanese practices. This style, which Kato (1975) calls the *miyage-banashi*, is attractive to Japanese readers but has the weakness that the American practices are not viewed on their own terms as part of the overall structure of American society. The travelogue approach scissors out little pieces and ignores the canvas.

In the mid-1960s, as Nagai began his critique of Japanese higher education, his view of American education became more sanguine and he stressed the relevance to Japanese education of the U.S. land-grant colleges and the quality of America's basic research (Nagai 1971). He had several occasions to teach at American universities, and in 1971 he was appointed director of the communication Institute of the East-West Center. That experience evoked his distaste for overmanagement and sharpened his sense that American intellectuals tend to see world events through ethnocentric lenses. Those themes appear in his critique of American education, *An Owl Before Dusk* (1975), prepared for the Carnegie Commission. Despite Nagai's growing pessimism about U.S. education, he concluded his volume with the statement that Japanese education "is in the midst of greater difficulties" (Nagai 1975, p. 45). Then, in 1974, Nagai became minister of education. His subsequent views on Japanese education have been more upbeat, and he has had little positive to say about American education.

In looking at American education, Nagai always sought ideas for improving Japanese education--for example, specialization, managerial techniques, and liberal arts colleges. That approach to American education became increasingly common over the postwar period. But by the late 1970s Nagai and others among his contemporaries concluded that America had little to offer.

Far less typical is Makoto Oda, a young leftist intellectual, who came to the United States in the early 1960s with few preconceptions other than his appreciation of the extraordinary and even scary influence of American civilization:

I wanted to see America not as an object to look at, but as something silently penetrating the lives of us Japanese. Our generation has grown up under the pressure of the constant cultural presence of America. I cannot formulate any theory about the United States without considering the "internalized America" that exists in the minds of Japanese. (cited in Kato 1975, p. 199)

So Oda tried to interpret and understand America on its own terms, feeling that somehow he might also be looking at an aspect of his own country. He sought to describe, not evaluate. During his U.S. sojourn he managed to participate in a wide range of American experiences, including student life at Harvard and the activities of black youths in nearby Boston. His final observations, written in the mid-1960s at the beginning of the Vietnam era, expressed hope that America was searching for a new way.

Hidetoshi Kato, writing in the early 1970s, suggested that Oda's open-minded approach would set a new trend in Japanese observations of America and its educational system. But, unfortunately, distressingly few Japanese intellectuals after Oda adopted his approach.

Other Academic Exchanges

Following the example of the Fulbright program, various agencies and organizations set up similar programs—for example, the Ford and Toyota foundations' fellowships for social scientists and the Japan Society for the Promotion of Science and National Science Foundation's programs, largely for natural scientists. Although Japanese scholars have tended to use these opportunities to take a year's rest in the United States or to polish manuscripts they were too busy to finish in Japan, many felt duty-bound to write something about American education. So the volume of academic and not-so-academic writing in Japan about American education has increased substantially in recent years.

According to the annual list of publications compiled by the National Diet Library, in 1963 there were only 17 entries on American education, and half of those were translations or summaries of U.S. publications. In 1982 the number was up to 89. The focus of most of the articles was limited and technical (see Appendix A). For example, I found articles on the credit system, competency-based education, the computerization of administrative tasks, and John Dewey. One article is so bold as to present "The Educational Situation in the USA During 1980 . . ."; but rather than offer an independent analysis, the writer presents views "according to *Time* and *Newsweek.*" The articles tend to focus on aspects of educational law, finance, administration, and history. Much that Americans take pride in and issues that have troubled them—such as school violence, busing, teacher and professor unionization, and racial prejudice—are ignored.

Although the exchange programs have enabled many young Japanese scholars to enter graduate degree programs in the United States, few of them have turned their attention to the U.S. educational system. I am aware of only eight Japanese dissertations that focus primarily on American education. All of them have rather narrow technical topics, and the data presented are typically derived from the administration of a standard psychological test (Appendix B). It is difficult to find even one Japanese scholar who in recent years has spent a full month in unstructured observation of a single American school. The distinguished Eisenhower fellowship has traditionally been awarded to prominent Japanese educators so that they could examine some facet of American education, but the only notable report to come out of this program was by Yoichi Maeda in 1963.

Teacher Exchanges

During the 1960s a program of Japanese and American teacher exchanges was initiated. The program had a most interesting genesis:

Responding to the pressure induced by a dynamic society, a group of prominent Japanese financiers turned their eyes to education. Taking a cue from philanthropic American businessmen, they wished to develop in themselves a sense of responsibility for society. In particular they were concerned with the hostilities which Japanese teachers have shown consistently to the established system in the postwar era. While resolving to be less conservative themselves, they also hoped to induce the teachers of Japan to become less radical. They thought they could achieve this by sending classroom teachers to the United States to correct their image of that country as a rapacious, capitalistic power, one which the Japanese businessmen themselves were accused of supporting. When the late Robert Kennedy visited Japan in 1963, the financiers took their problem to him. The senator introduced them to the Ford Foundation. The Foundation made an appropriate grant and entrusted it to the present writer, a professor from Teachers College, Columbia University, who, in turn, called upon the help of a colleague at Kyushu University. In the meantime, the Association for International Education was organized in Japan by the Japanese originators, and matching funds for activities in Japan were provided. In this way the Japanese-American Teacher Program, whose aim was to exchange teachers between Japan and the United States, was born. (Bereday and Masui 1973, pp. viii-ix)

Bereday and Masui's volume summarizes reports prepared by 150 teachers who participated in the early program during a three-year period. Few of the teachers made general comments about American society, which had been the original focus of the project. Rather, once in the United States, they had turned their attention to schools. They found much to admire in American education—the quality of school buildings and facilities, the initiative taken by individual teachers, the efforts to involve students actively in learning, the attention to differences in the abilities of children of the same age. Nevertheless, the teachers were disturbed by the lack of system in American education, the great diversity from one school district to another, the absence of moral education in the schools, and the great gap they often witnessed between the ideals that American educators announced and actual practices in classrooms. One detects a tone of envy in their accounts, yet also a sense of reaffirmed confidence in the Japanese way.

Recently, the Ministry of Education developed a sequel program that sends approximately 5,000 Japanese teachers overseas annually, mainly to the United States. Most of the teachers who go on the current tours view the trip as a reward for good work. Many of them cannot speak the language of the country they are visiting and go there in the summer, when the foreign schools are not in session. So it is doubtful that the trips add much understanding to Japanese images of American education.

Ryugaku (Overseas Study)

The enthusiasm expressed by Nagai about American liberal arts colleges has been a continuing theme in postwar Japan. Some Japanese colleges, such as Sophia University's International Division, Aoyama Gakuin, and Doshisha, actually modeled themselves on American liberal arts colleges. These same colleges were the first to set up area studies programs and Japanese-language instruction for foreign students. Over the past decade, as Japanese interest has grown in internationalism (which seems to mean interacting on a campus with foreign students), these colleges have become leaders in promoting the new trend. Other Japanese universities, such as Tsukuba and the new International University at Niigata, are following in their wake.

But increasing numbers of young Japanese, caught up in the fascination with "internationalism," are deciding that they might as well try the real thing, at least for a year. Many go overseas either during high school, for a year abroad, or during college, to earn an undergraduate degree. As it turns out, 80 percent decide to seek their internationalism in the United States. In 1980-81, 13,500 young Japanese were studying at American universities.

To attract and serve them, a minor industry of placement agencies and promotional literature has emerged in Japan. The monthly journal *Ryugaku Jiten*, for example, which caters to individuals planning an overseas study trip, projects a sanitized image of American higher education that includes cheerleaders (blond), libraries, boutiques, snappy professors giving well-prepared lectures, and challenging, small seminar classes. This image of American education is an old one, cherished by an affluent minority.

Children in American Schools

With Japan's growing affluence and the internationalization of its economy, increasing numbers of young people are coming to the United States for study, both by choice and because their parents are stationed here. More than 5,000 Japanese children currently are studying in Japanese government schools in America, and nearly twice that many are studying in ordinary American schools.

Their recent participation in American education has provided the opportunity for fresh insights. Whereas earlier generations of Japanese sojourners tended to end up at the better U.S. universities and to attend affluent schools near those institutions, the current wave of Japanese visitors has simply by virtue of its volume experienced a wider spectrum of American life. From this new generation have emerged many accounts, of which I will summarize two.

Iizumi (1981), the wife of a Japanese physicist, carefully recorded the experiences of her two children, who, respectively, attended a primary school and a junior high school on Long Island, New York. Mrs. Iizumi's account seeks to show the nature of U.S. society through its schools, and also to prepare parents who are considering putting their children into American schools. She observes that American schools are flexible and seek to provide an education suited to the ability of each child. She notes the pecu-

liarity of American humor in the schools from the first day, when
the principal tests her child's English and maturity by asking if the
child has any (pubic) hair—a relevant but admittedly shocking inter-
rogation for a first conversation. Much of her account focuses on
differences in school ritual between the United States and Japan
—for example, the absence of an opening-day ceremony, busing,
and ability grouping in classes, which she says is accepted as a
natural practice by the children and does not affect their friendships.
Mrs. Iizumi views American education as an expression of such
features of American society as its individualism, openness and
frankness in interpersonal relations, and diversity. She assures
Japanese parents that children can readily adjust to American schools
but is neutral on the question of whether American practices are
appropriate for Japan. Her style is refreshing and lively.

Many of the same themes appear in Kajita's (1983) more scholarly and systematic ethnography of a surburban Boston elementary
school. Kajita begins his study with an analysis of the relative financial support from the federal, state, and local levels; he concludes
that it varies considerably from school to school. For Kajita, each
school's budget, which results from a struggle with several governmental levels, is an interesting object of analysis. He believes that,
in contrast with Japan, where central authority is so strong, in the
United States, schools have more autonomy; thus they can have
more individual features such as in the format for report cards, the
furniture in classrooms, and the textbooks used. Kajita provides
detailed accounts of what happens in classrooms and is impressed
by major differences among U.S. teachers in teaching styles. Although some teachers use the open-classroom approach, which permits students free movement among work stations during a classroom period, he reports that parents do not seem to approve of it.
Kajita is impressed with opportunities for students to "show and
tell" their classmates about things of interest to them, and he ap-
plauds the encouragement provided for creative writing. He also
says that children adjust naturally to their ability-based groups.
Throughout his book he makes an effort to report what he sees,
without making judgments other than that many of the special
features of U.S. education seem to derive from the nature of American society and culture and therefore may not be appropriate for
Japan.

With the increasing numbers of Japanese children in the United
States, the Japanese public is gaining a clearer and more comprehensive understanding of U.S. education. Accounts by Japanese
authors tell the Japanese public that American schools are easier than
Japanese schools and thus Japanese parents need not worry about

their children's adjustment to an American school. Emphasizing the humane atmosphere in the U.S. schools, which seek to adjust to each individual child's needs, the accounts both admire this characteristic and suggest that a price is paid in educational efficiency.

AMERICANS IN JAPAN

Americans invited to Japan and books by U. S. authors on American education are additional means for the Japanese to learn about U.S. education. The Minshu Kyoiku Kyokai, or Institute for Democratic Education (IDE), has, since the Occupation period, played an important role in both of these respects. Over the last decade it has held bimonthly meetings to discuss "relevant" books written by foreigners and to listen to invited speakers, usually foreign. A recent list of the books and authors (Minshu Koiku Kyokai, 1983) selected for this influential forum reveals two salient features: Most of the books are on tertiary education, and most of the writers are American. Impressive is the ability of the IDE to identify hot American titles. But as one moves chronologically down the list, the topics and nationalities of the authors become more diverse, as if suggesting that America has less and less to offer the IDE group. The list provides a reasonable overview of the leading works on American education. But certain topics are left out— race, the debate on the importance of genes in academic performance, and class differences in admission to higher education, for example. Presumably those topics are not relevant to Japanese readers.

OFFICIAL REFERENCES TO U.S. EDUCATION

Japanese government publications provide another important perspective on U.S. education, and perhaps the most representative of these is the Ministry of Education's "Educational Standards in Japan," or White Papers, published approximately every five years.

The Ministry of Education's White Papers

Comparison of the White Papers of 1964, 1975, and 1981 is made easy by their retention of a common outline. They include an overview of enrollment trends, structure and curriculum, the supply of teachers and facilities, the level of educational expenditures, and new topics such as trends in educational reform. Both the 1964 and the 1975 White Papers contain extensive comparative references, usually of a statistical nature, to the United States, France, West

Germany, the United Kingdom, and the Soviet Union. Forty percent fewer foreign references appear in the 1981 addition, however.

One obvious reason for the decline in foreign references is the fact that Japan has caught up or surpassed its major foreign rivals in so many respects. The 1964 paper began by noting that Japanese educational expenditures were low and that the system suffered from major qualitative gaps. By 1981 Japan's public school expenditure as a percentage of national income was equal to or greater than that of all other countries, except the Soviet Union. And by 1981 the Japanese Ministry of Education was more confident about the quality of Japanese education.

The items stressed in the papers are indicative of the ministry's perception of foreign systems, or at least of its strategy in referring to foreign example. Several excerpts from the 1964 White Paper illustrate the strategy:

> In the U.S.A., full-time upper secondary schools are open to all, while in European countries, attempt is made to attain this goal by providing various kinds of full-time secondary school education or making it the duty of employers to give part-time supplemental vocational training to their employees. In our country, in spite of the considerable rise of the rate of entrants to upper secondary schools, there still remain not a small number of youth . . . who do not receive any sort of education. (pp. 168-69)

> In many countries, there is a tendency, along with the recent rapid scientific and technological progress, toward conducting new researches and practices which would change the basic organization of traditionally taught subjects as discussed above. Such improvements are especially marked in science and mathematics. (p. 45)

> The percentage of time devoted to the study of mathematics is lowest of all countries in the lower stage in Japan. (p. 48)

> The above two tables indicate that the proportion of educational expenditures devoted to higher education in Japan is lower at the present time than at the prewar period, and also lower than in any of the other four advanced countries. (p. 142)

After making this last comment, the 1964 White Paper noted increasing federal concern for education in the United States. It concluded by urging various changes in Japanese education, including greater attention to ability and aptitude differentials in teaching and student placement, the promotion of science and technology education, the expansion of both upper secondary and higher education, and more expenditures for education—changes that would enable Japanese education to reach the international standard.

The 1975 White Paper dropped the theme of expanding secondary and higher education, as Japan had surpassed most of the foreign examples. (In the graph showing trends in the expansion of higher education a logarithm scale was used so as to disguise the rapidity of Japan's expansion.) Instead, the paper devoted attention to preschool and graduate education, areas in which Japan numerically still lagged. It also noted that Japan had a smaller proportion of foreign students than other advanced societies.

The paper's discussion of reform in U.S. education dwelled on preschool education and the Head Start program, as well as the introduction of television and other technology into U.S. classrooms. It lauded the growth of U.S. community colleges and extension programs. Those topics were a clear expression of the Ministry of Education's programmatic goals and bore little relation to the big issue in U.S. education at that time, such as busing, teacher unionization, and federal funding.

The 1981 White Paper contained substantially fewer references to other countries' educational systems. It put more emphasis than the earlier reports on the success of Japanese education, which, it stated, now surpassed all but the Soviet Union in level of public support and the provision of preschool education, equaled the United States in participation at the tertiary level, and exceeded all other countries at the primary and secondary levels. Even in preschool education for four- and five-year-olds it described Japan as having caught up, though it acknowledged a lag in schooling for three-year-olds. The report glossed over other areas where Japan still lags, such as special education, and had nothing to say about mental illness and other maladies experienced by schoolchildren, which are frequently commented on in the Japanese press.

The major problem area considered was the quality of teachers and teaching; but the paper pointed out that the student-teacher ratio at the primary level, reported as 25, was close to that of other advanced countries, and it noted that although the proportion of female teachers was rising it was lower than in the other advanced societies. (Japanese teachers have traditionally been men.) The paper showed that the pay of Japanese teachers was reasonably competitive and the scope for career improvements in pay relatively high.

My review of the White Papers prepared by the Ministry of Education thus indicates that the ministry once had a keen interest in foreign examples because they could be used to promote the ministry's case for school expansion and increased finance. But by 1981 the Japanese system was quite competitive and therefore the ministry's interest in foreign examples had diminished.

The Prime Minister's Office

It is apparent from the White Papers that the Ministry of Education thinks of the nation's schools as administrative units. The reports have little to say about what goes on in the classrooms, how the personalities of children are developing, or what will happen to them after they graduate. This broader perspective gradually has become, apparently by default, the purview of other sections of the Japanese government. One of the most interesting centers addressing these broader issues is the Youth Section of the Prime Minister's Office, whose research is discussed by Carol Stocking in Chapter 7 of this volume.

The Politicians' View

As observed at the beginning of this chapter, Japanese views of U.S. education are shaped by politics. For many Japanese political figures, American education is a symbol for the reforms introduced during the Occupation. At that time some welcomed the reforms and others opposed them. This political symbolism was especially evident in the discussion of Japanese education during the 1950s. During the 1960s the politicians turned their eyes to higher education and the discussion became more pragmatic. It was in that political climate that American-educated party politician Takeo Miki became prime minister; and he was able to choose an intellectual with an American Ph.D. as his successor.

But over the past several years the political focus has once again shifted to youth and the schools. Japan's political leaders worry that young people lack basic values and a philosophy of life. They suggest that Japanese youth is beginning to suffer from the American disease. And they therefore conclude that Japan's problems may be due to the American features in Japanese education. Today it is common among politicians to search for the influences of American culture on Japanese education so that those influences—the lack of moral education, too many academic-track places at the secondary level, pornography—may be purged.

CONCLUSION

Japan has developed a considerable familiarity with American education, especially since World War II. The focus of Japanese observers is influenced by their institutional vantage points. Ministry of Education observers focus on finance, enrollments, and administration. Professors focus on the quality of academic life in the United States. Parents and students focus on events in the classroom and community. And politicians seem most concerned about the American diseases of drugs, violence, and sex.

Japanese observers systematically neglect certain features of U.S. education: the genetic debate, the American struggle to use schools as a means of promoting racial integration and the attendant problems, the orientation of blue-collar families to schools, and the relation of schools to American achievements in entertainment and sports. In general, the Japanese observers have a weak understanding of the link between American schools and the broader society. Thus they fail to place in proper perspective some of the troubled aspects of U.S. education, such as school violence and the drug culture.

The Japanese are acquiring a more diverse experience of American education, but this does not show up readily in the content or quality of their interpretations of American education. I have suggested that their interpretations continue to reflect two tendencies that crystallized after World War II. At that time the Japanese regarded American education, on the one hand, as expressive, individualistic, opulent, and creative and, on the other, as undisciplined, wasteful, and hedonistic. The main recent development has been to reverse the valence of the contrasting images so that, whereas American education was once perceived in a largely positive light, it now is seen in mainly negative terms. Political developments in Japan as well as Japan's international ascendence are behind this shift.

APPENDIX A: Typical Titles of Japanese Articles About U.S. Education Published in 1982

"Some Aspects of the Follow-Through Program"
"The Development of Community Colleges in the USA"
"The Treatment of Japan in American School Texts"
"The Establishment of the Credit System in American Junior High School"
"The Educational Philosophy of Dewey and the Formation of the Nation"

"The Exclusiveness of State Regulation on Teacher Selection: The Norwith Case"
"Accountability in Primary and Secondary Schools in the United States"
"Competency Based Education in the United States"
"The Educational Situation in the USA During 1980 According to *Time* and *Newsweek*"
"The Employment Conditions of American Professors"
"The Computerization of Administrative Tasks in American Universities"
"Music Education in American High Schools"
"The Great Books Program in American Universities"
"The First Years of the Normal Schools in Pennsylvania"

Source: National Diet Library (1983, pp. 29-32).

APPENDIX B: U.S. Ph.D. Dissertations by Japanese Scholars about American Education

Hara, Kimi. "A Cross-Cultural Comparison of Self Concepts and Value Orientations of Japanese and American Ninth Graders." Michigan State University, 1972.

Kambayashi, Kikuko. "The Expansion of Treatments of Japan in High School Textbooks in American History, 1951-1972." University of Michigan, 1975.

Sabie, Taha. "Foreign Students Coping with the American Culture at Eight Selected American Universities." George Peabody College for Teachers, 1975.

Shimada, Koji. "Education, Assimilation and Acculturation: A Case Study of a Japanese-American Community in New Jersey." Temple University, 1975.

Suzuki, Norihiko. "Transfer of American Business Education: International Business Educational Produce Life Cycle." Indiana University, Graduate School of Business, 1978.

Kataoka, Hiroko. "Motivations and Attitudes of Japanese-American Students Towards Learning the Japanese Language." University of Illinois at Urbana-Champaign, 1979.

Morioto, Takiko. "Teachers' Perceptions of Their Roles in Japan and the United States." University of California, Los Angeles, 1981.

Saito, Noriko. "A Comparison of Performance on Piagetian Tasks Among Japanese and Anglo-American Children Six Years of Age Who Were Exposed to One Language and Two Languages." University of Southern California, 1982.

REFERENCES

Bereday, George C., and Shigeo Masui. 1973. *American Education Through Japanese Eyes*. Honolulu: University Press of Hawaii.

Iizumi, Miyoko. 1981. *Nyuyooku Togai no Gakko de* (An Account of School Life in Surburban New York). Tokyo: Asahi Shinorama.

Kajita, Masami. 1983. *Bosuton no Shogakko* (A Boston School). Tokyo: Yukikaku.

Kato, Hidetoshi. 1975. "America as Seen by Japanese Travelers." In *Mutual Images: Essays in American-Japanese Relations*, edited by Akira Iriye, pp. 188-201. Cambridge, Mass.: Harvard University Press.

Ministry of Education. 1965. *Educational Standards in Japan 1964*. Tokyo.

Ministry of Education, Science, and Culture. 1976. *Educational Standards in Japan 1975*. Tokyo.

Minshu Kyoiku Kyokai. 1983. "IDE 30-nen no Ayumi" (30 years of IDE). *IDE: Gendai no Koto Kyoiku* 246 (November-December).

Mōmbushō. 1981. *Wagakuni no Kyoiku Sui jun 1980* (Educational Standards in Japan in 1980). Tokyo: Okurasho Insatsukyoku.

Nagai, Michio. 1971. *Higher Education in Japan: Its Take-off and Crash*. Tokyo: University of Tokyo Press.

_____. 1975. *An Owl Before Dusk.* Berkeley, Calif.: Carnegie Commission on Higher Education.

_____. 1976. *Education and Indoctrination: The Sociological and Philosophical Bases.* Tokyo: University of Tokyo Press.

Nagai, Michio, and Takeo Nishijima. 1975. "Postwar Japanese Education and the United States." In *Mutual Images: Essays in American-Japanese Relations*, edited by Akira Iriye, pp. 169-87. Cambridge, Mass.: Harvard University Press.

National Diet Library. 1983. *Annual Publications 1982.* Tokyo.

Nihon Seinen Kenkyusho. 1979. *Nichibeis einen Hikaku Chosa Hokokusho* (Report of the U.S.-Japan Comparative Survey of Youths). Tokyo.

Ryugaku Jiten '82 (Overseas Study '82). 1982. Tokyo.

PART VI
CONCLUSION

15
LEARNING FROM EACH OTHER
The Editors

The authors of this book are skeptical that education in the two societies is facing a major crisis. In their view the current crisis consciousness is largely a political invention. Both President Reagan of the United States and Prime Minister Nakasone of Japan have found education to be one of the safest issues they can exploit for political advantage.

Notwithstanding the artificiality of the crisis, neither country's educational system is perfect. In the current educational debates attention has been focused on the secondary schools. Critics say there is no clear rationale for the division of the lower and upper secondary levels, and much of the academic content at both levels is repetitious and boring. Confusion exists about the appropriate mix of academic and nonacademic subjects, as well as the mix of college preparation and life preparation, and there is uncertainty about the appropriate schooling for students with different aptitudes and perceptions. It might be said that the secondary schools are experiencing an identity crisis. Other areas are also troubling. In Japan the quality of university education is frequently criticized, and in the United States the status and education of teachers are of concern. How to resolve these problems is the major focus of contemporary debate in the two societies.

TRADITIONAL OBSTACLES TO LEARNING FROM EACH OTHER

The basic similarities in the two nations' educational situations suggest the usefulness of cross-national investigations. Whether useful insights will come out of such research depends on various factors. Historically, in the Japanese-American relationship two factors have had bearing: the mutuality of interest in each other's situation and the prevalence of common problems.

The Subjective Factor

As is well known, for the past 100 years, Japan has learned a great deal from American education, while the United States has remained indifferent to the educational system of this latecomer. Until recently, Americans took interest in Japanese education only as something that needed shaping and improvement, not as something to learn from. Thus, in what could best be described as one-way communication across the Pacific, the United States has been playing the part of teacher and Japan the part of learner.

During the 1870s, immediately after the Meiji Restoration, the new government launched a plan to establish a modern school system following the precedents set in advanced Western countries. Among them, the United States exerted the greatest influence because the majority of advisers on Japanese educational policy and most of the schoolteachers invited by the government were Americans. Their influence was felt not only on educational policy and the educational system but also on the content and teaching method. In the aftermath of World War II, the United States as winner held complete control over the second educational reform of the loser, Japan. A new educational system was fashioned after the U.S. example through the guidance of General Headquarters of the U.S.-dominated Occupation government.

In contrast, Japanese education has never exercised as profound an effect on American education. The current American interest in Japanese education may lead to a more reciprocal relationship. Nevertheless, up to the present, Japan is suffering from an excess of imports over exports in the fields of education, arts, and culture from its Pacific partner. It is thus ironic that in the economic sphere the question of America's unfavorable trade balance with Japan has become such a hot issue.

Differences in the two countries' attitudes toward each other are reflected in the depth of ordinary people's understanding of the other society's schools. A considerable number of the Japanese have some knowledge of U.S. education, but most Americans have only a faint idea of Japanese education, even though some U.S. experts have been in frequent contact with Japan. The perceptual mode of U.S. specialists on Japanese education also differs from that of Japanese specialists on the U.S. system. In comparison with the Japanese specialists, who tend to think of American education as the universal standard and seek to borrow directly its techniques, their American counterparts are apt to consider Japanese education as specially suited to its cultural and social context. The Japanese usually take notice of the assets of American education, whereas the Americans tend to focus on the weaknesses of the Japanese educational system. In addition, the Japanese specialists rely on literature about America published by American educationalists that coincides with their own views, while Americans develop their independent theories about Japanese education based on their own field surveys.

The Japanese inclination to follow the example of U.S. education and the American inclination to set an example for Japan naturally result from the historical relationship between the two countries. Both sides would better understand each other if they could be free from their respective biases.

The Objective Context

It is difficult for countries to learn from each other when they are at entirely different stages of development or have different ideologies. Thus, for advanced countries, education in developing countries is primarily a subject of anthropological interest and a target for assistance but not the substance from which lessons can be applied at home.

Although Japan and the United States were once decades apart in their objective situation, recently they have come much closer together. The demographic profile of both nations is assuming a similar form, with increasing proportions of old people and a modest decline in the school-age population. Both share a common commitment to a capitalist economy. Their rates of economic growth, after being so disparate during most of the postwar period, are converging in the 3 to 6 percent range. Because of the profound influence that American education has had in Japan, there are many similarities in the two educational systems. The similar rates of economic growth combined with a shared conservatism in fiscal policy mean that neither country is likely to allocate much new funding for educational innovation. Thus whatever educational reform takes place in the two countries is likely to be subject to similar constraints.

Major differences exist, however, between the two societies. The United States is much larger geographically and has a more diverse population, including many recent migrants who lack the language skills and motivation required for a demanding school experience. In contrast, Japan receives few immigrants, and its young children are better prepared for school and more motivated to learn. Another difference is the educational systems themselves. The American system is politically and administratively decentralized. Public schools are operated by some 30,000 local school boards. In addition, the United States has a large parochial system and numerous private schools at all grade levels. In most states, young people are expected to continue their education until age 16 and may if they wish continue to receive virtually free education until they complete high school. In Japan, although there are local school boards, the central government's more decisive role results in more uniform standards across the country and less disparity in per student educational expenditures from one area to another. Compulsory education extends only through the lower secondary level, and beyond that level private schools play an important role.

CONTRASTING IDEOLOGIES OF THE TWO SYSTEMS

More salient, however, than these structural characteristics is the way that the two nations think about education. The United States fosters a myth of limitless opportunity. Football players can earn more than corporation presidents, and the local shoe store of today has the possibility of becoming one of *Fortune's* Top 100 in 20 years. School is but one of several routes to success. For the individual who seeks the educational route, being a late bloomer is not necessarily an obstacle to upward mobility. Thus even when they enter college, many Americans have poorly developed intellectual skills. Most Americans are also relaxed about choosing their educational institutions, believing that what happens outside school and later in life may have more influence on their chances for success than what takes place in school. In contrast with the American belief in limitless opportunity, the Japanese assign great importance to a small number of career choices in the central government bureaucracy and the top corporations. They rank other careers in descending order and assume that an individual's educational performance will determine where he or she ends up in this hierarchy. Most Japanese parents seek to manage the lives of their children, from a surprisingly young age, so that the children will have the best chances of entering the top careers. Because admission to a prestigious university is known to be essential for gaining access to these attractive careers, parents are deeply concerned with the educational performance of their children. They exert every effort to ensure that their children earn good grades and enter the best schools. The large number of parents sharing this common belief results in severe academic competition. In contrast to Americans, Japanese children develop from an early age a realistic sense of the opportunities they can expect as they grow up.

There is considerable irony in these respective national ideologies. For despite the Japanese belief in an economic hierarchy, income differentials among adults in Japan are much less than in the United States. And there is no evidence to indicate that educational success in Japan is any more closely related to career success than in the United States. While Imperial university graduates are disproportionately visible in top Japanese positions, the same can be said for the graduates of America's most prestigious universities. In both countries the vast majority of graduates from those institutions settle for less elevated positions.

Still, these different perceptions of opportunity account for the much higher motivation of Japanese children, especially at the primary levels, to excel in school. They help to explain the greater tendency of Japanese children to remain in school and that of U.S. students to drop out and later drop back in.

But important changes are taking place in both the realities of social opportunity and the perceptions of these realities in the two societies. Coming from different directions, the two societies appear to be converging.

CONVERGENCE

Through much of the postwar period the United States has thought of itself as an economic giant with technological prowess beyond the reach of all other societies, including the Soviet Union. With this national self-confidence it has supported the steady expansion of service industries and the drift to postindustrialism. As a consequence, it has devoted less attention to industrial productivity, especially in the area of consumer goods. Because of the vastness of its domestic market, the United States until recently has been little concerned with expanding its share of the overseas market.

This American approach sufficed through the mid-1970s, but thereafter U.S. economic growth stalled and foreign imports began to eat away at the health of major corporations. In response to these developments the United States has reassessed its economic condition and launched active measures for reindustrialization and expansion of exports.

In the U.S. reassessment, schools have received much attention. How is it that America is educating only half as many engineers as Japan, its major industrial rival? And why have the test scores and writing abilities of America's young people steadily declined? Questions of this kind are behind the current concern in the United States to place greater emphasis on excellence than on equity, on math and science rather than on social studies, and on discipline and hard work rather than on creativity and learning adjusted to each individual.

Japan entered the postwar period as a devastated nation. Determined to build a new society, its leaders sought supreme sacrifices from the Japanese people. Based on hard work, the implementation of an export-oriented growth strategy, and the adoption of foreign technologies, the Japanese economy rapidly improved. By the 1970s Japan was effectively competing with the United States in many fields, and Japanese per capita income had risen to European levels.

But Japan's economic leaders perceived increasing competition from newly industrializing countries if Japan continued to concentrate on manufacturing heavy industrial products for export. In recent years, therefore, they have shifted their emphasis, on one hand, toward high-tech products as a means of sustaining their level of industrial exports and, on the other, toward leisure industries as a means of increasing domestic consumption and improving quality of life.

A less competitive educational system that allows young people to spend more time developing their own personalities and nonconventional skills seems increasingly desired by both Japan's leaders and the public. Increasing numbers of young people are opting out of the academic competition that leads to long work hours in traditional careers. Instead, they are seeking more control over their activities and greater scope for pursuing their own interests.

Whereas contemporary Japan wishes to liberalize its educational system to nurture a more diversified youth, the United States is concerned with developing a more competitive educational system that will provide basic academic skills to a broader spectrum of young people. This convergence has put educators from each nation on an equal footing; both are seeking to learn from each other. In their assessments of the other nation's systems, the following areas are likely to receive their attention.

PROMISING AREAS OF JAPANESE EXPERIENCE

American educators are showing increased interest in Japanese approaches to some of the problems of the American educational system.

The Correlates of Educational Competition

In the immediate postwar period the American myth of unlimited opportunity was introduced to Japan along with the rapid expansion of secondary-level educational opportunities. Over the next decade there was a quantum leap in the number of young Japanese seriously competing for entrance to top universities and elite careers. The pain and anxiety experienced by many of those youths after failing to achieve their cherished goals was severe and, in some cases, the catalyst for suicides. Over time new ancillary institutions have been established in Japan that supplement the role of formal schools in preparing young people for crucial educational examinations and help students to evaluate their abilities. The rationalization of educational competition has resulted in a lowering of youth anxiety.

As the U.S. economy become more nationally integrated and as youth aspirations rise, educational competition is likely to take on some of the characteristics of the Japanese "degreeocracy."

Promotion of Uniform Standards

Throughout the modern period Japan's central government has sought to define the educational objectives for different school and grade levels and the resources that schools require to realize those objectives. The government's statements of standards have had varying degrees of legal authority. During the postwar period its statements concerning curriculum have been called recommendations; those concerning facilities and resources have been used for administrative planning. In general, the Japanese standards specify an optimal level of performance for schools, whereas U.S. standards represent the minimum necessary for accreditation. Although Japan's centrally defined standards are never perfectly observed, they have served as a reference point in educational debate. The variety of Japan's school-level standards and the way in which they influence actual practice should be of interest to American educators who seek to raise the standards of American education.

Realization of Equitable School Finance

Among the variety of Japanese standards are several related to school expenditures. In the Japanese system local governments are primarily responsible for financing schools out of their tax revenues. To the extent that a local government has difficulty in collecting sufficient revenues, the central government supplements its income. The Japanese Diet has passed several laws authorizing additional expenditures for schools and schoolchildren who face hardships such as poverty, cultural deprivation, or being located in an isolated location. Expenditures per student in Japan are thus surprisingly equal. Some of these Japanese practices might be of interest to the governments of the larger U.S. states.

Mechanism for Subsidizing Private Schools

Recognizing that private schools play an important role in education, the Japanese central government provides extensive subsidies to private schools. Especially of interest is the Private School Promotion Foundation, which subsidizes private universities by meeting up to one-half of their personnel costs. The rationale for government support and the manner in which it is provided should be of interest to American leaders who believe that private educators deserve more support from government.

Cultivation of an Academic Climate

In the United States it is recognized increasingly that the school climate has a profound role in shaping the aspirations and performance of young people. In contrast to the strong emphasis on sports and "dating" that is characteristic of many U.S. secondary schools, Japanese secondary schools have a predominantly academic climate. The pattern of communication that takes place among teachers, the structure of student incentives, and the ways that different schools of a common region relate to each other are facets of Japanese education that deserve more careful documentation.

Curriculum and Pedagogy in Mathematics and Science

Recent international tests have demonstrated that Japanese secondary students know more math and science than do children of the same ages in most other industrial societies. The more demanding Japanese curriculum and Japanese teaching methods, which emphasize mastering the basics and student participation, help to account for Japan's high achievement in these areas. The total time the Japanese secondary school devotes to these subjects is no greater than in the United States, but time on tasks in Japan is much higher. What, then, is special about the Japanese curriculum and pedagogy?

Job Placement of School Graduates

Japan has the lowest youth unemployment rate of the industrial societies, whereas the United States has one of the highest rates. Japanese school and university administrators assume that they have a responsibility to help find employment for their students and thus actively cultivate relations with prospective employers. In addition, a variety of nationwide firms exists to administer tests to young people and mediate between employers and prospective school-age employees.

PROMISING AREAS OF AMERICAN EXPERIENCE

Just as Japanese education has developed certain practices that may be of interest to educators in the United States, so has the United States achieved notable results in several areas.

Individualization of Instruction

While sharing with Japan a commitment to equality, U.S. schools have been much bolder in developing educational strategies that take account of the ability of each student. Although controversy has arisen about the effects of these procedures, they should be of interest in Japan, where educators indicate increasing concern with the slow and fast learners.

Communication and Research Skills

American educators are less concerned with how much their students know than with how well they can apply and communicate their knowledge. Schools in the United States encourage many of their students to conduct their own research, write reports, and make presentations of their findings. Japanese schools are relatively weak in this regard.

Diversified School Climate

The American comprehensive high school has sought to encourage a great variety of activities within its confines. In addition to its academic program, it is likely to support a full program of athletics and graphic and performing arts. Many high schools also provide training in the industrial arts and in other life skills. The diversity of activities encouraged by the schools to explain America's prominence in such international contests as the Olympics and musical competitions. In general, Japan performs poorly in those competitions. How the American schools encourage such diversity should be of interest to Japanese educators.

School and University Image

Many American institutions, especially at the tertiary level, have been able to develop a distinct image and successfully project their image to the general public. Through their public relations effort, they are able to ensure stable admissions and continue to pursue the educational goals they value. The success of these schools in projecting their diverse images helps to diversify American higher education and fight the countervailing tendency of all institutions to be perceived as part of a single hierarchical order. Japanese education, given its concern to promote diversification, might learn from America's efforts at image production.

Procedures for University Admissions

Yet another area of sharp contrast between American and Japanese education is in university admissions. American universities employ several criteria in deciding admissions, only a few of which relate to academic achievement. This approach enables the institutions to recruit a diversity of student types and thus provide variety to campus life. At the same time, the arbitrariness of university admissions encourages students to apply to several institutions, thus alleviating some of the tension associated with explicit admissions criteria.

Lifelong Education

Whereas 90 percent of all students on Japanese campuses belong to the college-age cohort, fewer than half of college students in the United States are from this age group. A large proportion of America's university students are adults who have come back to school. Factors in the U.S. employment system and incentives offered by universities that account for the large numbers of adults who return for higher education should be of considerable interest to Japanese educators.

COMMON CONCERNS

Japan and the United States are struggling with common problems in yet other areas where neither has an obvious record of superiority.

Internationalization of the Curriculum

Despite the fact that the two nations are world leaders in trade and aid, their educational systems are notably ineffective in equipping their young people with the special skills that are needed for working in foreign settings. For example, in a recent international test of global understanding, college-age groups in both Japan and the United States were able to answer only half of the questions considered by a group of global experts as essential to international knowledge. Only 14 percent of U.S. high school students study a foreign language, and many U.S. colleges do not require their students to take foreign languages. The Japanese record on foreign languages is superior, but even so, few Japanese young people develop a speaking ability in the languages they study. How to increase the salience of foreign languages and international knowledge is a challenge faced by both societies.

Teacher Education and Status

Teachers in both societies, especially at the upper secondary level, are suffering from a serious morale problem. They are not accorded as much respect or receive as much income as they desire, and within the educational system they see limited opportunities for advancement. Under these circumstances many teachers of mathematics and science decide to resign and take up more lucrative positions in corporate laboratories. How to restructure the educational system so as to improve the morale and motivation of teachers is a common challenge.

Restructuring

Possibly the solution to many of the problems faced by these two societies will lie in a restructuring of secondary education. Since World War II both societies have utilized a similar structure involving three years of lower and three years of upper secondary education. Most children are obliged to take the academic track of the two levels in sequence. In many curricula, the two levels repeat each other. Structural alternatives to the current system might include a more comprehensive lower secondary school of up to five years, followed by a variety of upper secondary schools tailored to the occupational interests of young people and tied to adult institutions. Certainly some changes along these lines will be seriously considered by both societies.

CONCLUDING REFLECTIONS

It can be argued that, as formal education in the two societies is a common product of their industrialized economies, little variation exists between the two school systems. Rather, Japan and the United States have basically similar formal systems of education. To grasp the differences between the actual processes of education in the two societies, one must focus on nonformal education. Thus far the educational debates in the two societies have not given sufficient attention to the variety of educational experiences that occur outside of school, in the students' families, and the proprietary system (in Japan, especially the *juku*), nor to the role of the media, the excellent training provided by the military and many corporations for their employees, or the educational opportunities provided by museums and other public institutions.

Finally, in the comparative examination of Japanese and U.S. schools, much attention to date has been focused on the schools' formal structure, which again is shaped by universal economic exigencies. Yet the major differences in the schools may lie in their informal structure, the ongoing networks of human relations that are established among teachers, students, parents, and administrators. An accurate perception of these segments, which are rooted deeply in the respective cultures and social structures, requires thorough familiarity with the circumstances of each society, acquired through careful and intensive studies.

Each country will encounter considerable difficulty in borrowing ideas and practices from the other, and hasty transplantation may yield a bitter fruit. Nevertheless, to realize that a different mode or procedure is working smoothly in another society can help a country to gain a fresh view of the characteristics and problems of its own educational system. The examination by each country of the other's practices, instead of revealing a model to imitate, is likely to provide a mirror by which to reexamine its own cherished beliefs.

INDEX

abacus, 71, 127
academic achievement, Japan, 17, 122, 156, 161; United States, 52; international comparisons, 117
ad hoc Council on Educational Reform, 10, 154
American Occupation of Japan, 6, 9, 27, 121, 256, 276
aspirations and motivation, 24, 122, 127

baby boom, 98, 108

Carnegie Foundation for the Advancement of Teaching, 73, 91, 225
Central Council for Education, 7, 10, 154
centralization-decentralization, Japan, 20, 67; United States, 47, 49, 68, 181
Clark, Burton, 176
cooling-out effect, 31, 101
Council on Culture and Education, 10
counseling, 146, 221ff
credentialism, 27
Cummings, William K., 69, 121, 245
curriculum, Japan, 7, 62ff, 128, 248; United States, 70ff, 128; Japan-United States compared, 85, 138, 302

decline, Japan, 154ff; United States, 117, 171
delinquency, juvenile, 104, 107, 244, 263
discipline, 50, 248
drop-outs, 31, 90, 156

economy, Japan, 155, 244; United States, 297; international competition, 20, 47
educational crisis, 3; Japan, 8, 27; United States, 44, 47; origins, 47, 50; cyclical nature, 49
educational models, Japan, 47, 243, 262; United States, 3, 154, 244; European, 13; general, 3, 277; borrowing, 12, 252
educational quality, 35, 179, 300
educational reform, 3; Japan, current, 72, 153; prior, 4ff, 32, 38, 79, 81; United States, current, 17, 49-53; prior, 17, 45; general, 3; comparison, 19
educational stratification, Japan, 23, 24, 124, 159, 198, 207, 298; United States, 181, 284
educational system, Japan, general, 25, 35, 202; opportunities for graduates, 2, 197ff, United States, 46
enrollments, Japan, 155; United States, 173, 217; compared, 96
examination system, 7, 29, 38, 64, 160ff, 245, 250, 299; pressure, 30, 104, 133
excellence, 179, 300
extracurricular activities, 135

finance and expenditures, educational, 33, 103, 123, 155, 175, 177, 182, 302
Fundamental Law of Education, 80

homework, 137

ABOUT THE EDITORS

IKUO AMANO, professor of sociology of education at the University of Tokyo, formerly taught at Nagoya University. Two of Amano's recent books are *Kysusei Senmongakko* (The Old System's Specialized Colleges) and *Kyoiku to Sentaku* (Education and Selection).

EDWARD R. BEAUCHAMP is professor of comparative education at the University of Hawaii, at Manoa. He received his Ph.D. from the University of Washington in 1973 and is the author of *An American Teacher in Early Meiji Japan, Learning to Be Japanese*, and *Education in Contemporary Japan* and co-author of the forthcoming *A Sourcebook of Japanese Education*.

WILLIAM K. CUMMINGS, international science and technology resource analyst of the National Science Foundation, was a senior fellow at the East-West Center from 1983 to 1985. Two of his recent books are *Education and Equality in Japan* and *Changes in the Japanese University* (co-edited with Ikuo Amano and Kazuyuki Kitamura).

ROBERT EVANS, JR., Atran Professor of Labor Economics and chairman of the Department of Economics at Brandeis University, has long been active in the study of the labor economics and industrial relations of Japan and the United States. He is the author of papers on subjects as diverse as slavery, clipper ships, crime, and labor law, as well as work on Japan. In the last area he is the author of *The Labor Economies of Japan and the United States* and several journal articles. Evans was formerly a member of the Industrial Relations Section of the Massachusetts Institute of Technology and has three times been a visiting professor at the Economic Observatory of Keio University in Tokyo. He also is a longtime member of the School Committee in the town of Acton, Massachusetts.

SHOGO ICHIKAWA is director of Research Department II at the National Institute for Educational Research of Japan. Until 1970 he was associate professor of educational governance at the University of Hokkaido, Sapporo. Ichikawa is the author of numerous books on educational finance and governance and on lifelong education. His works in English include "Japan" in *Educational Policy: An International Survey* (edited by J. R. Hough) and "Finance of Higher Education" in *Changes in the Japanese University* (edited by W. K. Cummings et al.).

KAZUYUKI M. KITAMURA, professor of higher education in the Research Institute of Higher Education at Hiroshima University, spent the 1984-85 academic year as a Fulbright senior scholar and visiting associate at the Center for Studies in Higher Education at the University of California, Berkeley. Kitamura is the author of several books and numerous articles on Japanese higher education in Japanese and English. His most recent book is *The Internationalization of Higher Education in Japan—Japanese Higher Education Observed from Outside.*

VICTOR N. KOBAYASHI is professor, Department of Educational Foundations, University of Hawaii at Manoa, and affiliate research associate, East-West Center. His doctoral dissertation (1966) at the University of Michigan, "John Dewey in Japanese Educational Thought," won the Francis W. Parker dissertation prize from the John Dewey Society. His many published writings cover such topics as aesthetics, the implications of the ideas of Gregory Bateson for education, cinema and the humanities, and international education, as well as education in Japan.

JOHN W. MEYER is professor of sociology (and, by courtesy, education) at Stanford University and chairman of the Department of Sociology. He is co-author of *Environments and Organizations, National Development and the World System*, and *Organizational Environments* and has written a number of specialized monographs. Meyer has written numerous papers on the effects and structure of educational institution, comparative sociology, and formal organizations.

CAROL BOWMAN STOCKING is director of research programs at the Center for Clinical Medical Ethics, Pritzger School of Medicine, University of Chicago. She was the original project director of High School and Beyond, a longitudinal study of the U.S. high school classes of 1980 and 1982 sponsored by the National Center for Education Statistics. Her recent publications include an analysis and theoretical interpretation of inconsistent responses by handicapped students in the High School and Beyond data (*Characteristics of High School Students Who Identify Themselves as Handicapped*) and an essay on the relation between secondary and higher education in the United States (in *Schools and Universities*, edited by Burton Clark).

JOSEPH J. TOBIN is Assistant Professor of Human Development, University of Hawaii at Manoa. An anthropologist, he has published books and articles in both Japanese and English on American images of Japan.

MARTIN TROW is professor of sociology in the Graduate School of Public Policy and director of the Center for Studies in Higher Education at the University of California, Berkeley. He is the author or co-author of many books and essays, including *Union Democracy, Right-Wing Radicalism, The British Academics*, and *Students and Colleges: Interaction and Change*. He directed two National Surveys of Higher Education for the Carnegie Commission (1969) and the Carnegie Council (1975). He has been a fellow of the Center for Advanced Studies in the Behavioral Sciences at Palo Alto and a visiting member of the Institute for Advanced Study, Princeton. He is a member of the National Academy of Education and a trustee of Carleton College.

MAMORU TSUKADA is a doctoral student of sociology at the University of Hawaii at Manoa. He is an East-West Center degree participant. Tsukada holds a B.A. and an M.A. from Hiroshima University, Japan.

MORIKAZU USHIOGI, professor of the sociology of education at Nagoya University, was formerly on the faculty of the University of Tokyo. Among his many books are *Kindai Daigaku no Keisei to Henyo* (Development and Transformation of the Modern University), *Gakureki Shakai no Tenbo* (Transformation of the Highly Schooled Society), and *Kyoto Teikokudaigaku no Chousen* (Challenge of Kyoto Imperial University).

The Praeger Special Studies
Series in Comparative Education

General Editor: **Philip G. Altbach**

Published in Cooperation with the
Comparative Education Center,
State University of New York, Buffalo